electronic databases and publishing

electronic databases and publishing

and

publishing

edited by

albert henderson

Routledge
Taylor & Francis Group

LONDON AND NEW YORK

First published 1998 by Transaction Publishers

Published 2017 by Routledge
2 Park Square, Milton Park, Abingdon, Oxon, OX14 4RN
711 Third Avenue, New York, NY 10017, USA

Routledge is an imprint of the Taylor & Francis Group, an informa business

Copyright © 1998 by Taylor & Francis.
The chapters in this book originally appeared in various issues of *Publishing Research Quarterly*: chapters 1-20 in the Fall 1995 issue; chapters 21-23 in the Summer 1996 issue; chapter 24 in the Winter 1994/1995 issue; chapters 25-26 in the Summer 1995; chapter 27 in the Winter 1996/1997 issue; and chapter 28 in the Spring 1997 issue.

Library of Congress Catalog Number: 97–10966

Library of Congress Cataloging-in-Publication Data

Electronic databases and publishing / edited by Albert Henderson.
    p. cm.
  Includes bibliographical references.
  ISBN 1–56000–967–5 (pbk. : acid-free paper)
  1. Machine-readable bibliographical data. I. Henderson, Albert.
Z699.E62 1997
025.3'16—dc21   97–10966
                                   CIP

ISBN 13: 978-1-56000-967-2 (pbk)

Contents

Preface

T he true pioneers in electronic publishing put their bibliographic databases on tape and online in the 1960s. Nearly all of them had a long experience with compiling information for distribution in printed form and a strong market connection. The buyers of database information services were largely technical libraries with information mandates based on a baby boom economy and spurred by the Soviet Union's *Sputnik* and man in space Yuri Gagarin. The excuse Western scientists gave to embarrassed politicos for Soviet success in space was that Soviet information resources were unified and orderly while Western resources were chaotic. One industry spokesman complained that it was easier to repeat $100,000 worth of research rather than to try and find out what had been done. As a result of *Sputnik*, government support for information science and academic libraries flowed freely for a little over a decade, making possible tremendous advances in technology, in retrieval techniques, and in sophisticated coverage. Advances in information technology and market conditions have encouraged many more participants to underwrite the development of databases that now extend into the arts, social sciences, business, and popular interests.

One of the interesting sidelights of electronic databases is the capacity to enumerate records with relatively simple programs. We have exploited that feature only to a small degree. The present collection of essays develops two themes. First, production statistics accompanied by statements of editorial coverage provide a fairly accurate reflection of research output/publishing as itemized by many of the major disciplinary bibliographic databases. The urgent priority of information resources in the 1960s encouraged a comprehensive servicing of the formal research literature as published in journals and monographs. Some of our authors have given us counts of subject words, languages, origins, types of publication, and so forth, over several decades. Included are some databases that are not strictly bibliographic, such as the CMG database of college courses, which illuminates some of the changes in college textbook publishing. Second, we see in production statistics and comments a shift in emphasis as database publishers respond to the impoverishment of a marketplace whose information mandate is history.

Information seekers will find the many tables of practical use, inasmuch as they provide a unique form of guidance to how much of what may be found within each database. Regrettably, we were no more able to standardize the tabular presentations than we were able to secure the participation of all database publishers. As we go to press, many invitations remain extended to major publishers. We trust that coverage of these databases will eventually appear in *Publishing Research Quarterly*, supplementing the present volume. Analysts of publishing, of science policy, and of higher education will find information that they can relate to expenditures, human resources, and other indicators of education, research, and technology activity.

Albert Henderson

1

Database Publishing Statistics

Martha E. Williams

Database statistics have been a long-standing interest of mine because of their relationship to the conversion of traditional abstracting and indexing journals from paper-based products to electronic computer-readable databases. In the late 1960s, in order to keep track of databases as they became publicly available, I began collecting literature about bibliographic databases. By 1973 I had sufficient information to warrant developing a directory of data about databases wherein the same types of data about the different databases would be collected to permit comparisons on the same bases. In 1974 I founded and edited the first edition of *Computer-Readable Databases* (*CRDB*) and offered it to the American Society for Information Science for publication. (See Williams & Rouse 1976.) I continued to edit and produce the camera-ready copy of *CRDB* for a sequence of publishers over the years (American Society for Information Science; Knowledge Industry Publications, Inc.; American Library Association; and its copublisher in Europe for *CRDB*, Elsevier Science Publishers) and published database statistics in those volumes. In 1987 *CRDB* was acquired by Gale Research, Inc. For several years Gale published *CRDB* with Kathleen Young Marcaccio as editor and with Martha E. Williams as founding editor. In the latter capacity I analyzed the database data collected by Gale and produced an annual article entitled "The State of Databases Today" (see e.g., Williams 1995 c), which Gale published as the foreword to the directory. In 1993 Gale ceased publishing the *CRDB* per se and merged it with two other directories. *The Gale Directory of Databases* was formed in 1993 by the merger of three database directories acquired by Gale Research, Inc.: *Computer-Readable Databases*, founded by editor Martha E. Williams in 1975 and acquired by Gale in 1987; *The Directory of Online Databases*, founded by Cuadra Associates in

1979 and acquired by Gale in 1992; and *The Directory of Portable Databases,* founded by Cuadra/Elsevier in 1990 and acquired by Gale in 1992. The *Gale Directory of Databases* is published twice a year in two volumes (see Nolan 1995). The statistics presented herein are based on the analyses I do for Gale Research of data published in the *GDD* plus data from the *Information Market Indicator Reports* (*IMI Reports*).

Data cover the worldwide database industry and are independent of the media in which databases are distributed and accessed. To maintain continuity with prior database statistics and to build a continuing comprehensive set of comparable database statistics, entries are coded by Gale specifically for my analyses even though these special codes do not appear in print. The statistics indicate the growth of the database industry as represented by the increase in number of database records, online searches, databases, database entries in *GDD*, database producers, and database vendors. I look at databases in terms of geographic region and producer status where producer status refers to the societal sector of origin—Government; Commerce/Industry (for-profit); Not-For-Profit (NFP), which includes Academe; and Mixed sectors. I also consider databases in terms of the form or representation of the data, the subject matter or intellectual content of the data in the database, and the medium for access and/or distribution. Data relative to early years, and some of the current data are taken from some of my other publications and are also included in the "State of Databases Today" articles. Because of page limitations, I include here a brief snapshot of the major statistics about databases over the twenty-year period 1975–1994.

Databases

Databases are characterized as word-oriented, number-oriented, and also, in more recent years with the introduction of multimedia technology, as audio (for databases including sound data), image (for databases including pictorial or graphic data), and video (for moving picture data). Some data are world-wide and some are for the United States only and are noted as such.

From 1975–1994 databases have grown by a factor of 28.2 (from 301 to 8,776), producers have grown by a factor of 13 (from 200 to 2,778), and vendors have grown by a factor of 15.1 (from 105 to 1,691) (see Fig. 1). The number of records contained in the databases has grown more dramatically. In 1975 the 301 databases contained about 52 million records. The 8,776 databases in 1994 contained some 6.3 billion records, a growth by a factor of 120.5 (see Fig. 2). The average number of databases per producer in 1994 was 3.0, and the average number of records per database was 791,954. Naturally, the range is very wide, from a few thousand records to tens of millions of records per database. In 1994 there were 367 databases that contained more than a million records. If one excludes those very large databases, the average database entry contains 109,593 records and the average database contains 99,640 records.

Looking at databases in terms of form of representation, 72 percent of data-

FIGURE 1
Growth in Number of Vendors, Producers, Database Entries, and Databases, 1975–1994

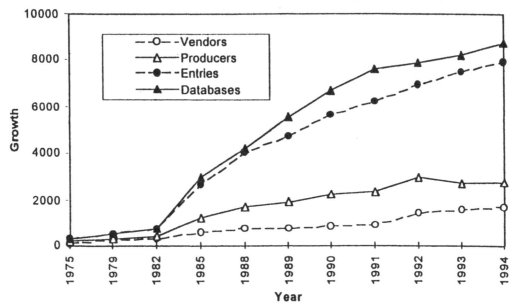

FIGURE 2
Number of Database Records, 1975–1995

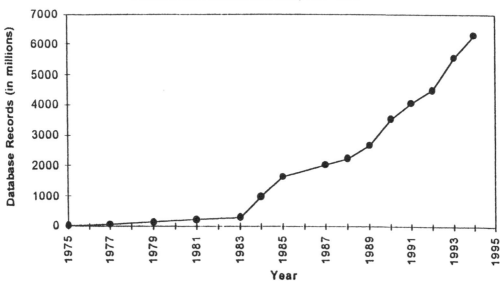

bases in 1994 were of the word-oriented type (bibliographic, full-text, patent/trademark, directory, and dictionary); 18 percent were number-oriented; 5 percent were image- or picture-oriented; 2 percent were audio- or sound-oriented; and the remaining 3 percent included various electronic services and software (where software databases are those that include manipulable and/or downloadable software for use on the user's local personal computer or work station). Within the word-oriented databases, the full-text databases have grown the most in recent years. From 1985 through 1994 bibliographic databases grew by 67 percent and full-text databases grew by 547 percent. There are now more than 3,462 full-text databases, and much of the growth is due to the great increase in full-text databases on CD-ROM.

When looking at computer databases in terms of eight major subject classes —science/technology/engineering, business, health/life sciences, social sciences, humanities, law, news/general, and multidisciplinary—we find the class with the largest number of databases is business (32 percent); second, science/technology/engineering (19 percent); third, law (12 percent); and fourth, health/life sciences (9 percent). The remaining four classes make up 28 percent.

When classed by medium for access or distribution (online, batch, CD-ROM, diskette, magnetic tape, and handheld), the majority (57 percent) are accessed online, 5 percent are still available in batch mode; 20 percent are on CD-ROM; 10 percent are on diskette; 7 percent are available on magnetic tape, and 1 percent are handheld. It is worth noting that the use of magnetic tape for local mounting of databases is making inroads and supplanting the use of online in certain markets—especially in academe.

Databases are produced throughout the world. The percentage of databases produced in the United States has increased greatly since 1979. From 1975 through 1979 the U.S.:non-U.S. ratio was about 1:1, but from 1979 to 1985 it increased steadily and from 1985 through 1993 was about 2:1. In 1994 the non-U.S. fraction increased more than the U.S. fraction so that the ratio became 63 percent U.S. and 37 percent non-U.S. This change is partially due to the political changes in the formerly communist countries and expansion of commerce in the Pacific Rim. Producer status has also changed considerably from the late 1970s, when governments were responsible for 56 percent of databases and not-for-profits and commerce/industry each produced 22 percent. In 1994 commerce/industry was responsible for 76 percent; governments, 14 percent; and not-for-profits, including academic, 10 percent.

There are many ways to measure database success, but this discussion is limited to measuring the success of a database as an entity in the marketplace, and there we must look at usage and revenues. Payments are made for database use, and use is measured in several ways: on the basis of the amount of time spent online in searching a database; number of items retrieved, viewed, printed, downloaded, or otherwise accessed; number of searches conducted (the term *search* may be defined in accordance with the specific content of the database); packages of searches; use of computer ports for unlimited access during specific hours; subscriptions of many different types; and so on. This discussion is restricted to looking at database success in the marketplace where the market is the information center/library market in the United States. The databases are those that are available via the major vendors of word-oriented databases in the United States. These data are taken from the IMI Reports, which cover fourteen major vendors of word-oriented databases, for example, Mead Data Central (LEXIS, NEXIS), DIALOG, ORBIT, and WEST.

In 1974 there were approximately 750,000 searches conducted on fourteen vendor systems by users in the United States in the information center/library market. In 1982, there were about ten times as many searches, or 7.5 million; and in 1993, 58.3 million. Thus, in twenty years the number of searches increased by a factor of 78. Over the same time period baud rates changed from 300 to 1,200 to 2,400 to 9,600 to 14,400 to 28,880 and higher. Although different searching organizations have upgraded their modems at different times, and some have upgraded several times, the overall time per search decreased by more than 50 percent and the amount of material being searched in databases increased 10–25 fold depending on the specific database and how many backfiles stayed online. At the same time the charges levied per connect hour and per information unit delivered or accessed also increased. Files got bigger, prices for connect time and information units delivered went up, baud rates speeded up, search features were improved, front ends and interfaces became easier to use, searcher efficiency increased, and average search time decreased, but the average cost per search did not change much. The net result of these simultaneous changes over the years from 1978 through 1993 was very little change in the average cost per search in dollars of the day, but in CPI-adjusted dollars, the average cost per search went down considerably.

A closer look at this segment of the online database market, the information center/library market, shows that connect hours have increased by a factor of nearly 10, from 1978 with 780,000 hours to 1993 with more than 7 million hours. Revenues to the online vendors have increased by a factor of 28.6, from $40 million to $1.145 billion.

Usage and revenues have not been shared equally among vendors—far from it. Of the fourteen vendors monitored by the *Information Market Indicators* survey in 1993, three vendors (Mead Data Central [LEXIS/NEXIS], West, and DIALOG) had 81 percent of the use and 93 percent of the revenues. (See Williams 1995a.)

Producers whose databases were up on the 14 vendor systems numbered 360 in 1993, and the distribution of connect hours among them was disproportionate. The top three producers in 1993, Mead, West, and OCLC (all are also online vendors, and each in its producer status experienced use of more than 100,000 hours per quarter), had databases that amounted to 70 percent the total market usage. If one adds the National Library of Medicine (NLM) to this high-use group of producers whose databases generate more than 100,000 hours per quarter, then that group is responsible for 76 percent of the total market use among the 360 producers. Mead, West, OCLC, and NLM were the only producers to have more than 100,000 hours per quarter. The next 13 each had more than 10,000 hours per quarter, representing 13.5 percent of the hours; the next 35 producers each having at least 1,000 hours per quarter, made up 6.5 percent; 73 producers with at least 200 hours per quarter made up 1 percent; and the remaining 235 producers, each of whom had fewer than 200 hours per quarter, accounted for less than 3 percent.

Revenues associated with the same 360 producers are similarly distributed. The top 2 producers in terms of revenue were Mead and West; together they accounted for 64 percent of the revenues. The third producer was Chemical Abstracts Service, but the distance between the second and third is considerable and hence Chemical Abstracts should not be grouped with Mead and West. There were, however, 14 producers each of which generated at least $1 million per quarter. Although Mead and West each generated more than $75 million, the remaining 13 high-revenue producers each generated between $1 and $5 million per quarter and accounted for 11 percent of the revenue. The remaining revenues were distributed very much like the connect hours.

The revenues of the next 35 that generated more than $100,000 each, account for 4 percent of the revenues; 68 producers who generated more than $25,000 per quarter made up 1 percent of the market, leaving 241 producers who generated less than $25,000 per quarter making up 19 percent of the market. Individually these small producers do not account for much revenue, but as a group they represent $219 million, which is 19.12 percent of the total market ($1,145,000,000). The online database market is still growing, and the differences between the large and small players continue to become more extreme.

Often search intermediaries complain about the cost of online searching and tend to think that all database producers are making money at their expense. Few understand the high expenses associated with database production: that most databases do not enjoy a high enough level of use to produce sufficient online revenue to support their creation, and that a database is often largely supported by the corresponding print product. The foregoing statistics on database use and revenues should make these facts of life quite clear. Desirable as it may be to have an abundance of free information, as is available currently through the Internet, there still remains the need for quality information with the type of added value that many of the abstracting and indexing publishers as well as the publishers of numeric and transactional databases provide. The collection of information and the adding of value is done at considerable cost to database publishers and they must be compensated. Perhaps the announcement of the existence of various databases through the Internet and the free offering of sample databases will help to expand the market for online databases. The Internet provides many options for database publishers, and there is little doubt that innovative publishers will make effective use of it to the benefit of users and themselves.

Note

1. Portions of this article appear in Williams, 1995b, c.

References

Nolan, Kathleen Lopez, ed. 1995. *The Gale Directory of Databases*. Detroit: Gale Research.

Williams, Martha E. 1995a. *Information Market Indicators: Information Center/Library Market*, issue 47. Monticello, IL: Information Market Indicators, Inc.

Williams, Martha E. 1995b. Highlights of the Online/CDROM Database Industry: The Information Industry and the Role of the Internet. In *Proceedings of the 16th National Online Meeting*. Medford, NJ: Learned Information.

Williams, Martha E. 1995c. The State of Databases Today: 1995. In *The Gale Directory of Databases*. Detroit: Gale Research.

Williams, Martha E., and Sandra H. Rouse, comps. and eds. 1976. *Computer-Readable Databases (CRDB): A Directory and Sourcebook*. Washington, DC: American Society for Information Science.

2

Secondary Information Services—
Mirrors of Scholarly Communication:
Forces and Trends

Richard T. Kaser

It has been said that the "direct purpose" of scientific research is the "acquisition, accumulation, and integration of scientific information."[1] By communicating their observations, thoughts, and results, scientists as well as practitioners of the arts create a body of knowledge that their peers and proteges can build upon. In the process, they leave a "paper trail" of documentation, mostly in the form of formal papers (such as the one you are reading) published in scholarly journals (such as the one you are holding in your hands).

But as any researcher knows, the process of finding the papers on a specific topic at the moment when they're needed can be like finding a needle in a haystack (or more contemporaneously, a specific document on the Internet) because there are tens of thousands of journals published each year, and hundreds of thousands of papers. Historically, this is the point where secondary services enter the picture. By systematically obtaining, reviewing, and selecting important papers for coverage, secondary information services catalog and often index this literature so that it can be identified, located, and obtained later. In many cases, secondary services also summarize the information contained in a paper in the form of an abstract—which can be likened to a review—so that potential users can zero in on papers that are most directly related to their current topics of interest.

Titles, topics, sources, summaries—by any other names, these are the stuff of secondary information services. As means of helping scientists, researchers, and other scholars locate published information, these pointers to journals, books, conference proceedings, monographs, and other primary sources of information have been an integral part of the scientific communication process for more than three hundred years.

As a by-product of their cataloging, critiquing, and reviewing effort, secondary services also help to "measure" the formal output of scholarly communication activity. By tracking the number of papers abstracted and indexed, for example, one can see how the literature has grown over the past several decades. Furthermore, one can see reflected in these statistics all manner of social, political, economic, technological, and even philosophical currents that have shaped and are continuing to mold the development and evolution of scholarly communications.

The Secondary Services' Scorecard

The National Federation of Abstracting and Information Services (NFAIS) in Philadelphia has tracked the growth of secondary services for more than thirty-five years. Figure 1 shows the number of abstracts published by twelve leading publishers of secondary information in selected years since 1957.[2]

The most noticeable thing these data illustrate is that the scientific literature has been growing and growing and growing. In 1957 these twelve organizations combined published just about 555,000 abstracts. Twenty years later they were publishing four times as many: 2.24 million. And today, the number is hovering at approximately 3.7 million. Table 1 shows the growth rates that these particular secondary publishers have experienced. As if these numbers are not astounding enough, it should be noted that all NFAIS members who reported their statistics in 1993 (with forty-six organizations reporting) are currently publishing about 14 million abstracts a year. All told, their cumulative databases contained more than 217 million records at the end of 1993.

The numbers alone do not explain why the literature has grown to such magnitudes, how the organizations who catalog, index, and abstract it have managed to keep up, and what is responsible for the recent tapering off in the growth rate in coverage. Many factors must be considered in order to understand what the numbers actually represent. And for a full consideration of the issues, we must draw in many fields and disciplines, starting with a lesson from history.

The Evolution of Scholarly Communication

Though it can be argued that the systematic collection and recording of human knowledge traces back five thousand years to Mesopotamian clay tablets and papyrus scrolls in Egypt, though there were already large libraries in existence two millennia ago, and though printing technology itself is nearly two thousand years old, it is generally acknowledged that the European adoption of the printing press, starting in 1450, ushered in a new era of information capture and dissemination, launching the world into the Information Age.

Prior to this point, the only way that knowledge could be shared was if a learned person visited another learned person, penned a letter, or tediously drafted a manuscript by hand. The lack of any better communications tech-

FIGURE 1
Number of Abstracts Published per Year 1957–1993, Selected Publishers

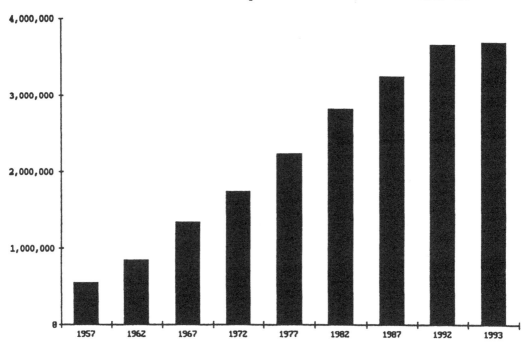

nologies than these severely limited the ability of individuals not only to communicate but to build on one another's ideas. The printing press revolutionized our opportunity to exchange information. Scholars could now augment their private discussions and personal correspondence with occasional published works in the form of books. But in the process of expanding our ability to communicate, the printing press also created problems of its own. No sooner did printing technology catch on, than there was too much literature for any single person to read.

The year 1655 can be considered as the turning point. In that year a man named de Sollo had the brilliant idea of summarizing everything of importance currently in print and publishing the summaries in a new kind of journal. The *Journal de Scavans*, survived only thirteen issues (for reasons I shall get to later), but nonetheless it established the precedent for all of the abstracting and indexing services published to this day.

Working on a somewhat different tack, scholars themselves would—over the next hundred years—invent and perfect a shortened form of information presentation that by its very nature made the results of serious research more accessible to others working in the field. The emerging format was the article published in a scholarly journal, which between 1665 and 1790 grew from thirty-five serial titles to just over four hundred.[3] But even four hundred was too many for some fields! And by the year 1800, abstracting services had emerged to cover the literature in chemistry. Abstracting journals for medi-

TABLE 1
Growth in the Publication of Abstracts, 1957–1992

Year	Number (000s)	Growth Rate (%)
1957	554	
1962	851	54
1967	1,343	58
1972	1,748	30
1977	2,240	28
1982	2,824	26
1987	3,252	15
1992	3,671	13
1993	3,699	1

cine, biology, and most other academic disciplines followed. By 1900, there were five thousand scientific journals being issued and 136 abstract journals to cover them.[4] But the world hadn't seen anything yet.

A scant fifty years later, it would take an astounding thirty thousand primary journals to record a single year's worth of scientific progress. Now, more than ever, the scientific community could not live without the finger of secondary information services pointing at the individual articles. But, being mostly not-for-profit operations, the world's abstracting and indexing services were having their own problems keeping up.

Political Currents

It was the Spanish Inquisition that put a halt to de Sollo's noble experiment to summarize all available information in print. It seems the authorities of the time did not take kindly to having the full-texts of their decrees condensed and summarized. So the *Journal de Scavans* ceased publication rather quickly after start-up.

By 1958, it was a different story, but it was politics nonetheless that lit a fire under the secondary services in the United States. Sputnik had been launched, the Cold War was raging, and the U.S. government was taking a particular interest in science, technology, and the information services that were recognized to be a critical factor not only for the advancement of science but for national security. This was the statement that changed the history of secondary information services in the United States:

The White House—Dec. 7, 1958. "The President [Eisenhower] today approved a plan designed to help meet the critical needs of the Nation's scientists and engineers for better access to the rapidly mounting volume of scientific publication. Acting upon the recommendations of his Science Advisory Committee, the President directed the National Science Foundation . . . to provide or arrange for the provision of, indexing, abstracting, translation, and other services leading to a more effective dissemination of scientific information."[5]

With these words, President Eisenhower launched a development cycle that transformed the way in which secondary information services operated, ultimately giving birth to electronic publishing, online information retrieval, and even the first computer networks that, in a different political era, would become known as the information highway.

Now you know the reason why the annual output of American abstracting and indexing services doubled between 1957 and 1967. As for how they did this . . .

Technology's Saving Grace

What the printing press wrought, it ultimately took the computer to control. During the 1960s, secondary information services in the United States stretched the computer technology of the day to its maximum limits, pioneering the development of large, often cumbersome, but effective computer-assisted record management and photocomposition systems. According to Malcolm Rigby, who worked at the National Oceanographic and Atmospheric Administration at the time:

> By 1960, BIOSIS, Meteorological Abstracts, Armed Services Technical Information Agency (ASTIA), and others were experimenting with or [were] operational in publishing permuted title indexes using IBM 1401 computers and other tabulators or computers. Bibliographies were also being prepared with automated equipment. By 1973 almost all [secondary services in the U.S.] were using electronic equipment to produce many printed products and authority files of subjects, chemicals, and authors.[6]

It was advances such as these that helped the secondary services catch up with the backlog of journals waiting to be abstracted and indexed at the time. It also supported the services in broadening their scope in an era when scientific disciplines were themselves broadening and becoming more interdisciplinary. The tremendous growth in the number of abstracts published during the 1960s and 1970s is testimony to the miraculous effectiveness of data processing in handling large volumes of information efficiently and also to the concerted effort—regarded as a part of national security—to make secondary services as comprehensive as possible.

Economic Factors

Technological improvements to the production and expansion of editorial content came at a price. Though some early automation efforts received a modicum of support from the National Science Foundation, professional societies, or other sources, for the most part it was initially the subscriber to secondary journals who had to pay for the cost of faster and more comprehensive publication of these pointers to research results.

In 1971, Robert Collison, speaking on behalf of the library community, commented on the situation by saying: "Comprehensiveness, as an editorial policy, is here to stay since it obviously serves both national and international interests. The question remains concerning who should pay for such a policy which involves a steady rise in costs each year, since the world's output of periodicals is rapidly increasing."[7] Collison went on to suggest various sources of funding in addition to traditional subscribers (who in those days still consisted of individuals as well as libraries). His list of potential funding sources included the government, international bodies, professional societies, and industrial organizations. As other scenarios, he also predicted that libraries might have to start sharing subscriptions rather than maintain comprehensive collections of secondary journals. But it was when he suggested that "industry should pay" that he really hit the nail on the head. Over the next twenty years, it would often be industry (and not the traditional academic library) that would pay the lion's share for developing, producing, and distributing a new generation of secondary information services—though clearly government agencies and professional societies continued to underwrite the development as well.

Something Other than Print

Unbeknown to and unfathomed by the developers of the first automated production systems, they were simultaneously laying the foundation for a new kind of information access. The data tapes used to instruct the computer's peripheral photocomposition systems on placing abstracts, bibliographic citations, and index entries on the printed page could also be searched by the computer to find information in these "databases" on a particular subject.

At this point a merger of political incentives and industrial research needs drove technological innovation. In Palo Alto, California, a small division of the Lockheed Space and Missile Company, a prominent government defense and space program contractor, had—by the early 1970s—developed powerful computer programs to support the search and retrieval of scientific and technical information stored in bibliographic databases. The only thing Lockheed lacked in the early 1970s was the databases.

As "by-products" of the editorial production process, the computer tapes from secondary publishing endeavors immediately filled the gap. The online information retrieval service that resulted from the merger of Lockheed's information-handling technology and secondary information databases would soon become famous as Dialog—now Knight-Ridder Information Services. And over the next twenty years, its heaviest users would be information centers in industrial labs, serving scientists engaged in industrial R&D activities.

Why did the interest in scholarly research literature suddenly shift from its traditional home in the university to the university's traditional nemesis—the commercial sector? It was because at this time science itself was shifting. To borrow a phrase from the era, little science was becoming big science. Scholarly research was stretching out from its traditional academic environment. Though the academic community still wrote and published the majority of the papers printed in journals and referenced by secondary services, it was the industrial scientist who seemed to have developed the greatest hunger for accessing this published literature. And the desired means of access was quickly shifting from print to online.

Online information retrieval, priced by the amount of usage and not by the annual subscription, never became a large line item in most university library's acquisition budgets. On the other hand, large pharmaceutical, petroleum, and medical technology companies became big online consumers. Their insatiable desire for more timely information and more powerful information-handling systems would drive developments at secondary services and online vendors alike for the next two decades. The secondary services kept growing and growing in the 1980s and 1990s, the growth fueled, and to a great extent paid for, by industrial research needs. Meanwhile, at colleges and universities throughout the world, something else was happening.

The Birth of the Cyber College

Concurrent with the developments in the aerospace industry in the late 1960s, the U.S. Department of Defense was also about to make history. In 1969, DoD launched ARPANET, a strategic computer networking capability designed to assure access to computer resources should the United States undergo a devastating nuclear attack. Because colleges and universities bought their computers from the same suppliers as government agencies, the networking technology was imbedded in the hardware they obtained. Over the next two decades, the collective genius of the academic community would put this Cold War technology to peaceful and productive use, in the process building a worldwide system that would eventually be known as the Internet.

While industrial users were busy reaping the results of traditional scientific communication formats (the journal article and its associated abstracts), the academic community was rapidly revolutionizing a fundamental aspect of the scholarly communication process. In addition to the formal means of communication at a scholar's disposal (letters, conferences, books, and journals), scholars were now able to "talk" directly and informally with one another, share data, and exchange research results almost instantaneously by sending electronic messages on the Net—which they did with growing enthusiasm. In the ivy-covered halls (now underlain with fiber-optic cable) there was even increasing discussion about whether this new means of communication would ultimately create a paradigm shift in the way scholarly work occurs. Some even went so far as to suggest that perhaps scientific publishers would no longer be necessary in the brave new cyber world ahead.

Sociological Factors

But old habits, as they say, die hard. After twenty-five years of "internetworking," the paradigm of scholarly publishing in printed journals (and subsequent reference in secondary services) has not shifted to any great extent. Though some experiments with electronic journals have been conducted—and a few successes have been noted—publication of papers by faculty in printed journals still remains a critical element in the academic reward system and a powerful factor in the academic community's self-assessment models. As a recent paper observed:

> Many studies have demonstrated that there is a strong correlation between citation counts [i.e., the number of papers published by a particular faculty and subsequently referenced in other printed publications] and ratings of academic excellence as measured by other means, for example, receipt of honors, receipt of research funding, editorships of major journals and peer group ratings.[8]

In other words, despite the Internet, a scholar must still publish (in print) or perish (even if actively networked to colleagues online). And it is this publication tradition, institutionalized in the form of a printed paper, that still fuels not only primary journals but secondary information services in their coverage of an ever-expanding literature base.

Information Implosion?

Why then, in Figure 1, do we see the rate of growth in number of published abstracts suddenly tapering off in recent years? Last year—for the first time since NFAIS started collecting statistics on secondary information services in 1957—the total number of published abstracts declined, from a base of 14 million in 1992 to 13.6 million in 1993, a 3 percent decrease.[9] Could it be that in a demonstration of the laws of physics some critical mass has been achieved and now expansion is turning into contraction?

There is actually no reason to believe that the literature itself is suddenly shrinking. But there is reason to wonder about the ongoing ability of primary publishers to continue to publish it all—at least not on the traditional economic basis of paid subscriptions. And there is reason to question whether it is economically viable for secondary services to continue to take as their mission the 1960s concept of providing comprehensive coverage of the published literature. If so, it would not be the first time organizations dedicated to providing information access have had to draw the line. Take libraries, for example.

When Economic Push Comes to Shove

In the 1970s and 1980s U.S. university libraries began to reassess their long-standing collections-management tradition of maintaining comprehensive resources, turning instead to the sharing of library materials through interlibrary loan. The impetus for this departure—at least the reason that is most often cited—was the rising cost of maintaining subscriptions to serial publications, most notably primary scholarly journals.

From 1978 to 1988 the weakening of the U.S. dollar abroad, increasing paper costs, and other economic forces had driven the average cost of journal subscriptions, by some estimates, from $50 to more than $118,[10] with individual titles ranging as high as $1,000 or more, depending on the subject matter of the journal. In 1978 the University of California at Riverside reported paying, on average, $30.40 for a book and $146.21 for a journal subscription, with journal subscriptions consuming 60 percent of the library's total acquisitions budget.[11] These price levels are often blamed for the resulting "economic crisis" in libraries.

The crisis in libraries actually had begun in the 1960s, due to the same escalation in the volume of scientific literature that the secondary services had experienced. As the volume of published scholarly literature expanded, university libraries expanded their serials collections accordingly—consistent with the philosophy that a good library was a complete library. Later, when subscription costs rose, the philosophy came under question.

Though some blamed rapidly escalating acquisitions costs on the fact that those who had stepped in to help cope with the mounting volume of scholarly papers were commercial publishers with higher profit expectations than earlier scholarly presses, the problem that confronted libraries was not just a pricing matter but also a budgeting issue. While the number of papers published by the academic community was rising at an exponential rate, library budgets to acquire the papers were hardly keeping pace with the double-digit inflation that prevailed at the time. Because the cost of maintaining complete holdings of expanding numbers of journal titles outstripped library budgets, librarians had to turn to other ways of meeting their historical mission of providing patrons with access to a full set of materials.

They turned to "resource sharing." By combining resources with, at first, libraries in the general vicinity and, then, libraries in neighboring regions, college libraries were able more selectively to acquire journals, with the knowledge that if a patron selected a journal the immediate library did not have in the stacks, one of the affiliated libraries would have it available for loan. So successful were these efforts that by 1995, OCLC—which offers an international library networking facility—had handled the transactions for 56 million interlibrary loan requests since 1979, 7 million alone in 1994. And—representing the parallel development of sophisticated document delivery networks—the British Library is reported to have processed more than 3 million requests for document copies in 1993.

The Snowball Effect

Though one can observe that it was rising subscription prices that may have spawned—and at least encouraged—the development of library consortia, sophisticated interlibrary loan networks, and the associated emergence of document copy services, these solutions to library management issues also fueled further price increases from publishers. By sharing resources with one another, libraries have successfully been able collectively to buy fewer journal subscriptions. And in response to declining subscription bases, primary publishers not only have continued to raise prices but are currently seeking new revenue streams to compensate for lost subscription revenues.

Among the new revenue streams that primary publishers are currently investigating are the establishment of subscription fees, new licensing fees, and other contractual arrangements with secondary publishers. However, it is unlikely that secondary publishers will be able to pay subscription fees for the more than 50,000[12] journals they review, abstract, and index without raising prices of their own services to subscribers and users.

More Economic Forces at Play

Libraries, of course, have not been the only ones to have felt the pinch of economic pressures in recent years. The 1990s were not kind to many organizations, including secondary publishers, whose printed subscriber bases have been declining for several decades and whose electronic revenues from online distribution, unfortunately, proved highly sensitive to recessionary conditions. As industrial users—who had largely supported database improvements and online developments in the 1980s—underwent acquisition, merger, downsizing, and right-sizing, information acquisition was not spared in the cuts. Though this critical funding base that once contributed to the ongoing expansion of some secondary services did not go away entirely, for many years it ceased to grow at its historic rates, thus undermining development efforts just at the time when secondary publishers were finding it necessary to retool their production systems.

In other cases, erosion in the electronic subscriber bases has occurred from the adoption of CD-ROM databases (often provided at substantially lower overall effective prices than traditional online access or even printed subscriptions) at colleges, universities, and teaching hospitals. In an ironic development, CD-ROM technology has helped to expand the number of users for the databases produced by secondary services, but CD-ROM revenues have not effectively substituted for the lost online (and print) revenues that their adoption has encouraged.

More important, CD-ROM and other electronic technologies have allowed small start-up companies to create less comprehensive but more focused information products targeted to segments of users once served only by large secondary publishers. Though no single entrepreneur can undermine a comprehensive secondary service's total subscription or user base, a number of services collectively have chipped away significant usage. In addition, recent government funding cuts, as well as shifts in industrial R&D supported by government contracting, have in some cases also undermined the direct or indirect funding of certain databases.

Encumbered to some extent by proprietary (often labor-intensive) production systems and interfaces developed during previous generations of computer technology, secondary services and traditional online vendors found themselves scrambling in the 1990s to reestablish the technological lead they once held in electronic publishing. Many secondary services—who have weathered their own downsizing and right-sizing efforts in recent years—are now reengineering their production processes in order to take advantage of off-the-shelf, state-of-the-art applications as means of reducing costs and making a full recovery from the recession they have weathered to date. Traditional online services are also scrambling to update their powerful expert systems to operate with the look and feel of today's PC-based applications.

Where once catching up with the technology was driven by the need of secondary services to keep up with the primary literature, today's secondary services are more inclined to stabilize their coverage of the literature in order to free resources for keeping up with the technology. By stabilizing the coverage, secondary services are, of course, also reacting to very real economic pressure they feel to contain costs.

The recent announcement by some secondary services that they will be expanding their coverage in the future,[13] may be a sign that growth in the number of abstracts published will resume after the effects of the recession are over. But selectivity in coverage seems more likely to be the norm in future years, and the tremendous growth rates experienced in the past are not likely to occur again. Why not?

Print—A Terminal Technology?

As more and more information transfer occurs in electronic form, the notion of comprehensive coverage of the scholarly literature–though noble–becomes less and less viable. Within secondary services it has long been known that the vast majority of those 14 million abstracts published each year (by U.S. services alone) are never read by anyone, but they are included in the publication just in case they might turn out to be useful to later research. In 1971 one observer, reflecting on the price of comprehensive secondary services, noted:

> It is reasonable for the editor to say that each abstract costs the subscriber only a fraction of a penny, while the user can say with equal reason that each abstract costs him a very much larger sum. Both are correct, since the editor is talking about the total number of abstracts, while the subscriber is referring only to those that have been of use to him personally.[14]

Despite assertions such as these, comprehensive coverage was possible only for the very economics reasons implied in the foregoing statement. The cost of including an abstract and indexing pointers to a journal article published in a narrow field (or, for that matter to a journal article whose immediate impact might not necessarily be felt) was viable only because the cost of including that reference could be spread across the entire subscription base of the printed publication.

The keyword is *print*. Printing technology—and its associated subscription-based distribution method—works because subscribers do, in fact, help pay for information that they individually do not consume. The costs of gathering, selecting, assembling, printing, and distributing a publication are spread across all users. Though one can argue that this is not absolutely fair, the net effect is that it reduces the cost of any particular piece of information to any given user, thus making information more affordable to everyone—a notion that makes realistic our societal ideals as to the importance of literacy, education, and scholarly communication.

In an electronic environment, however, users suddenly (and often gleefully) expect to pay only for the particular piece of information they make direct use of in answering their immediate question. This is an economic assumption entirely different from the model that drove the proliferation of printed books, journals, and secondary services. Though at first blush electronic access to information tends to sound as if it will have some great humanistic effect—perhaps even eliminating the perceived barriers between "information haves" and "information have nots" electronic access may actually in the long run prove to be less egalitarian than print.

As more and more access to not only secondary information but primary journals occurs in an electronic context—where users pay only for the information they actually take out of the database or, for that matter, pay only for the article in a primary journal that they actually read—who pays for the articles that are published and the pointers that are developed that apply to only a few individuals working in a narrow discipline or whose value is not appreciated until years after the initial publication? One might argue that publishers should simply establish information unit prices that take the overall usage of the database or journal literature into account. But what user is going to want to pay, say, $100 for an abstract or $1,000 for a single journal article?

"Terminal" technologies are inventions that simply cannot be improved upon. Though print certainly has its format, access, and storage limitations, as an economic model for the distribution of information, it is quite likely the world will never know a better, more fair, or more egalitarian information technology than the printing press. As print gives way to today's political pressures and societal demands for electronic dissemination of information (or in lieu of that, document delivery instead of subscriptions), comprehensive publication of scholarly papers and comprehensive coverage of the scholarly literature may well no longer be economically viable.

Because U.S. secondary services were the first electronic publishers in the world, their performance may be a model for judging what the impacts of electronic information transfer are in the long run. In the tapering off of the number of abstracts being produced by secondary publishers in recent years, we may actually be seeing the early consequences of information dissemination in an electronic world. If so, the Darwinian laws of natural selection and survival of the fittest would seem to be fully operational in the new world order.

Implications for Scientific Communication

It is at this point a given that over the coming years secondary publishers will exert more selectivity in the journals they choose to include in their coverage. The first journals to go will be obscure titles that account for only one or two articles of note per year. Interdisciplinary coverage of journals outside the core field of the secondary service would make the next most likely target for cutbacks, to the extent that such coverage is actually marginal. And finally—if worse comes to worst, and there's no reason to believe this has happened to date—the services would be inclined to cut back within their own core discipline to the journals that are most productive in terms of high-quality material. Or, alternatively, they might actually extend coverage of the crème de la crème journals to be more thorough at least on this aspect of the literature.

Though one might lament that this will mean that important papers published in unlikely sources will not get the exposure they deserve in the community nor be made accessible as a result, greater selectivity is the natural result of cost pressures, at least some of which are due to the differences in print and electronic distribution economic efficiencies. On the other hand, one might also argue that though greater selectivity in coverage might hurt a few users, it will benefit most users in the form of lower prices for individual records than would otherwise be necessary to recoup costs.

Changes in coverage that secondary services are being forced to implement today may be the harbinger of changes that are coming to the primary journal-publishing community as well. User demand for delivery of journal articles online is spurring primary journal publishers to deliver their products directly to users in electronic form . . . one article at a time. Though primary publishers may attempt to retain subscription-based pricing models for this delivery option, users will continue to demand per-article pricing at affordable levels. And if primary publishers do not provide per-article pricing, interlibrary loan and document delivery services will only continue to flourish, creating further erosion in subscription bases.

Ultimately, it seems that primary publishers will reach the same conclusion as secondary publishers. To support electronic distribution demands, they will have to start limiting the number of papers they accept for "publication" in the first place. Though this development might be hailed by some as representing a newfound emphasis on quality rather than quantity in the scholarly publishing and academic rewards tradition, it might initially result in more professors perishing than publishing, as publication becomes more competitive than it already is. Or it is also possible that the Internet might fill the gap, providing a self-publication outlet for more speculative or marginal research results, leaving "the press" to handle the core material.

As for libraries? In the future, librarians may actually get their dream of a world consisting of large electronic archives. But once all information is available in electronic form and readily accessible from every PC equipped with a modem, one might begin to wonder what need there is for libraries at all.

What about Scholars?

Primary publishers, secondary publishers, libraries . . . economic, political, and technological currents. In all of these practical deliberations it's far too easy to give the impression that we have all forgotten what we do or why we do it. Libraries are trying to survive. Primary and secondary publishers are trying to survive. And—though they have gone relatively unmentioned here—scholars too are trying to survive.

In an age when scholars are hardwired to one another on the Internet, does it matter that a research project has to wait for a paper to come via interlibrary loan or document delivery rather than being immediately accessible? Does it matter that the primary journal is still printed on paper when the bulk of day-to-day scientific communication is taking place online? Does it matter that some of the primary-journal contents are not going to get reviewed and indexed because the secondary services cannot afford to expand their coverage any further? The answer, of course, is yes—to all of the above. Yes, it does matter. And the people it matters to are the scholars who are doing the communicating in the first place and who not only want but need their work to get the widespread exposure it deserves. They are also the ones who need to locate and read about the work of others—a process that these days is perhaps just as practically or more expediently done via one-on-one communication on the Internet as by the traditional route of primary and secondary publication usage.

Old Models in a New Age?

Traditionally speaking, the scientific communication process has often been described as a neat, linear progression of events. Information moves along the "chain" from authors to journals to abstractors and indexers to library shelves and back to authors again. But it is a model founded on the economics of print distribution, communications capabilities that predate the telephone, and the assumption that computing technology is not in the hands of individuals.

Though it is very likely that NFAIS will continue to collect statistics on the number of abstracts published by secondary services well into the next millennium, it is also likely that more and more of the documents included in these numbers will be delivered to the user in electronic form, without the users necessarily stopping by the library first to pick them up and without necessarily getting them directly from the primary journal publisher.

If in this process economic forces actually result in the literature explosion of the past turning into literature implosion, some scholars may find that the Internet is, in fact, their last refuge for effective communication with one another, particularly if they are working in a narrow field or in an area where their colleagues are widely distributed throughout the world. Such a future, blending the best of the past with the best of today's technology, is, in the end, perhaps not a bad destiny to predict for the scholarly community as a whole.

Notes

1. A. I. Mihhailov, A. I. Chernyi, and R. S. Gilliarevskii, *Scientific Communications and Informatics* (Arlington, VA: Information Resources Press, 1984), p. 3.
2. The publishers included here are those for whom NFAIS has continuous data; they represent a cross-section of government, not-for-profit, and commercial publishers active in the field of secondary information: American Psychological Association, BIOSIS, Chemical Abstracts Service, Defense Technical Information Center, Ei (Engineering Index), INSPEC, Institute for Scientific Information, Institute for Paper Science, National Agricultural Library, National Library of Medicine, and Smith-Kline Beecham.
3. Bruce M. Manzer, *The Abstract Journal, 1790–1920* (Metuchen, NJ: Scarecrow Press, 1977), p. 117.
4. Ibid., p. 107.
5. Anne Wheaton (Associate Press Secretary to the President), White House press release, December 7, 1958, reprinted in *Abstracting & Indexing Services in Perspective* (Philadelphia: National Federation of Abstracting and Information Services, 1983), p. 186.
6. Malcolm Rigby, "The History of NFAIS," *Abstracting & Indexing Services in Perspective* (Philadelphia: National Federation of Abstracting and Information Services, 1983), p. 9.
7. Robert Collison, *Abstracts and Abstracting Services* (Santa Barbara, CA: American Bibliographic Center Press, 1971), p. 77.
8. Charles Openheim, "The Correlation between Citation Counts and the 1992 Research Assessment Exercise Rating for British Library and Information Science University Departments," *Journal of Documentation* (London: ASLIB, 1995), p. 19.
9. For the twelve organizations whose data are shown in Figure 1, there was a modest 1 percent increase.
10. Ronald Aike, "Periodical Prices 1986–1988 Update," *Serials Librarian* 15, (Haworth Press, 1988), p. 51.
11. James C. Thompson, "Confronting the Serials Cost Problem," *Serials Review*, Spring 1989, p. 42.
12. In a 1994 NFAIS member survey, twenty-two secondary services reported monitoring 47,400 journals as part of their effort to abstract and index the scholarly literature.
13. The Institute for Scientific Information, Derwent, and Elsevier Science have all announced expansion of their coverage in 1995.
14. Collison, *Abstracts and Abstracting Services*, p. 77.

3

Resources for Research and Learning: The Databases of the Research Libraries Group

Linda P. Lerman and Joan M. Aliprand

The Research Libraries Group, Inc. (RLG), is a not-for-profit membership corporation of universities, archives, historical societies, museums, and other institutions devoted to improving access to information that supports research and learning. Founded in 1974 by three universities—Columbia, Harvard, and Yale—and the New York Public Library, RLG became a pioneer in developing cooperative solutions to problems in the acquisition, intellectual control, preservation, and delivery of research information.[1]

RLG offers users access to the Research Libraries Information Network (RLIN) database of bibliographic records, the CitaDel® files of article citations and abstracts, and several specialized research files. All of RLG's databases are accessible worldwide via the Internet (as well as by other communications pathways).

RLG offers three online search services for access to its database: Eureka™, RLIN®, and Zephyr®.

- **Eureka** is easy to use, with context-sensitive help as needed. Its design accommodates a wide range of users, providing guidance for novices without holding back the experienced. Eureka can be reached over the Internet from any terminal or PC that uses VT100 emulation, and can be integrated into library and campuswide information networks (thus supplementing local resources with RLG's).

- **RLIN** was RLG' s first online service, and has been in worldwide use for more than twelve years. A library and archival support system designed primarily for use by trained librarians, RLIN is renowned for its powerful searching capabilities, which include Boolean logic (*and, or, not*) and the ability to refine further a search result by every data element in the bibliographic record. Although Eureka has its own searching commands, RLIN search syntax is also allowed, thus augmenting Eureka's capability.

- **Zephyr** is RLG's Z39.50[2] server, which works with compatible client software running on the user's system to provide access to RLG's resources. Zephyr allows the RLIN bibliographic database and CitaDel files to be accessed using the command syntax of the client system, usually a library' s public access catalog.

RLG member institutions, other institutions, and individuals around the world did 17,420,000 searches of RLG's databases in the academic year 1993/94, and issued 63,560,000 individual commands. More than 18 million searches are projected in 1994/95, with a marked increase in access via the Internet.

Bibliographic Files

The RLIN bibliographic database consists of eight files based on type of material:

AMC (*Archival and Manuscripts Control*): descriptions of archival collections of literary and historical documents, including public records, manuscripts, personal papers, oral histories, and other primary source materials in various formats.

BKS (*Books*): records for printed items cataloged individually, including microform reproductions, government documents, and art and book auction catalogs.

MAP (*Maps*): records for printed and manuscript maps and globes.

MDF (*Computer Files*): records for machine-readable data files, including literary texts, statistical files, and computer programs.

REC (*Recordings*): records for musical and nonmusical sound or historical recordings, including speeches, oral histories, and interviews.

SCO (*Scores*): records for manuscript and printed music, and libretti.

SER (*Serials*): records for items with a recurring pattern of publication (periodicals, newspapers, journals).

VIM (*Visual Materials*): records for photographs, motion pictures, videos, and graphics, including drawings, blueprints, and posters.

These eight files can be used for searching, cataloging, acquisitions, and interlibrary loan through the RLIN library and archival support system. Through Eureka and Zephyr, for searching, they appear as one single bibliographic file (BIB).

The files are updated daily through online cataloging and by regular additions of records, either delivered to RLG on tape or sent by file-transfer protocol (FTP) over the Internet. Contributors to the files are leading research libraries, both academic and public, special libraries, archival repositories, and museums. RLG augments these contributed resources with records describing specialized materials, for example, from the British Library's Incunabula Short Title Catalogue database.

The RLIN bibliographic database retains all records as individual, discrete records containing the contributing library's cataloging; it does not have a "master record" structure. To eliminate the presentation of multiple records for the same title on displays, RLG introduced *record clustering*. Records for the same bibliographic entity are grouped together (*clustered*) by algorithm, and all records in a cluster share access points. One record, that with the highest level of cataloging, is algorithmically chosen as the representative record for the cluster, and is used on certain displays. Only the AMC file (because of the unique nature of archival material) is unclustered.

Because the RLIN bibliographic database consists of individual records grouped into clusters, file size may be reported as *records* (that is, records owned by individual institutions) or as *titles* (corresponding to the clustered groupings of records). In the record/cluster comparison of March 1993, there were 3.05 records per cluster in the BKS file; in the other files, records per cluster ranged from 1.14 to 1.81.

The RLIN bibliographic database contains more than 72 million records in more than 365 languages. Table 1 gives annual counts (in March of each year) of the number of records in each file, as well as the sum total.

Non-Roman Scripts

A unique feature of RLIN is full support for all non-Roman scripts considered essential by the Library of Congress: the combined Chinese/Japanese/Korean (CJK®) character set, and Hebraic and Arabic scripts.[3] RLIN also supports Cyrillic script. RLG was a leader in the automation of East Asian scripts, and is a founding member of the Unicode® Consortium. RLIN CJK was released in September 1983, followed by Cyrillic in 1986, Hebraic script in 1988, and Arabic script in 1991.

The RLIN bibliographic files contain more than one million records with CJK data, including records created for the Chinese Rare Books Project, a cooperative effort of libraries in China and North America. Substantial numbers of Hebraic and Arabic script records have been entered by libraries with preeminent collections of Judaica and Middle Eastern material. The Library of Congress uses RLIN to catalog East Asian monographs and material in Hebraic and Arabic scripts.

Cyrillic script has not been used extensively by U.S. libraries, but two projects with Russian institutions are under way. The Russian State Archival Service (Rosarkhiv), in conjunction with the Hoover Institution at Stanford University, is using RLIN to make information about Russian archival material available

TABLE 1
RLIN Bibliographic Files: Number of Records by File

FILE	Annual Count			
	March 1992	*March 1993*	*March 1994*	*March 1995*
AMC	354,798	380,971	395,137	415,505
BKS	45,147,921	50,962,363	56,414,102	61,215,533
MAP	220,342	236,221	268,307	288,762
MDF	28,098	33,575	35,711	34,867
REC	1,263,643	1,342,217	1,459,163	1,526,314
SCO	985,978	1,069,650	1,177,210	1,231,568
SER	3,434,572	3,633,365	3,921,268	4,191,696
VIM	175,388	188,413	227,645	257,732
Annual Total	51,610,740	57,846,775	63,898,543	69,161,977

worldwide. Bibliographies from the Institute of Scientific Information in the Social Sciences (INION), a unit of the Russian Academy of Sciences, are a CitaDel file (described below).

Authority Files

Four authority files provide online references to the standard headings used in RLIN bibliographic records. These files are accessible both through Zephyr and through the RLIN library and archival support system.

- The *Name Authority File* (NAF) provides the most current information on standard headings for names, uniform titles, and series authorized by the Library of Congress. NAF is updated daily.

- The *Subject Authority File* (SAF) contains authorized Library of Congress subject headings and is updated weekly.

- The *Avery Reference File* (ARF) contains headings used in the *Avery Index to Architectural Periodicals*[4] (a CitaDel file described below). This file was originally a special database known as AREF. When ARF was created from AREF in June 1994, unnecessary references were omitted, causing the drop in number of records between 1994 and 1995. ARF is updated daily.

- The *Art and Architecture Thesaurus* (AAT), an online version of the thesaurus published by the Getty Art History Information Program, contains terms for art and architecture of the Western world from antiquity to the present, as well as terms for archival description. A unique feature of AAT on RLIN is the display of the hierarchical relationships between terms. AAT is updated annually.

TABLE 2
RLIN Authority Files: Number of Records by File

FILE	Annual Count			
	March 1992	*March 1993*	*March 1994*	*March 1995*
NAF	4,784,927	5,112,397	5,112,397	5,784,224
SAF	286,246	309,671	329,447	365,820
AREF / ARF	44,046	48,499	54,315	50,941
AAT	19,449	20,074	27,278	27,278
Annual Total	5,134,668	5,490,641	5,859,781	6,228,263

Table 2 gives the number of records in each file for the years 1992–1995 (measured each March).

CitaDel Files

RLG also offers a range of files containing citations to journal articles, papers in conference proceedings, and other similar material. Document delivery is a feature of this service, hence its name CitaDel: Citations and document Delivery. Table 3 lists its files. Subject coverage ranges from the generic (for example, *Inside Information,* and *Newspaper Abstracts*), to broad topics (*PAIS— Public Affairs Information Service* and *Life Sciences with Bioengineering*), to specialized (*Avery Index to Architectural Periodicals* and *History of Science and Technology*).

CitaDel files are not created by RLG but obtained from external sources; these include

- commercial companies (e.g., University Microfilms, Inc.; Cambridge Scientific Abstracts);

- major information sources (e.g., Library of Congress; British Library's Document Supply Centre); and

- other nonprofit institutions and organizations (e.g., Avery Architectural & Fine Arts Library, Columbia University; Tozzer Library, Harvard University; History of Science Society; Society for the History of Technology).

RLG began adding citation files to its resources in September 1990, with *Ei Page One,* covering engineering and technology. RLIN was the initial access mechanism; the CitaDel files are now available via Eureka. Table 4 shows the size of the CitaDel files for the past three years.

TABLE 3
CitaDel Files: Acronyms and Names

File Identifier	File Name
ABI	ABI/INFORM – Global Edition
ANL	Anthropological Literature
AVE	Avery Index to Architectural Periodicals
DSA	Dissertation Abstracts
EIP	Ei Page One
ENV	Environmental Sciences
FLP	Index to Foreign Legal Periodicals
GPI	U.S. Government Periodicals Index
HAP	Hispanic American Periodicals Index
HLA	Handbook of Latin American Studies
HST	History of Science and Technology
IIN	Inside Information
LIF	Life Sciences with Bioengineering
MRB	Marine Biology – including.Aquatic Sciences & Fisheries Abstracts
NPA	Newspaper Abstracts
PAI	Public Affairs Information Service (PAIS)
PRA	Periodical Abstracts – Research II Edition
RAS	Russian Academy of Sciences Bibliographies
SCP	Scientific Conference Papers
WLI	World Law Index

General Features of CitaDel Access

CitaDel files are searched through Eureka. Access options for a specific file depend on the content of the records (determined by the file supplier). Records in all CitaDel files can be searched by author name and by title, either as a phrase or using keywords; author names and titles are also browsable. If records include subject headings, these can be searched as a phrase (complete or truncated) or with keywords. Subjects as phrases can also be browsed. Abstracts, if present, can be searched using keywords.

Six of the CitaDel files have online document-ordering capability, and extension of this to other files is being planned. The user has a choice of delivery methods: Ariel® (the Internet document transmission software developed by RLG), fax, or regular mail. Ariel provides delivery of documents anywhere in the world at the same price as regular mail. Table 5 contains additional information about the CitaDel files.

TABLE 4
CitaDel Files: Number of Records by File

FILE	Annual Count		
	March 1993	*March 1994*	*March 1995*
ABI	369,840	516,746	676,674
ANL	-	88,963	96,963
AVE	131,588	147,967	166,983
DSA	1,222,377	1,284,736	1,336,456
EIP	1,324,162	1,645,217	1,989,104
ENV	-	478,070	542,672
FLP	69,979	80,692	106,939
GPI	-	-	10,891
HAP	-	178,301	184,527
HLA	-	11,436	21,780
HST	6,071	67,255	76,666
IIN	-	1,438,838	2,508,223
LIF	-	1,003,661	1,143,162
MRB	-	407,295	462,146
NPA	2,058,242	2,611,966	3,183,360
PAI	257,625	271,818	287,888
PRA	1,091,067	1,486,216	1,879,965
SCP	-	595,135	667,795
WLI	43,522	48,898	52,326

The CitaDel Files in Detail

ABI/INFORM—Global Edition (ABI). To support the needs of scholarship, RLG has mounted the larger Global Edition of *ABI/INFORM*, with maximum coverage, from 1986 to present. The file covers all aspects of business, not only topics such as banking, marketing, real estate, and taxation but also other aspects such as the environment, human resources, public administration, and transportation. Sources of articles include business magazines, management and professional publications, academic journals, trade and specialty publications, and international titles. Copies of articles may be ordered online from the file's creator, University Microfilms, Inc.

Anthropological Literature (ANL). *Anthropological Literature,* one of the most important tools for anthropology, covers articles and essays in anthropology and archaeology from 1984. The file is produced by Tozzer Library of Harvard University (which will supply items through normal interlibrary loan procedures).

TABLE 5
CitaDel Files: Summary Information
(Number of records as of April 10, 1995)

CitaDel File	Number of Records	Coverage from	Update Frequency	Records per Update	Features
ABI	683,042	1986	Weekly	1,200	Abstracts; Subject access; Online article ordering
ANL	98,963	1984	Quarterly	2,000	Subject access; ILL from Tozzer Library
AVE	167,637	1977	Daily	55	Subject access
DSA	1,343,001	1861 & 1962 *	Monthly	3,500	Abstracts;* Subject access
EIP	2,002,915	1986	Weekly	6,000	Online article ordering
ENV	562,038	1983	Monthly	5,000	Abstracts; Subject access
FLP	106,939	1985	Quarterly	2,200	Subject access
GPI	20,261	1993	Quarterly	2,500	Subject access; Online article ordering
HAP	184,527	1970	Annually	9,000	Subject access
HLA	21,780	1990	Annually	5,700	Abstracts; Subject access
HST	76,666	1976 & 1987 *	Annually	6,700	Abstracts (some); Subject access
IIN	2,557,803	October 1992	Weekly	19,000	Online article ordering
LF	1,143,162	1983	Monthly	8,000	Abstracts; Subject access
MRB	462,146	1983	Monthly	5,500	Abstracts; Subject access
NPA	3,203,425	1989	Weekly	10,000	Abstracts; Subject access; Online article ordering
PAI	289,200	1980	Monthly	4,000	Abstracts (some); Subject access
PRA	1,896,532	1986	Weekly	5,000	Abstracts; Subject access; Online article ordering
RAS	unknown *	1992	Bimonthly	unknown *	Subject access; Cyrillic script option
SCP	667,795	1988	Bimonthly	6,500	Includes conference announcements plus papers
WLI	52,326	1976	Quarterly	1,000	Abstracts; Subject access
Total	15,469,764				

* See text for details

Avery Index to Architectural Periodicals (AVE). Records describe articles in more than 1,000 periodicals in the fields of architecture and related disciplines (including city planning, landscape architecture, and historic preservation). Coverage is from 1977, but there is partial coverage for older materials. The Avery Library of Columbia University uses RLIN for creation and maintenance of this file; consequently, the *Avery Index* available through Eureka is updated daily. Access points used in the records are maintained in the *Avery Reference File* (described above, under Authority Files).

Dissertation Abstracts (DSA). Records describe doctoral dissertations and master's theses in all areas of academic research from more than 550 universities (including almost all North American graduate schools as well as many European universities). Coverage of dissertations is from 1861; abstracts have been included since 1980. Master's theses were added in 1980, with abstracts included from 1988 on. *Dissertation Abstracts* is produced by University Microfilms Inc., which sells microfilm copies of most of the dissertations and theses.

Ei Page One (EIP). *Ei Page One* is the most comprehensive source for articles and papers on engineering, technology, and related sciences. More than 5,400 national and international engineering journals are indexed, and more than half the citations are for papers from conferences. Access to citations is by author, title (phrase and keywords), and author affiliation. Journals and conference proceedings from all major engineering societies, commercial publishers, research and development organizations, university presses, and government agencies are covered. *Ei Page One* appears earlier and has more than 50 percent more records than *Compendex*Plus*, Engineering Information's other database for the engineering field. Copies of articles may be ordered online from Article Express.

Environmental Sciences (ENV). A comprehensive and multidisciplinary database in the environmental sciences and pollution management, this file covers 1,500 core journals, monographs, and conference proceedings, and provides selective coverage of an additional 5,500 sources. Citations include abstracts that are indexed by keywords. Cambridge Scientific Abstracts, which supplies this file, is the source for three other CitaDel files, *Life Sciences with Bioengineering, Marine Biology including Aquatic Sciences & Fisheries Abstracts,* and *Scientific Conference Papers.*

Index to Foreign Legal Periodicals (FLP). The *Index to Foreign Legal Periodicals,* a product of the American Association of Law Libraries and the Law Library, University of California at Berkeley, covers international law (public and private), comparative law, and the national law of countries with a legal system not based on common law (i.e., countries other than the United States and member nations of the British Commonwealth). More than 450 legal journals are indexed, as well as essay collections, Festschriften, and conference reports. Boalt Express is an independent document delivery affiliate of the Law Library.

U.S. Government Periodicals Index (GPI). This is the standard index to all articles of significant research, reference, or general-interest value found in key periodicals published by agencies of the U.S. government. Access points include author, title, and subject, as well as the Government Printing Office and Superintendent of Documents reference numbers. Copies of documents may be ordered online from the file's creator, Congressional Information Service, Inc.

Hispanic American Periodicals Index (HAP). An international panel of librarians and scholars selects and indexes articles from more than 400 scholarly journals in the social sciences and humanities published in Latin America or treating Latin American and U.S. Hispanic topics. Articles in English, French, German, Italian, Portuguese, and Spanish are included. The *Hispanic American Periodicals Index* is compiled by the Latin American Center, University of California at Los Angeles, which has an independent document delivery service.

Other CitaDel files related to Hispanic and Latin American studies are *Handbook of Latin American Studies* and *World Law Index, Part 1: Index to Hispanic Legislation*.

Handbook of Latin American Studies (HLA). The *Handbook of Latin American Studies*, compiled by the Hispanic Division of the Library of Congress, indexes books, book chapters, and conference papers, as well as articles from more than 800 social science and 550 humanities journals. Many records (60 percent to 75 percent) contain evaluative annotations.

History of Science and Technology (HST). The *History of Science and Technology* (an exclusive CitaDel file) is a composite of two print publications that index the history of science and technology and allied historical fields: *Current Bibliography in the History of Technology* (published annually in the journal *Technology and Culture*) and *ISIS Current Bibliography*. Coverage is from 1976 for citations on the history of science, and from 1987 for those on the history of technology. Citations reflect the contents of more than 600 journals and partial contents of several hundred more, as well as conference proceedings, books, book reviews, and dissertations. Some records include abstracts (which are indexed by keywords).

Inside Information (IIN). *Inside Information* provides author and title access to articles in 10,000 journals, those that are most requested from the British Library's Document Supply Centre. The journals indexed are mainly North American and European titles, and most are in English. Copies of articles may be ordered online from the file's creator, the British Library's Document Supply Centre.

Life Sciences with Bioengineering (LIF). This file from Cambridge Scientific Abstracts provides comprehensive coverage of the medical and biological sciences. More than 1,000 core sources—monographs, conference proceedings, and journals—are fully indexed; another 5,800 secondary sources are selectively indexed. Records include abstracts that are indexed by keywords.

Marine Biology—including Aquatic Sciences & Fisheries Abstracts (MRB). Sponsored by four United Nations organizations, this Cambridge Scientific Abstracts file is the primary database for marine science research. Topics range from aquaculture to underwater acoustics. Citations (which include abstracts) describe articles from more than 6,500 core journals and from secondary sources such as monographs, conference proceedings, and items of so-called *gray literature*. Nine hundred core titles are indexed fully; the remainder, selectively.

Newspaper Abstracts (NPA). Newspaper Abstracts is the source for articles from 27 major regional, national, financial, and ethnic newspapers, including *New York Times, Wall Street Journal, Washington Post, Los Angeles Times*, and *USA Today*. Copies of articles may be ordered online from the file's creator, University Microfilms, Inc.

Public Affairs Information Service (PAI). Public Affairs Information Service, also known as *PAIS*, is one of the world's most widely used indexes. It covers the entire spectrum of public and social policy issues, with an emphasis on factual and statistical information. Records describe articles in more than 1,400 periodicals, and thousands of government documents, statistical directories, reports, pamphlets, conference proceedings, and books, published anywhere in the world. Languages used are French, German, Italian, Portuguese, and Spanish, as well as English. Most records include an abstract.

Periodical Abstracts—Research II Edition (PRA). The *Research II Edition*, with coverage from 1986, is the most complete version of this comprehensive index to popular and academic journals. Records (which include abstracts) describe articles from more than 1,650 general-interest, academic, and business journals, and transcripts of more than 30 news-oriented television programs. Copies of articles may be ordered online from the file's creator, University Microfilms, Inc.

*Russian Academy of Sciences Bibliographies (RAS).*This new CitaDel file was created in summer 1995 and will be available by the time this article appears. It represents an amalgamation of the bibliographies compiled by INION, the Russian Academy of Sciences' Institute of Scientific Information in the Social Sciences. Records describe articles in more than 10,000 periodicals, as well as books, manuscripts, and dissertations. This file covers publications in the humanities and social sciences worldwide, with particular emphasis on the Commonwealth of Independent States and other Eastern European countries. The anticipated initial size is 1.5 million records. Between 15,000 and 20,000 records will be added bimonthly. Document delivery is planned.

Scientific Conference Papers (SCP). This Cambridge Scientific Abstracts file constitutes the premier source of information on scientific, technical engineering, and medical sciences conferences, and the resulting proceedings. Citations for the conferences themselves and individual conference papers are drawn from the conferences' final programs or abstract publications. Records for conferences name the sponsoring organizations, the location of the meeting, and ordering information for publications. Citations for papers include the first author's affiliation, if available.

World Law Index (WLI). The first part of the *World Law Index*, the *Index to Hispanic Legislation,* is compiled by the Hispanic Law Division of the Law Library of the Library of Congress. It contains records describing the national laws, decree-laws, regulations, and the like taken from official legal gazettes of twenty-nine countries: the Spanish-speaking countries of Latin America, plus Haiti, Brazil, the Philippines, Portugal, Spain, and nations from the Portuguese-African region. Abstracts in English are included in records and are indexed by keywords. Microfilm copies of source documents may be ordered from the Photoduplication Division of the Library of Congress.

Research Resources

Several specialized databases that support research in specific scholarly fields are currently accessible through the RLIN library and archival support system.

- *RLG Conspectus® Online* is a subject-based assessment tool for comparing and analyzing existing collection strengths and current collection development. In addition to RLG libraries, it also contains collection evaluation data for members of the Association of Research Libraries participating in the North American Collections Inventory Project, the Library of Congress, the British Library, and other major institutions. The Conspectus is arranged hierarchically by subject divisions, categories, and subject descriptors. Access points include subject, institution, Library of Congress classification number, and collection level.

- The *English Short Title Catalogue* (described below).

- *SCIPIO*, the Art Sales Catalog Database, describes not only art auction catalogs but catalogs of rare book sales. Sales catalogs are valuable sources of information on the provenance of art objects and books, patterns of collecting, and the contemporary art market. The SCIPIO file cites catalogs of sales from as early as 1599 to auctions scheduled but not yet held.

Table 6 gives statistics for the English Short Title Catalogue and SCIPIO for the past four years.

English Short Title Catalogue

The *English Short Title Catalogue* (or *ESTC*), an international union catalog of British, British colonial, and other English-language materials printed before 1801, is an invaluable research tool for scholars of English literature and culture. Each record contains an authoritative description for a specific publication and a list of the institutions holding copies of it.

The *ESTC* database, which has been available on RLIN since 1982, currently contains more than 400,000 records. It is updated daily by the ESTC Editorial Offices at the British Library and at the Center for Bibliographical Studies and Research, University of California at Riverside. More than 1,000 libraries around the world have reported their holdings to the Editorial Offices.

In 1995 the original *Eighteenth-Century Short-Title Catalogue* (for the period 1701–1800) was augmented with 75,000 records describing earlier publications (from the beginning of English printing in 1473 to 1700). These added records

TABLE 6
Selected Special Databases: Number of Records by File

FILE	Annual Count			
	March 1992	*March 1993*	*March 1994*	*March 1995*
ESTC	343,568	367,310	382,222	396,533
SCIPIO	112,184	118,466	124,231	130,645

include 70 percent of the items listed in the short-title catalog compiled by Pollard and Redgrave (1976)[5] and half of those in Donald Wing's extension (1994):[6] the standard reference works for early English printing.

Indexes to the *ESTC* database include place of publication, printer or publisher name, and the date(s) in the imprint. Table 7 gives a breakdown by imprint date, grouped by decade. Because the ESTC Editorial Offices are still actively adding records, this table is not a comprehensive overview of all English letterpress publications to 1800. Furthermore, some imprint statements may include multiple dates (resulting in multiple entries in the index); for example, multivolume works published over several years, or when the date on the title page is not the actual date of publication. The last category in the table, 180–, includes titles with the imprint date 1800, as well as multivolume works that completed publication between 1800 and 1809.

In March 1994 the Consortium of European Research Libraries (CERL) chose RLG to provide database support for its Hand Press Book project. The scope of the HPB database is European printing to 1830. The eventual size of this database is estimated as 4.5 million entries. RLG expects to complete the initial phase of the HPB project, access to the HPB database for CERL member libraries, in late 1995.

Conclusion

The Research Libraries Group, celebrating its twentieth anniversary in 1995, is known worldwide for its research resources and its leadership in the application of automation to facilitate scholarship. Researchers and librarians can access the bibliographic and citation resources described in this article over the Internet, to find out what exists and where it is located.

TABLE 7
ESTC: Imprint Dates by Decade

Decade Span	Records	Decade Span	Records
147-	31	164-	14,105
148-	92	165-	9,201
149-	183	166-	7,087
150-	260	167-	7,149
151-	364	168-	10,996
152-	525	169-	8,391
153-	696	170-	18,629
154-	961	171-	22,846
155-	993	172-	19,613
156-	1,023	173-	19,889
157-	1,400	174-	21,338
158-	1,869	175-	24,790
159-	2,206	176-	29,569
160-	2,792	177-	35,702
161-	3,430	178-	42,129
162-	3,544	179-	67,569
163-	4,120	180-	9,950

Notes

RLIN® (Research Libraries Information Network), CJK® (RLIN' s Chinese, Japanese, and Korean script capability), the RLG Conspectus® (RLG's online measure of collection strength and collection commitments), Ariel®, CitaDel®, Eureka™, and Zephyr™ are all service marks of The Research Libraries Group, Inc. Unicode® is a registered trademark of Unicode, Inc.

1. A current list of RLG members appears in RLG's World Wide Web Page, at URL http://www-rlg.stanford.edu.
2. ANSI/NISO Z39.50 is the *Information Retrieval Application Service Definition and Protocol Specification*, published by the National Information Standards Organization.
3. The Library of Congress coined the acronymn *JACKPHY* for the principal languages—Japanese, Arabic, Chinese, Korean, Persian (or Farsi), Hebrew, and Yiddish—that are written in the essential scripts. RLIN's non-Roman script support, which also includes Cyrillic, is called *JACKPHY Plus*.
4. The *Avery Reference File* and the *Avery Index to Architectural Periodicals* are operating programs of the Getty Art History Information Program and the Avery Architectural & Fine Arts Library, Columbia University.
5. A. W. Pollard and G. R. Redgrave, comps., *A short-title catalogue of books printed in England, Scotland, & Ireland, and of English books printed abroad, 1475-1640*. The second edition, revised and enlarged, was begun by W. A. Jackson and F. S. Ferguson, and completed by Kathleen F. Pantzer. (London: Bibliographical Society, 1976–91).
6. D. G. Wing, comp., *Short-title catalogue of books printed in England, Scotland, Ireland, Wales, and British America and of English books printed in other countries 1641-1700*; the second edition, newly revised and enlarged, was edited by John J. Morrison and Carolyn W. Newlson, and Matthew Seccombe, assistant editor (New York: Modern Language Association of America, 1994).

4

The OCLC Online Union Catalog: An Incomparable Library Resource

Mark Crook

The OCLC Online Union Catalog (OLUC) is arguably the world's foremost bibliographic database in terms of number of participating libraries, depth and breadth of coverage, and ongoing quality control programs.

It has been available to libraries via the OCLC Online System since 1971. This database is essentially a merged, electronic catalog of the bibliographic and holdings information of 6,702 member libraries. Members of OCLC are participating libraries that agree to do all their current cataloging online or by tapeload.

Members as of March 1, 1995, include the following libraries by type: 1,748 academic; 132 research; 872 public; 76 state; 105 state/municipal government; 111 processing centers; 457 law; 450 medical; 534 corporate; 165 theological; 593 federal; 142 school; 531 community/junior college; and 960 others. Overall, more than 20,000 libraries in 61 countries use the Online Union Catalog for acquisitions, cataloging, resource sharing, and reference purposes.

In 1991 the OLUC became available to end-users of libraries through the OCLC FirstSearch service as the WorldCat database. In 1994 WorldCat ranked fifth in total usage of all online databases consulted in the information industry.

As of June 30, 1994, the OLUC contained more than 29 million records and grows at a rate of approximately 31,000 records a week. The records describe books, journals, audiovisual media, maps, archives/manuscripts, sound recordings, music scores, and computer files. A typical record contains a physical description of an item and information about its intellectual content. Also attached to each record in the OLUC is a list of member libraries that hold the item, arranged alphabetically by state or country. The 29 million records in the OLUC have more than 524 million location listings attached to them.

The OLUC has been built with an online shared cataloging system in which participating institutions retrieve and use bibliographic records contributed by other libraries, and enter records for items not already cataloged. Once a library catalogs an item and adds it to the OLUC, the cataloging record becomes available to other libraries for a variety of uses. The database now supports more than 60 related services, tools, and products, ranging from online reference databases to interlibrary loan services.

On average, users succeed in locating records in the OLUC for 94.6 percent of the current items they wish to catalog and must enter new records for only 5.4 percent.

The OLUC grows at a rate of approximately 1 million records every six months. These records are created through the cooperative efforts of OCLC participating libraries, which contribute the preponderance of records, and the Library of Congress, the National Library of Medicine, the U. S. Government Printing Office, and other national libraries (such as the British Library, the National Library of Canada, and the National Library of Australia).

In 1993/94, participating libraries used the OLUC to catalog approximately 23.2 million items online and 18.5 million by tapeloading. That same year, libraries used the OLUC to transact 7.1 million interlibrary loans. The OLUC also supported 134 union lists of serials for 12,856 libraries and 52 specially designed groups totaling 5,379 libraries that used the OLUC for resource sharing.

All OCLC-participating libraries are required to follow specified cataloging standards when contributing information to the OLUC. Ongoing quality-control programs at OCLC and member institutions are aimed at improving catalog listings—eliminating multiple listings for the same item and encouraging compliance with cataloging standards.

OCLC established the Enhance program in 1983. It allows designated libraries to correct or add information to bibliographic records as they catalog materials. The program now includes 118 institutions. In 1993/94, Enhance libraries corrected approximately 100,000 records in the OLUC.

OCLC's Online Data Quality Control Section conducts an aggressive quality control program. Section staff correct some 18,000 records in the OLUC each month. The section also directs software-driven global database quality improvement projects, which have corrected more than 8 million records since 1991.

The CONSER (Cooperative Online Serials) Program has been operational on the OCLC database since 1975. Members of CONSER include 19 OCLC-member libraries, the Library of Congress, the National Library of Medicine, the National Agricultural Library, the National Library of Canada, and OCLC, which provides the host system. CONSER members build and maintain a comprehensive machine-readable database of authoritative bibliographic information for serial publications. The CONSER database, which resides in the OLUC, consists of approximately 500,000 serials records.

The U.S. Newspaper Program, under the aegis of the National Endowment for the Humanities, is creating a computerized catalog on the OLUC of the more than 300,000 newspapers published in North America since 1690. OCLC acts as a liaison with the National Endowment for the Humanities (NEH), the Library of Congress, and other agencies for ongoing project administration and planning. In addition to the online newspaper database, OCLC also publishes on microfiche union lists of newspapers cataloged under the program. To date, 38 states are in various stages of converting to machine-readable form basic bibliographic information for newspapers, ranging from *Publick Occurrences* (1690) to *USA Today*.

The Major Microforms Project, initiated by the Research Libraries Advisory Committee to OCLC, is enabling libraries to catalog significant microform holdings. OCLC developed the capability to collect the cataloging records for these sets (often rare or out-of-print materials) and to make cataloging available offline to any library needing it.

The Linked Systems Project (LSP) involves computer-to-computer links between the Library of Congress, the Research Library Information Network, and OCLC. Ninety-three OCLC member libraries, the Library of Congress Serial Record Division, and OCLC's Online Data Quality Control section transmit new or edited Authority records to the Library of Congress.

The OCLC Online System uses eight cataloging formats derived from the Library of Congress MAchine-Readable Cataloging (MARC) formats for communication of bibliographic information in machine-readable form. Bibliographic records entered into the database must conform to one of these formats, but each one has a great degree of flexibility, as can be seen from the variety of materials that they encompass See Screen Display of a typical MARC record. MARC records contain a physical description of an item and information about its intellectual content. A list of member libraries that hold the item is attached to each record in the database. Individual libraries are represented by a unique three-character symbol that is alphabetically arranged by state or country.

Table 4 provides a frequency distribution of these formats in the OLUC. By far, books make up the largest percentage of the OLUC. Books are defined as any separately published, monographic printed items (books, pamphlets, textual sheets and broadsides, sets of activity cards, etc.), published atlases, theses and dissertations, original microform publications, and individual technical reports. A serial is a publication in any medium, issued in successive parts bearing numerical or chronological designations, and intended to be continued indefinitely. Examples of serials include magazines, newspapers, annual reports, yearbooks, proceedings, and numbered monographic series. Sound recordings include both musical and nonmusical recordings on any media, such as vinyl LPs, CDs, player-piano rolls, reel-to-reel tape, and cassettes. Audiovisual media are items such as conventional motion pictures, filmstrips, slides, transparencies, and video recordings. Three-dimensional materials such as electronic toys and calculators, puzzles, models, dioramas, games, and kits are also embraced by this format. Scores are music in print form (including scores and broadsides), manuscripts of music, songbooks with words only, studies and exercises, score theses, and microform publications of music. Maps are any cartographic material except for atlases (which are considered to be books). Published maps and manuscripts, globes, map theses, microform publications of maps, navigational charts, and LANDSAT images are all examples of records in the map format. Archives/Manuscripts encompass manuscripts of textual material and reproductions of textual manuscripts—letters, wills, business ledgers, and so on. Computer files represent both data stored in machine-readable form and the programs used to process that data. Included in this format are computer programs, interactive fiction diskettes, theses and dissertations in machine-readable form, electronic magazines, and numeric, representational, or text files stored on magnetic tape, disk, or other electronic medium.

Tabular Data

Table 1 shows the distribution of OLUC records by date of publication. The oldest item identified in the database is a terra cotta cone with a Babylonian inscription, cataloged by Dartmouth University (OCLC # 3244509). Through OCLC, libraries have merged their catalogs electronically, making available to libraries and, ultimately, to their patrons, resources that no single institution could possess. Records in the OLUC represent four millennia of recorded knowledge from approximately 2150 B.C. to the present.

Table 2 highlights the distribution of OLUC records by place of publication. Created, assembled and nurtured by libraries for libraries and their patrons, the OLUC reaches more than 20,000 libraries of all types in 60 countries.

Table 3 depicts the rich linguistic diversity of the OLUC. As a result of OCLC's international presence and a higher representation of non-U.S. publications, a higher percentage of records denote items in languages other than English.

Table 4 lists the number of records for each format in the OLUC.

Table 5 lists the number of bibliographic records of composers and authors in the OLUC. Mozart and Bach continue their neck-and-neck race as the most popular personal author in the OLUC; since 1988, Mozart has supplanted Bach as number one. Shakespeare continues as the most frequently occurring writer in the OLUC.

Table 6 lists the most frequently occurring (10,000 or more) topical subject headings (MARC tag 650) in the OLUC. In 1994 there were more than 6 million unique Library of Congress subject headings in the OLUC. To obtain the results in this table, geographic subfields ($z) and trailing form headings ($x) were dropped. A frequency count was then done on the remaining subject heading string.

TABLE 1
Date Ranges of Records in OLUC, 1 January 1995

Imprint Date Range	Number of Records	Percentage of OLUC
2000 B.C. - 1449	3,725	0.0
1450-1699	305,572	1.0
1700-1749	152,243	0.5
1750-1799	328,162	1.1
1800-1849	799,219	2.7
1850-1899	1,945,625	6.6
1900-1909	1,032,330	3.5
1910-1919	731,284	2.5
1920-1929	894,434	3.0
1930-1939	1,039,248	3.5
1940-1949	1,079,315	3.7
1950-1959	1,703,963	5.8
1960-1969	3,199,334	10.9
1970-1979	5,676,842	19.3
1980-1989	7,343,861	25.0
1990-	3,112,242	10.6

TABLE 2
Frequency Distribution of Records in OLUC by Place of Publication, 1 March 1995

Place	Number of Publications	Place	Number of Publications	Place	Number of Publications
Place Unknown	4,599,867	Portugal	71,191	Kenya	13,434
New York	2,827,055	Alabama	70,403	New Brunswick	13,319
United Kingdom	2,576,196	Utah	69,387	Belarus	12,937
West Germany	1,557,631	Eire	64,752	Latvia	12,071
France	1,323,353	Oklahoma	64,177	Panama	11,308
District of Columbia	1,204,942	South Carolina	64,033	Estonia	11,183
California	1,016,653	British Columbia	63,610	Northern Ireland	10,992
Illinois	679,732	Norway	63,237	Various Places	10,224
Massachusetts	662,421	Egypt	61,850	Dominican Republic	9,864
Michigan	557,068	Finland	58,862	Bangladesh	9,817
Italy	555,723	Turkey	56,726	Sri Lanka	9,789
Pennsylvania	516,104	Colombia	51,920	Iceland	9,764
USSR	491,109	South Africa	51,778	Luxembourg	9,423
Ontario	444,357	New Mexico	49,301	Uzbekistan	9,292
Spain	405,607	Chile	49,165	Syria	8,322
Japan	387,556	Hong Kong	48,116	Burma	8,129
United States, place unknown	371,918	Maine	48,026	Kazakhstan	8,084
Texas	327,786	Thailand	47,981	Iraq	8,059
Ohio	302,172	Hawaii	47,977	Honduras	7,702
India	296,842	New Hampshire	47,502	Armenia (Republic)	7,537
Netherlands	275,876	Massachusetts	45,879	Zimbabwe	7,184
Virginia	268,519	Greece	45,022	Czech Republic	7,174
New Jersey	266,079	Rhode Island	44,557	Georgia (Republic)	7,161
Australia	260,786	Nebraska	44,360	Nepal	7,072
Minnesota	253,787	Arkansas	41,927	Morocco	6,919
People's Republic of China	239,344	Romania	41,863	El Salvador	6,729
Switzerland	229,130	Venezuela	41,495	Saudi Arabia	6,700
Mexico	212,740	Bulgaria	40,641	Algeria	6,693
Maryland	209,372	North Dakota	39,980	Paraguay	6,622
Quebec	198,252	Pakistan	39,005	Nicaragua	6,539
Wisconsin	197,030	Peru	38,685	England	6,355
Connecticut	196,861	Alberta	35,624	Azerbaijan	6,162
Brazil	171,853	Lebanon	34,518	Liechtenstein	6,157
Colorado	171,818	Iran	34,241	Tunisia	6,143
Sweden	165,162	New Zealand	33,555	Tanzania	6,056
Florida	164,347	Vermont	32,565	Jordan	5,731
Poland	158,800	Philippines	29,788	Moldova	5,680
Taiwan	157,337	Uruguay	29,234	Papua New Guinea	5,600
North Carolina	156,186	Canada, province unknown	29,119	Newfoundland	5,555
Argentina	152,729	Cuba	28,771	Ethiopia	5,488
Indiana	149,472	Wales	28,405	Haiti	5,419
Missouri	144,383	Alaska	26,537	Ghana	5,165
Austria	137,327	South Dakota	26,199	Jamaica	5,054
Israel	135,428	Ecuador	24,410	Zaire	4,303
United Kingdom, place unknown	134,064	West Virginia	21,896	Zambia	4,238
Scotland	127,146	Nigeria	21,310	Senegal	4,094
Tennessee	125,702	Vietnam	20,987	Kyrgyzstan	4,016
Georgia	124,498	Manitoba	20,694	Kuwait	3,862
Belgium	1 19,199	Wyoming	20,408	Fiji	3,715
Washington	116,420	Puerto Rico	20,124	Cameroon	3,633
Denmark	103,620	Guatemala	20,062	Korea (North)	3,619
Kentucky	96,736	Montana	19,145	Croatia	3,611
Czechoslovakia	94,032	Bolivia	18,852	Albania	3,486
Oregon	91,357	Costa Rica	17,844	Uganda	3,409
Korea, South	91,320	Malaysia	17,257	Trinidad and Tobago	3,392
Iowa	90,462	Nova Scotia	16,966	Monaco	3,365
Yugoslavia	84,302	Delaware	16,239	Sudan	3,326
Indonesia	83,227	Idaho	16,180	Barbados	3,205
Hungary	81,637	Nevada	14,951	Cyprus	2,992
Kansas	78,417	Saskatchewan	14,835	Ivory Coast	2,781
Louisiana	75,025	Singapore	14,809	Tajikistan	2,609
Arizona	73,286	Lithuania	13,793	Malawi	2,572

Table 2 (cont'd)

Place	Number of Publications	Place	Number of Publications	Place	Number of Publications
Botswana	2,529	Pacific Islands	1,172	Gabon	646
Libya	2,407	Somalia	1,056	Oman	638
New Caledonia	2,396	Macau	1,040	Solomon Islands	611
Turkmenistan	2,393	French Polynesia	1,002	Central African Republic	602
Madagascar	2,248	Reunion Islands	996	Vanuate	596
Vatican City	2,064	Mali	939	Ireland	568
Prince Edward Island	2,063	Surinam	935	Seychelles	556
Guyana	1,976	Bermuda Islands	909	Western Samoa	552
Mauritius	1,955	Swaziland	902	Bhutan	539
Slovenia	1,849	Kiribati	894	Chad	536
Mozambique	1,801	Congo (Brazaville)	877	Bahrain	516
Afghanistan	1,781	Martinique	864	American Samoa	508
Guam	1,765	Benin	848	Equatorial Guinea	491
Angola	1,724	Bahamas	843	Argentina	472
Lesotho	1,709	Guadeloupe	803	Saint Lucia	448
Liberia	1,666	Burundi	798	Bosnia and Herzegovina	419
Northwest Territories	1,625	Togo	787	Brunei	397
Slovakia	1,585	Mongolia	785	Grenada	396
Burkina Faso	1,422	Yukon Territory	783	Antigua and Barbuda	384
United Kindom, misc.	1,399	United Arab Emirates	779	Faroe Islands	381
Netherlands Antilles	1,391	Laos	778	Cape Verde	312
Cambodia	1,376	Belize	761	Tonga	307
Virgin Islands	1,375	Mauritania	757	Dominica	257
Rwanda	1,362	Yemen	727	Guinea-Bissau	241
Singapore	1,289	Qatar	726	British Virgin Islands	241
Niger	1,279	Gambia	703	French Guiana	229
Malta	1,272	Guinea	700		
Namibia	1,189	Macedonia	699		

TABLE 3
Languages Represented in OLUC, 1 January 1995

Language	Number of Records	Language	Number of Records
		Ukranian	38,288
		Romanian	37,781
English	19,709,750	Finnish	36,400
French	1,863,282	Hindi	35,388
German	1,824,453	Persian, Modern	32,545
Spanish	1,317,888	Yiddish	29,763
Not Applicable	799,656	Vietnamese	27,630
Russian	610,757	*Undefined*	*23,488*
Italian	539,922	Catalan	22,496
Chinese	429,547	Urdu	22,379
Japanese	351,203	Bengali	21,364
Latin	293,632	Multilingual	17,957
Portuguese	265,372	Slovak	17,170
Dutch	178,983	Tamil	15,262
Hebrew	156,792	Lithuanian	14,000
Arabic	150,127	Slovenian	13,473
Polish	148,189	Sanskrit	13,057
Swedish	124,061	Welsh	12,912
Korean	88,280	Greek, Ancient	12,607
Danish	83,295	Afrikaans	10,623
Indonesian	80,546	Latvian	10,410
Czech	76,887	Icelandic	10,094
Hungarian	70,190	Matathi	9,718
Serbo-Croatian	69,815	Armenian	9,576
Norwegian	54,906	Telugu	9,058
Turkish	51,034	Gujarati	8,180
Greek, Modern	50,943	Malay	7,803
Bulgarian	40,560	Estonian	7,714
Thai	39,352	Panjabi	7,179

Table 3 (cont'd)

Kannada	7,087	Syriac	725
Irish	6,163	Maithili	706
Malayalam	6,016	Indic (Other)	694
Burmese	5,915	Hausa	646
Tibetan	5,296	Newari	641
Belorussian	4,951	Southern Sotho	631
Ottoman Turkish	4,463	Slavic (Other)	564
Oriya	4,223	Sudanese	554
Macedonian	4,026	Papiamento	542
Austronesian (Other)	3,880	Anlgo-Saxon	540
Albanian	3,845	Wendic	534
Georgian	3,829	Egyptian	524
Sinhalese	3,821	Provençal	516
Nepali	3,812	Breton	506
Azerbaijani	3,474	Malagasy	506
Uzbek	3,132	Bashkir	505
Tagalog	3,053	Mayan Languages	497
Papua-Australian	2,994	Prakrit	467
Swahili	2,766	Xhosa	448
Church Slavic	2,624	Central American	444
Kazakn	2,446	Rhaeto-Romance	427
Javanese	2,281	Miscellaneous	421
Sindhi	2,251	Faroese	401
Niger-Kordofania	2,073	Konkani	396
Basque	1,855	Chuvash	371
English, Middle	1,674	Navajo	360
Esperanto	1,655	Bhojpuri	356
Gallegan	1,611	Cree	352
Creoles and Pidgins	1,570	Dakota	349
French, Middle	1,551	Maori	340
Mongol	1,516	Braj	330
Romance (Other)	1,483	Ojibwa	318
Hawaiian	1,465	Quechua	314
Pushto	1,334	Tswana	302
Kirghiz	1,303	Uigur	294
Gaelic (Scots)	1,291	Coptic	279
Sino-Tibetan (Other)	1,231	Nilo-Saharan (Other)	279
Yoruba	1,188	Nyanja	272
Assamese	1,143	Somali	270
South American Indian	1,131	Judaeo-Arabic	265
Ladino	1,125	Kashmiri	253
Frisian	1,094	Manipuri	251
Tajik	1,068	Balinese	248
Cambodian	1,054	Northern Sotho	244
French, Old	1,041	Aramaic	240
Romany	1,008	Caucasian (Other)	236
Pali	989	Kurdish	228
Shona	962	Nahuatlan	224
Turkmen	960	Ethiopic	223
North American Indian	958	Dogri	220
Finno-Ugrian (Other)	935	Baluchi	209
Eskimo	867	Tahitian	207
Rajasthani	833	Afro-Asiatic	202
Moldavian	804	Cherokee	199
German, Middle High	795	Kinyarwandi	198
Tatar	791	Tsonga	194
Ahmaric	783	Ndebele (Zimbawe)	188
Turko-Tataric (Other)	782	Luganda	185
Germanic (Other)	769	Twi	183
Langue D'oc	768	Lahnda	180
Lao	762	Igbo	179
Zulu	739	Choctaw	173

Table 3 (cont'd)

Ilocano	172	Himachali	47
Bemba	167	Manx	47
Mandingo	163	Achinese	46
Akkadian	162	Ossetic	46
Scots	159	Tigre	46
Athapascan Languages	145	Chechen	44
Samoan	138	Judaeo-Persian	44
Mohawk	137	Sumerian	44
Kongo	136	Luo	42
Dravidian (Other)	134	(Kenya and Tanzania)	
Khasi	134	Kachin	41
Muskogee	134	Mende	40
Pahlavi	126	Efik	39
Iranian (Other)	122	Mon Khmer (Other)	38
Algonquian	119	Araucanian	37
Karakalpak	113	Herero	36
Cebuano	112	Mossi	36
Kikuyu	108	Kamba	35
Berber	106	Lozi	35
Guarani	106	Salishan Languages	35
Awadhi	104	Tonga (Nyasa)	35
Maltese	104	Chinook Jargon	34
Apache	101	Magahi	34
Buginese	101	Ndonga	32
Iroquaian Languages	99	Umbundu	32
Karen	97	Avesta	31
Micmac	97	Kurukh	31
Lapp	96	Nubian	31
Bambara	94	Indo-European (Other)	30
Lingala	94	Palauam	30
Minangkabau	92	Temne	30
German, Old High	90	Ponape	29
Dutch, Middle	89	Tumbuka	29
Venda	88	Basa	28
Aymara	86	Fanti	28
Ewe	85	Kabyle	28
Otoman Languages	77	Chagatai	26
Swzazi	77	Hiligaynon	26
Rundi	76	Iban	26
Manobo	73	Sango	26
Siouan Languages	72	Duala	25
Samaritan Aramaic	71	Acholi	24
Fijian	70	Delaware	24
Interlingua	69	Marshall	24
Luba	69	Arawak	23
Marwari	69	Artificial (Other)	23
Gothic	68	Aleut	22
Munda (Other)	68	Carib	22
Wolof	67	Celtic Group	22
Zapotec	63	Pampanga	22
Cornish	61	Songhai	22
Fulah	61	Kuanyama	21
Chamorro	58	Makasar	21
Rarotongan	58	Akan	20
Tonga (Tonga Islands)	58	Fang	20
Gilbertese	57	Tsimshian	20
Galla	55	Kawi	19
Blackfoot	54	Masai	19
Madurese	53	Mongo	19
Cheyenne	52	Zuni	19
Ga	51	Avaric	18
Tigrina	48	Ekajuk	18

Table 3 (cont'd)

Serer	18	Arapaho	10
Dinka	16	Baltic (Other)	10
Grebo	16	Semitic (Other)	10
Lamba	16	Khosian (Other)	9
Persian, Old	16	Kusaie	9
Shan	16	Ugaritic	9
Wakashan Languages	16	Nzima	8
Bikol	15	Sogdian	8
Cushitic (Other)	15	Yap	8
Kpelle	15	Bini	6
Lunda	15	Pangasinan	6
Niuean	15	Vai	6
Tivi	15	Votic	6
Bamileke Languages	14	Chibcha	5
Ijo	14	Ewondo	5
Truk	14	Osage	5
Yao	14	Sukuma	5
Gondi	13	Aljamia	4
Gayo	13	Tereno	4
Kanuri	13	Elamite	3
Adangme	12	Khotanese	3
Caddo	12	Nyamwezi	3
Haida	12	Sidamo	3
Hiri Motu	12	Waray	3
Nyoro	12	Luiseno	2
Selkup	12	Walamo	2
Tlingit	12	Afrihili	1
Dyula	11	Banda	1
Fon	11	Hupa	1
Nyankole	11	Kutenai	1
Susu	11	Wasno	1

TABLE 4
Formats of Materials Cataloged in OLUC, 1 January 1995

Format	Total Records	Percentage of OLUC
Books	25,430,527	84.3
Serials	1,582,777	5.2
Sound Recordings	969,959	3.2
Audiovisual Media	788,332	2.6
Scores	752,712	2.5
Maps	352,757	1.2
Archives/Manuscripts	236,549	0.8
Computer Files	58,307	0.2

TABLE 5
Frequency Distribution of Top 100+ Composers and Authors in OLUC

Name	Number of Citations	Name	Number of Citations
Mozart, Wolfgang Amadeus (1756-1791)	28168	*Thackeray, William Makepeace (1811-1863)*	3503
Bach, Johann Sebastian (1685-1750)	27449		
Shakespeare, William (1564-1616)	23989	*Verne, Jules (1828-1905)*	3473
Beethoven, Ludwig van (1770-1827)	23135	*Wilde, Oscar (1854-1900)*	3283
Brahms, Johannes (1833-1897)	12802	Bernstein, Leonard (1918-1990)	3280
Haydn, Joseph (1732-1809)	12515	Weber, Carl Maria von (1786-1826)	3275
Handel, George Frideric (1685-1759)	11388	Shostakovich, Dmitrii Dmitrievich (1906-1975)	3267
Schubert, Franz (1797-1828)	11211		
Dickens, Charles (1812-1870)	10659	*Longfellow, Henry Wadsworth (1807-1882)*	3265
Tchaikovsky, Peter Ilich (1840-1893)	10124	Grieg, Edvard (1843-1907)	3252
Schumann, Robert (1810-1856)	8514	*Doyle, Arthur Conan (1859-1930)*	3250
Andersen, Hans Christian (1805-1875)	8505	*Milton, John (1608-1674)*	3236
Wagner, Richard (1813-1883)	8172	Rimsky-Korsakov, Nikolay (1844-1908)	3225
Verdi, Giuseppe (1813-1901)	7888	*Ruskin, John (1819-1900)*	3185
Scott, Walter (1771-1832)	7763	Berlioz, Hector (1803-1869)	3159
Mendelssohn-Bartholdy, Felix (1809-1847)	7388	Foster, Stephen Collins (1826-1864)	3101
Liszt, Franz (1811-1886)	7332	*Lytton, Edward Bulwer (1803-1873)*	3031
Goethe, Johann Wolfgang von (1749-1832)	7317	*Hawthorne, Nathaniel (1804-1864)*	3028
Chopin, Frederic (1810-1849)	6762	Bizet, Georges (1838-1875)	2977
Debussy, Claude (1862-1918)	6392	Hindemith, Paul (1895-1963)	2936
Dvorak, Antonin (1841-1904)	6046	*Shaw, Bernard (1856-1950)*	2929
Vivaldi, Antonio (1678-1741)	5944	Purcell, Henry (1659-1695)	2887
Twain, Mark (1835-1910)	5532	*Scribe, Eugene (1791-1861)*	2877
Kipling, Rudyard (1865-1936)	5391	*Gardner, Erle Stanley (1889-1970)*	2806
Strauss, Richard (1864-1949)	5361	Faure, Gabriel (1845-1924)	2779
Stevenson, Robert Louis (1850-1894)	5253	Mahler, Gustav (1860-1911)	2773
Dumas, Alexandre (1802-1870)	5196	Sibelius, Jean (1865-1957)	2773
Prokofiev, Sergey (1891-1953)	5090	*Ingraham, Prentiss (1843-1904)*	2745
Rossini, Gioacchino (1792-1868)	5030	*Carroll, Lewis (1832-1898)*	2728
Balzac, Honore de (1799-1850)	4979	*Conrad, Joseph (1857-1924)*	2709
Ravel, Maurice (1875-1937)	4816	Strauss, Johann (1825-1899)	2682
Hugo, Victor (1802-1885)	4796	*London, Jack (1876-1916)*	2660
Luther, Martin (1483-1546)	4713	*Tennyson, Alfred (1809-1892)*	2625
Defoe, Daniel (1661-1731)	4420	*Swift, Jonathan (1667-1745)*	2617
Stravinsky, Igor (1882-1971)	4415	*Eliot, George (1819-1880)*	2612
Irving, Washington (1783-1859)	4249	*Goldsmith, Oliver (1728-1774)*	2606
Cooper, James Fenimore (1789-1851)	4179	Britten, Benjamin (1913-1976)	2554
Bartok, Bela (1881-1945)	3991	*Hardy, Thomas (1840-1928)*	2508
Telemann, Georg Philipp (1681-1767)	3985	*Ovid (43-17 or 18)*	2487
Grimm, Jacob (1785-1863)	3918	Gershwin, George (1898-1937)	2482
Voltaire (1694-1778)	3916	*James, Henry (1843-1916)*	2454
Saint-Saens, Camille (1835-1921)	3822	Gounod, Charles (1818-1893)	2451
Puccini, Giacomo (1858-1924)	3757	Franck, Cesar (1822-1890)	2436
Rachmaninoff, Sergei (1873-1943)	3747	*Grimm, Wilhelm (1786-1859)*	2413
Poe, Edgar Allan (1809-1849)	3709	*Faulkner, William (1897-1962)*	2393
Donizetti, Gaetano (1797-1848)	3686	Vaughan Williams, Ralph (1872-1958)	2366
Cervantes Saavedra, Miguel de (1547- 1616)	3684	*Zola, Emile (1840-1902)*	2364
Schiller, Friedrich (1759-1805)	3587	*Byron, George Gordon (1788-1824)*	2361
Tolstoy, Leo (1828-1910)	3578	Mussorgsky, Modest Petrovich (1839-1881)	2349
Moliere (1622-1673)	3547	*Dryden, John (1631-1700)*	2344
Christie, Agatha (1890-1976)	3542	*Marx, Karl (1818-1883)*	2332
Dante Alighieri (1265-1321)	3513	*Asimov, Isaac (1920-1992)*	2312

TABLE 6
Subject Headings in OLUC, March 1995

Popular music	75,241	Law reports, digests, etc.	13,921
Education	47,586	Housing	13,734
Geology	45,123	Industrial management	13,502
Piano music	29,466	Political science	13,441
City planning	28,251	Paleontology	13,201
Communism	26,092	Vocational education	13,153
Agriculture	25,912	Ethics	13,097
Law	25,731	Finance, Public	13,039
Botany	25,102	Conduct of life	13,016
Symphonies	24,944	Mines and mineral resources	12,954
Missions	24,941	Gospel music	12,910
Agriculture -- Economic aspects	24,750	Water-supply	12,846
World War, 1939-1945	24,570	Criminal procedure	12,822
Rock music	24,329	Birds	12,764
Jazz	23,149	Natural history	12,745
Economics	20,802	Family	12,597
Organ music	20,581	Civil procedure	12,391
Regional planning	20,223	Forests and forestry	12,166
Hymns, English	20,175	Marriage	12,118
Operas -- Vocal scores with piano	19,641	Vocational guidance	12,101
Socialism	19,509	Trade-unions	12,024
World War, 1914-1918	19,407	Commercial law	11,869
Feature films	19,249	Jews	11,635
Indians of North America	18,759	Slavery	11,520
Registers of births, etc.	18,083	Art, Modern -- 20th century -- Exhibitions	11,494
Ethnology	17,966	Water resources development	11,317
Architecture	17,861	Finance	11,262
Banks and banking	17,306	Operas -- Librettos	11,254
Operas	16,977	Folk music	11,168
Operas -- Excerpts	16,679	Cookery, American	11,133
Cookery	16,506	Women	11,118
Labor laws and legislation	16,485	Education, Higher	11,109
Folklore	16,127	Interpersonal relations	11,105
Taxation	16,104	Real property -- Maps	10,909
Christmas music	15,833	Personnel management	10,837
Christian life	15,751	Frontier and pioneer life	10,786
Sonatas (Piano)	15,683	Sociology	10,732
Songs (Medium voice) with piano	15,346	Public opinion	10,730
Criminal law	15,108	Labor supply	10,730
Songs (High voice) with piano	15,008	Women -- Employment	10,697
Children's stories	14,795	World War, 1939-1945 -- Campaigns	10,641
Large type books	14,757	School management and organization	10,615
Country music	14,574	Agriculture and state	10,588
Art	14,498	Management	10,557
Sermons, American	14,498	Fairy tales	10,539
Songs with piano	14,191	Corporation law	10,245
Civil rights	14,160	Local government	10,212
Philosophy	14,157	Psychology	10,149
Railroads	14,073	Budget	10,095
Orchestral music	14,012	Parent and child	10,068
Reading (Elementary)	13,984	Children's songs	10,019
Music	13,977		

5

EMBASE—The *Excerpta Medica* Database: Quick and Comprehensive Drug Information

Kim Briggs and Ian Crowlesmith

E xcerpta Medica—which since the mid–1970s has become increasingly better known as the online database EMBASE—actually began life as the
Excerpta Medica Foundation, an international nonprofit organization established in the Netherlands in August 1946 by a group of Dutch medical practitioners. The principal aim of the foundation was "to further the progress of
medical knowledge by making information available to the medical and related professions on all significant basic research and clinical findings reported
in any language throughout the world."

The chosen medium was the abstract journal, and to this end original articles
published in well over 1,000 scientific journals were screened, evaluated, and
classified, and abstracts were prepared (where necessary, translated) and indexed for publication in a series of 15 separate abstract journals that were
organized by medical discipline. This proved to be a popular format, and in
the course of the next twenty to thirty years, the number of titles expanded to
more than 40.

By the mid-1960s, it had become clear that a series of manually published
and independently indexed abstract journals could no longer survive unchanged
in the modern world. As was the case for many similar services, automation
provided the key not only to integration of indexed and classified information
into a single database but also to faster processing. From this new computerized production system, EMBASE—as the Excerpta Medica database became
known—has been available online via the major database vendors since 1974,
and is the source of all other EMBASE products (e.g., the EMBASE CD-ROM
Series and EMSCOPES Customised Services).

EMBASE Today

EMBASE is today probably best known for its extensive coverage of the drug-related literature. However, it is and always has been a broadly based biomedical database and provides comprehensive coverage in the following areas:

- Drug research in humans and animals: this covers all phases of drug development, from initial identification or synthesis through market introduction to postmarket surveillance, and includes pharmacology, pharmaceutics, and toxicology.

- Clinical and experimental medicine in all medical specialties, including related disciplines such as psychiatry, physiotherapy, and biomedical engineering and instrumentation.

- Basic biology relevant to human medicine: coverage ranges from anatomy and physiology through virology and microbiology all the way to biochemistry, molecular biology, biotechnology, and genetics.

- Public, occupational, and environmental health; special attention is also given to health policy and management.

- Among a number of specialized topics, forensic science and "drug dependence" (the abuse of illicit drugs, medications, alcohol, and other substances) are also worthy of mention.

Less extensive coverage is provided in the following areas: nursing, dentistry, veterinary medicine, psychology, and alternative medicine. However, articles on these topics are covered if they fall within the range of journals screened for the core topics of EMBASE.

In each of the twenty-one years since its inception in 1974, EMBASE has grown by a quarter of a million items or more, and currently contains over 6 million records (Table 1). Since 1990 more than 350,000 items, drawn from almost 3,500 journals published in 110 countries, have been added each year. Until the early 1990s almost 60 percent of EMBASE records had abstracts; thereafter, as a result of a change in policy to include all author abstracts, this percentage rose in 1994 to almost 80 percent (see also Table 1).

Journal coverage is international, with particular emphasis on European titles (Table 2); the number of EMBASE items derived from these titles is shown in Table 3. An alternative method of assessing the international coverage is by means of the language of the original article: more than twenty percent of the articles covered by EMBASE were originally published in a language other than English, though this percentage is currently running at 10 percent, reflecting the predominance of English as the language of scientific publication, even in countries in which this is not the first language. In all, almost forty languages are represented in EMBASE; the top twenty-three are listed in Table 4.

Traditionally, EMBASE has covered original articles and "significant communications" relevant to its scope; in the past, some journals were covered selectively. By the end of the 1980s, selective coverage was limited to a set of some 600 journals, which are screened for information relevant to drugs, and in 1990 the different types of article were systematized into eight item types, of which articles reporting original results account for 70 percent, (Table 5).

Indexing Using EMTREE, the EMBASE Thesaurus

One of the most powerful features of EMBASE is the thesaurus EMTREE. The EMBASE thesaurus originated in the early 1960s; the subject indexes from the abstract journals were pooled and a single authority list of index terms was defined. Beginning with 25,000 terms, this grew by up to 10,000 terms a year until, by 1990, it comprised some 250,000 preferred subject index terms and nearly 300,000 synonyms. It was toward the end of this period that, for practical reasons, a subset of the most frequently used terms was identified, and formed the basis of the currently used thesaurus, EMTREE, which as well as acting as an authority list also defines the structure and relationships between terms. First introduced in 1988, EMTREE reached its definitive form in 1991, with some 35,000 preferred subject index terms. Since then it has grown at between 500 and 1,500 terms a year, and currently comprises just fewer than 38,000 preferred terms (including nearly 20,000 drugs and chemicals) and more than 150,000 synonyms, the majority of which are nongeneric drug names: the trade names, laboratory codes, and chemical names of the drug preferred terms (Table 6).

EMTREE forms the basis of EMBASE's indexing system. It is organized around some 9,000 EMTREE codes, which facilitate structure searching, and is in addition linked to 210 EMTAGS codes and over 16,000 CAS registry numbers. These codes together account for a significant proportion of the searchable information attached to an average EMBASE item (Table 7). In addition, the subject indexing—divided into drug and medical (nondrug) terms—is enhanced with subheadings (links), drug trade names, and manufacturer names, and—for new concepts, particularly new drugs and chemicals—candidate terms (Table 8).

Although many of the above enhancements have been added to EMBASE only within the past ten years, data have where possible (e.g., by generation of codes) been backposted to earlier segments of the database.

EMBASE Currency

Last (but not least) it must be mentioned that EMBASE is currently one of the most up-to-date bibliographic biomedical databases available. Fully indexed citations and complete author abstracts are distributed to vendors within, on average, fifteen working days (three weeks) after receipt of the journal; this is the culmination of steady improvement over several years (Figure 1).

List of EMBASE Products and Services

EMBASE is disseminated on a variety of media: online, tape, CD-ROM, and print. A summary of products and services is given in Table 9.

TABLE 1
Growth of EMBASE and Abstract Coverage, 1974–1994

Year	Items	Abstracts (%)
1974	237392	137769 (58.0%)
1975	221127	133130 (60.2%)
1976	225794	131863 (58.4%)
1977	238377	133317 (55.9%)
1978	244012	136787 (56.1%)
1979	248121	146218 (58.9%)
1980	242177	150943 (62.3%)
1981	249807	147105 (58.9%)
1982	254657	144486 (56.7%)
1983	225173	136815 (60.8%)
1984	255044	143194 (56.1%)

Note: Year is publication year of original item; additional items with publication years 1973 and earlier are omitted from this overview. Items with publication year 1994 are still being added to EMBASE due to delayed receipt of 1994 journals in 1995.

TABLE 1 (continued)

Year	Items	Abstracts (%)	
1985	275175	171044	(62.2%)
1986	238213	135577	(56.9%)
1987	218367	137039	(62.8%)
1988	269693	178212	(66.1%)
1989	310058	185483	(59.8%)
1990	387361	213970	(55.2%)
1991	349902	215365	(61.6%)
1992	348754	228009	(65.4%)
1993	362754	249595	(68.8%)
1994	357174	284658	(79.7%)

TABLE 2
Journals Covered in EMBASE, 1991–1995

Country	1991	1992	1993	1994	1995
United States/Canada	1126	1064	1112	1105	1149
Europe	1789	1643	1715	1736	1753
Japan	212	184	188	188	190
Rest of the World	418	379	389	369	376
Total	3545	3270	3404	3398	3468

TABLE 3
EMBASE Items by Journal Country, Selected Years, 1975–1994

Country	1975		1980		1985		1990		1994	
United States/Canada	74951	(34.8%)	86966	(36.1%)	117760	(42.9%)	165217	(42.9%)	159558	(45.5%)
Europe	121619	(56.4%)	132460	(54.9%)	134178	(48.8%)	192079	(49.9%)	169548	(48.3%)
Japan	9450	(4.4%)	11638	(4.8%)	14803	(5.4%)	14925	(3.9%)	12710	(3.6%)
Rest of the World	9645	(4.5%)	10005	(4.2%)	8061	(2.9%)	12694	(3.3%)	9053	(2.6%)
Total	215665		241069		274802		384915		350869	

TABLE 4
Original Language of EMBASE Articles, Selected Years, 1975–1994

Language	1975	1980	1985	1990	1994	Total [1]	
English	67.6%	73.5%	79.0%	83.8%	89.5%	4,718,816	79.0%
German	9.5%	7.9%	6.1%	5.1%	3.3%	364,848	6.1%
French	7.1%	5.6%	4.3%	3.5%	2.6%	270,084	4.5%
Japanese	2.4%	2.5%	3.4%	1.7%	1.8%	144,288	2.4%
Russian	3.9%	2.6%	1.4%	1.6%	0.1%	116,264	1.9%
Italian	2.6%	2.8%	2.2%	1.5%	0.7%	115,497	1.9%
Spanish	1.6%	1.0%	0.8%	1.1%	0.8%	66,425	1.1%
Polish	1.3%	0.7%	0.5%	0.1%	0.1%	31,260	0.5%
Dutch	0.7%	0.6%	0.5%	0.7%	0.4%	31,612	0.5%
Portuguese	0.6%	0.4%	0.1%	0.2%	0.2%	17,898	0.3%
Czech	0.4%	0.4%	0.4%	0.2%	0.1%	16,035	0.3%
Chinese	0.0%	0.1%	0.2%	0.2%	0.3%	10,119	0.2%
Hungarian	0.3%	0.2%	0.0%	0.1%	<0.1%	9,302	0.2%
Bulgarian	0.3%	0.2%	0.1%	<0.1%	<0.1%	9,205	0.2%
Danish	0.2%	0.3%	0.3%	<0.1%	<0.1%	8,324	0.1%
Rumanian	0.2%	0.2%	0.1%	<0.1%	<0.1%	6,944	0.1%
Serbocroatian	0.2%	0.1%	0.1%	0.1%	<0.1%	6,890	0.1%
Swedish	0.3%	0.2%	0.1%	<0.1%	<0.1%	6,532	0.1%
Slovak	0.2%	0.2%	0.1%	0.1%	<0.1%	6,181	0.1%
Norwegian	0.2%	0.2%	0.1%	<0.1%	<0.1%	4,984	0.1%
Hebrew	0.1%	0.1%	0.1%	<0.1%	<0.1%	3,180	0.1%
Korean	<0.1%	0.1%	<0.1%	<0.1%	<0.1%	3,075	0.1%
Turkish	<0.1%	<0.1%	<0.1%	0.1%	0.1%	2,946	<0.1%

* As of April 1995; only the most frequently occurring twenty-three languages are shown.

TABLE 5
EMBASE Item Types, 1990–1994

Tag	Definition	1990		1991		1992		1993		1994	
60	article	257983	(66.6%)	242966	(69.4%)	241316	(69.2%)	253149	(69.8%)	257203	(72.0%)
1	review	18121	(4.7%)	19223	(5.5%)	22243	(6.4%)	24996	(6.9%)	24479	(6.9%)
2	short survey	10266	(2.7%)	9423	(2.7%)	9433	(2.7%)	9795	(2.7%)	11140	(3.1%)
61	conference paper	47037	(12.1%)	39169	(11.2%)	39731	(11.4%)	37975	(10.5%)	32322	(9.0%)
3	editorial	8670	(2.2%)	6394	(1.8%)	5309	(1.5%)	5640	(1.6%)	5543	(1.6%)
8	letter	26964	(7.0%)	19099	(5.5%)	16504	(4.7%)	17295	(4.8%)	15865	(4.4%)
63	note	16850	(4.3%)	11758	(3.4%)	11687	(3.4%)	11211	(3.1%)	7933	(2.2%)
62	erratum	2078	(0.5%)	2321	(0.7%)	2789	(0.8%)	2884	(0.8%)	2847	(0.8%)

TABLE 6
Growth of EMBASE Thesaurus and EMTREE, Selected Years, 1975–1995

Nr of preferred terms	1975	1980	1985	1990	1995
EMBASE thesaurus (unstructured authority list)	100,000	150,000	200,000	250,000	–
EMTREE (structured thesaurus)	–	–	–	25,000	37,827

TABLE 7
Searchable Codes per EMBASE Item, 1991–1994

Searchable codes	1991 [1]	1992	1993	1994
EMTREE codes	18.9	24.6	25.6	26.4
EMTAGS codes	7.9	8.7	8.7	8.7
CAS registry numbers	1.9	2.3	2.5	2.6

* Additional EMTREE codes and CAS registry numbers introduced in 1992–1994 are also searchable on most online hosts.

TABLE 8
Searchable Terms per EMBASE Item, 1991–1994

Searchable terms	1991	1992	1993	1994
Drug index terms & links [1]	3.9	5.1	5.3	5.8
Medical index terms & links	9.9	12.8	13.3	13.6
Trade names & manufacturers [2]	0.23	0.25	0.25	0.28
Total (searchable terms per item)	14.0	18.2	18.9	19.7

[1] Because approximately two-thirds of all EMBASE items are "drug items" (items with at least one drug index term), the averages for "drug items" are some 50 percent greater.
[2] Between 10 and 15 percent of all items list at least one trade name or manufacturer; for such items, an average of 2.2 trade names or manufacturers are indexed.

TABLE 9
EMBASE Products and Services

EMBASE Products
      EMBASE
      EMBASE Alert
      EMBASE CD-ROM Series
      Excerpta Medica Abstract Journals
      Core Journals
      EMSCOPES Services
      EMDOCS, the EMBASE Document Delivery Service
User Aids and Services
      EMTREE Thesaurus
      EMBASE List of Journals Indexed
      EMBASE User Manual
      Quick Reference Guides
      Free Training Seminars
      Profile Newsletter
      Help Desks

FIGURE 1
EMBASE Currency, 1990–1995

6

Growth and Change in the World's Biological Literature as Reflected in BIOSIS Publications

Bernadette Freedman

In the early 1920s there was informal and then formal discussion among biologists for several years about the need for a comprehensive abstracting journal for all of biology. The Society of American Bacteriologists had established *Abstracts of Bacteriology* in 1916 (publication started in 1917), and an organizing group of editors of American botanical journals had begun publication of *Botanical Abstracts* in 1918 (both were instigated mainly as replacements for the German abstracting journals that had been cut off by World War I). Even this early in the century, however, biologists from every subdiscipline felt that the literature was growing rapidly and becoming unmanageable. In 1923 the Union of American Biological Societies was inaugurated with the purpose of establishing a biological abstracting journal. This purpose became a reality when the Rockefeller Foundation committed an initial ten-year grant to defray editorial expenses for this endeavor. On December 31, 1925, *Abstracts of Bacteriology* and *Botanical Abstracts* were merged into *Biological Abstracts*.

The company that currently calls itself BIOSIS was incorporated as the not-for-profit organization called Biological Abstracts, Inc., in Washington, DC, early in 1927, shortly after the appearance of the first issue of *Biological Abstracts* in December 1926. The purpose of the corporation, as stated in its articles of incorporation, is "to advance and further the increase, dissemination and use of the knowledge, principles and techniques involved in theoretical and applied biology" by a variety of activities, the first of which is "issuing professional and technical publications." It was in October 1964 that the trustees approved BioSciences Information Service of Biological Abstracts (BIOSIS) as the new official name of the organization, to distinguish it from the publication, *Biological Abstracts* (BA).

By April 1928, the first editor in chief of *BA*, Jacob R. Schramm, was able to report to the Board of Trustees that a worldwide network of more than 3,000 collaborating biologists was preparing abstracts on a volunteer basis from approximately 6,000 serials (Steere, 1976). In its first full year of publication (1927), *BA* contained 12,628 items. In 1928, volume 2 contained 20,124 items. By 1994, *BA* and its companion print product, *Biological Abstracts/Reports, Reviews, Meetings,* contained 551,320 items. Except for a five-month suspension of publication in 1938 caused by a lack of funding, *BA* has been published continuously since its inception. Today, fewer than 50 volunteer abstractors provide only a fraction of the enormous content of *BA*. Most biological research journals now include an abstract for each published article, and BIOSIS uses these in *BA* as originally published. See Table 1 for comprehensive historical data about the content of *BA*.

Growth of *BA* and Creation of a Companion Product

In just five years, between 1958 and 1962, the annual number of items in *BA* grew from 42,575 to 100,858. Still there were more items available to BIOSIS than could be included. In 1965, BIOSIS introduced a second print product, *BioResearch Titles,* which was initially designed to cover the backlog of abstracts that could not be published in *Biological Abstracts.* In 1967 this publication's title was changed to *BioResearch Index.* In 1980 the title was changed again to what it is today, *Biological Abstracts/Reports, Reviews, Meetings (BA/RRM),* and its content was broadened to complement *BA* by supplying unique coverage of international meeting literature, review papers, books, and research reports. See Table 2 for comprehensive historical data about the content of *BA/RRM.* For the purpose of this table and all discussions in this paper, we use the name *BA/RRM* to encompass all three product names.

When "symposia" became a keyword in *BA* in 1960, the coverage it described was meetings that were published in the form of full research articles. With the start of *BioResearch Titles,* we were able to accommodate a rapidly growing segment of the biological literature—meeting and symposia abstracts (i.e., proceedings published only as collections of abstracts). As Table 2 shows, however, we did not specifically segregate meetings from the other title-only coverage in *BA/RRM* until 1985.

As the pace of biological research accelerated through the 1960s and 1970s, the need for rapid exchange of research information grew concomitantly. Often, the slowness of traditional refereed journal publication could not (and still does not today) meet that need. Moreover, researchers exchange important information in face-to-face contacts. Although many of the presentations at meetings may eventually be published as refereed research articles, the immediate record of these proceedings is usually only the set of meeting abstracts. The number of professional meetings and size of their proceedings have grown steadily as a result. BIOSIS must be selective about meeting coverage. We attempt to provide continuity from year to year by covering a predefined set

TABLE 1
Biological Abstracts: Publication Record, 1926–1994

YEAR	VOL.	ABSTRACTS PER VOL.	ABSTRACTS PER YEAR	TOTAL ABSTRACTS TO DATE	PAGES OF ABSTRACTS PER VOL.	PAGES OF ABSTRACTS PER YEAR	PAGES OF INDEXES PER VOL.*	PAGES OF INDEXES PER YEAR*	TOTAL PAGES PUBLISHED*
1926**	none			1,878					
1927	1	12,628	12,628	14,506	1,288	1,288	301	301	1,589
1928	2	20,124	20,124	34,630	1,912	1,912	488	488	2,400
1929	3	23,071	23,071	57,701	2,164	2,164	540	540	2,704
1930	4	30,052	30,052	87,753	2,862	2,862	669	669	3,531
1931	5	30,060	30,060	117,813	3,016	3,016	734	734	3,750
1932	6	26,186	26,186	143,999	2,679	2,679	747	747	3,426
1933	7	22,917	22,917	166,916	2,410	2,410	575	575	2,985
1934	8	21,531	21,531	188,447	2,506	2,506	656	656	3,162
1935	9	20,658	20,658	209,105	2,276	2,276	720	720	2,996
1936	10	22,870	22,870	231,975	2,402	2,402	580	580	2,982
1937	11	20,074	20,074	252,049	2,254	2,254	414	414	2,668
1938	12	17,124	17,124	269,173	1,591	1,591	305	305	1,896
1939	13	18,108	18,108	287,281	1,810	1,810	343	343	2,153
1940	14	17,090	17,090	304,371	1,651	1,651	311	311	1,962
1941	15	28,804	28,804	333,175	2,315	2,315	449	449	2,764
1942	16	23,491	23,491	356,666	2,381	2,381	417	417	2,798
1943	17	25,999	25,999	382,665	2,497	2,497	441	441	2,938
1944	18	23,369	23,369	406,034	2,453	2,453	420	420	2,873
1945	19	23,498	23,498	429,532	2,546	2,546	448	448	2,994
1946	20	21,782	21,782	451,314	2,282	2,282	470	470	2,752
1947	21	26,560	26,560	477,874	2,593	2,593	515	515	3,108
1948	22	26,265	26,265	504,139	2,644	2,644	445	445	3,089
1949	23	30,725	30,725	534,864	3,162	3,162	597	597	3,759
1950	24	38,371	38,371	573,235	3,595	3,595	676	676	4,271
1951	25	38,422	38,422	611,657	3,398	3,398	712	712	4,110
1952	26	37,355	37,355	649,012	3,264	3,264	664	664	3,928
1953	27	33,498	33,498	682,510	3,178	3,178	634	634	3,812
1954	28	30,036	30,036	712,546	2,961	2,961	611	611	3,572
1955	29	30,057	30,057	742,603	2,987	2,987	685	685	3,672
1956	30	36,080	36,080	778,683	3,613	3,613	824	824	4,437
1957	31	40,060	40,060	818,743	3,606	3,606	880	880	4,486
1958	32	42,575	42,575	861,318	3,539	3,539	1,106	1,106	4,645
1959	33	47,547			3,977		1,314		
	34	15,012	62,559	923,877	1,335	5,312	408	1,722	7,034
1960	35	72,532	72,532	996,409	6,082	6,082	2,027	2,027	8,109
1961	36	87,022	87,022	1,083,431	8,131	8,131	2,344	2,344	10,475
1962	37	25,225			2,542		683		
	38	24,514			1,909		663		
	39	25,530			2,033		710		
	40	25,589	100,858	1,184,289	1,950	8,434	736	2,792	11,226
1963	41	25,157			2,029		722		
	42	24,316			1,927		697		
	43	25,604			1,980		823		
	44	25,785	100,862	1,285,151	1,923	7,859	864	3,106	10,965
1964	45	107,103	107,103	1,392,254	8,428	8,428	3,654	3,654	12,082
1965	46	110,119	110,119	1,502,373	8,927	8,927	4,425	4,425	13,352
1966	47	120,102	120,102	1,622,475	10,387	10,387	5,331	5,331	15,718
1967	48	125,027	125,027	1,747,502	11,256	11,256	5,360	5,360	16,616
1968	49	130,024	130,024	1,877,526	11,864	11,864	6,582	6,582	18,446
1969	50	135,010	135,010	2,012,536	13,091	13,091	7,252	7,252	20,343

TABLE 1 (continued)

YEAR	VOL.	ABSTRACTS PER VOL.	ABSTRACTS PER YEAR	TOTAL ABSTRACTS TO DATE	PAGES OF ABSTRACTS PER VOL.	PAGES OF ABSTRACTS PER YEAR	PAGES OF INDEXES PER VOL.*	PAGES OF INDEXES PER YEAR*	TOTAL PAGES PUBLISHED*
1970	51	140,025	140,025	2,152,561	13,753	13,753	7,308	7,308	21,061
1971	52	140,020	140,020	2,292,581	13,948	13,948	8,302	8,302	22,250
1972	53	70,006			6,855		4,255		
	54	70,000	140,006	2,432,587	6,829	13,684	4,357	8,612	22,296
1973	55	70,028			7,060		4,284		
	56	70,008	140,036	2,572,623	7,077	14,137	4,431	8,715	22,852
1974	57	70,006			7,494		3,350		
	58	70,018	140,024	2,712,647	7,514	15,008	3,378	6,728	21,736
1975	59	70,004			7,492		3,487		
	60	70,008	140,012	2,852,659	7,487	14,979	3,442	6,929	21,908
1976	61	70,000			7,270		3,723		
	62	70,004	140,004	2,992,663	6,876	14,146	3,160	6,883	21,029
1977	63	72,500			7,113		3,214		
	64	72,512	145,012	3,137,675	7,093	14,206	3,117	6,331	20,537
1978	65	74,503			7,329		3,097		
	66	74,502	149,005	3,286,680	7,326	14,655	3,061	6,158	20,813
1979	67	77,496			7,715		3,499		
	68	77,496	154,992	3,441,672	7,787	15,502	3,729	7,228	22,730
1980	69	82,500			8,728		4,088		
	70	82,500	165,000	3,606,672	8,582	17,310	3,993	8,081	25,391
1981	71	85,008			8,885		4,204		
	72	85,008	170,016	3,776,688	8,717	17,602	4,178	8,382	25,984
1982	73	87,504			9,111		4,374		
	74	87,504	175,008	3,951,696	9,009	18,120	4,262	8,636	26,756
1983	75	92,508			9,661		4,489		
	76	92,508	185,016	4,136,712	10,125	19,786	4,645	9,134	28,920
1984	77	96,504			10,660		4,870		
	78	96,504	193,008	4,329,720	10,828	21,488	4,920	9,790	31,278
1985	79	110,004			12,260		4,449		
	80	110,004	220,008	4,549,728	12,175	24,435	4,369	8,818	33,253
1986	81	117,504			13,237		4,502		
	82	117,496	235,000	4,784,728	13,302	26,539	4,568	9,070	35,609
1987	83	124,742			14,028		4,821		
	84	125,258	250,000	5,034,728	14,166	28,194	4,887	9,708	37,902
1988	85	128,970			14,710		5,102		
	86	131,030	260,000	5,294,728	14,946	29,656	5,139	10,241	39,897
1989	87	132,776			13,563		5,247		
	88	137,224	270,000	5,564,728	14,063	27,626	5,639	10,886	38,512
1990	89	133,412			13,830		5,460		
	90	141,588	275,000	5,839,728	13,504	27,334	5,303	10,783	38,117
1991	91	137,120			14,485		5,673		
	92	142,880	280,000	6,119,728	14,912	29,397	5,754	11,427	40,824
1992	93	141,050			15,110		5,774		
	94	138,950	280,000	6,399,728	15,139	30,249	5,921	11,695	41,944
1993	95	137,850			15,203		6,170		
	96	143,131	280,981	6,680,709	16,024	31,227	6,140	12,310	43,537
1994~	97^	185,780			17,176		7,777		
	98^^	171,075	356,855	7,037,564	16,648	33,824	7,888	15,465	49,289

* 1927–1978: Index pages counted in the Cumulative Index.
 1979–1994: Index pages counted issue-by-issue.
** Startup year: December was the first and only issue in 1926.
^ First *BA* volume to include cite-only items (no abstracts provided); there were 37,125 cite-only items in it.
^^ Included 32,163 cite-only items.
~ Due to an unexpected surplus of material, 4,747 items with abstracts and 1,128 cite-only items were omitted from the printed *BA* and put only in the online database, *BIOSIS Previews*.

TABLE 2
Biological Abstracts/RRM: Publication Record, 1965–1994

YEAR	VOL.	CONTENTS SUMMARIES ITEMS PER VOL.	MEETINGS & BOOKS ITEMS PER VOL.	TOTAL ITEMS PER VOL.	TOTAL ITEMS PER YEAR	TOTAL ITEMS TO DATE	CONTENTS SUMMARIES PAGES PER VOL.	CONTENTS SUMMARIES PAGES PER YEAR	MEETINGS & BOOKS PAGES PER VOL.	MEETINGS & BOOKS PAGES PER YEAR	TOTAL PAGES OF ITEMS PER VOL.	TOTAL PAGES OF ITEMS PER YEAR	PAGES OF INDEXES PER VOL.	PAGES OF INDEXES PER YEAR	TOTAL PAGES PUBLISHED
1965^	1	·	·	20,001	20,001	20,001	·	·	·	·	···	···	···	···	···
1966	2	·	·	60,016	60,016	80,017	·	·	·	·	···	···	···	···	···
1967^	3	·	·	68,081	68,081	148,098	·	·	·	·	···	···	···	···	···
1968	4	·	·	84,001	84,001	232,099	·	·	·	·	···	···	···	···	···
1969	5	·	·	85,000	85,000	317,099	·	·	·	·	···	···	···	···	···
1970	6	·	·	90,000	90,000	407,099	·	·	·	·	2,519	2,519	4,141	4,141	6,660
1971	7	·	·	90,000	90,000	497,099	·	·	·	·	2,077	2,077	4,868	4,868	6,945
1972	8	·	·	100,000	100,000	597,099	·	·	·	·	2,305	2,305	5,399	5,399	7,704
1973	9	·	·	100,007	100,007	697,106	·	·	·	·	2,307	2,307	5,602	5,602	7,909
1974	10	·	·	100,300	100,300	797,406	·	·	·	·	2,399	2,399	4,274	4,274	6,673
1975	11	·	·	100,000	100,000	897,406	·	·	·	·	2,394	2,394	4,313	4,313	6,707
1976	12	·	·	100,000	100,000	997,406	·	·	·	·	2,796	2,796	3,840	3,840	6,636
1977	13	·	·	105,136	105,136	1,102,542	·	·	·	·	2,928	2,928	3,915	3,915	6,843
1978	14	·	·	56,500			·	·	·	·	1,562		2,006		
	15	·	·	56,500	113,000	1,215,542	·	·	·	·	1,550	3,112	1,994	4,000	7,112
1979	16	·	·	60,000			·	·	·	·	1,637		2,086		
	17	·	·	60,000	120,000	1,335,542	·	·	·	·	1,671	3,308	2,247	4,333	7,641
1980^	18	·	·	62,502			·	·	·	·	3,910		2,474		
	19	·	·	62,502	125,004	1,460,546	·	·	·	·	3,951	7,861	2,367	4,841	12,702
1981	20	·	·	65,004			·	·	·	·	4,153		2,513		
	21	·	·	65,004	130,008	1,590,554	·	·	·	·	4,133	8,286	2,481	4,994	13,280
1982	22	·	·	70,008			·	·	·	·	4,546		2,620		
	23	·	·	70,008	140,016	1,730,570	·	·	·	·	4,566	9,112	2,629	5,249	14,361
1983	24	·	·	75,000			·	·	·	·	4,757		2,710		
	25	·	·	75,000	150,000	1,880,570	·	·	·	·	4,796	9,553	2,785	5,495	15,048
1984	26	·	·	83,508			·	·	·	·	5,344		3,114		
	27	·	·	83,508	167,016	2,047,586	·	·	·	·	5,369	10,713	3,099	6,213	16,926

TABLE 2 (continued)

YEAR	VOL	CONTENTS SUMMARIES ITEMS PER VOL	MEETINGS & BOOKS ITEMS PER VOL	TOTAL ITEMS PER VOL	TOTAL ITEMS PER YEAR	TOTAL ITEMS TO DATE	CONTENTS SUMMARIES PAGES PER VOL	CONTENTS SUMMARIES PAGES PER YEAR	MEETINGS & BOOKS PAGES PER VOL	MEETINGS & BOOKS PAGES PER YEAR	TOTAL PAGES OF ITEMS PER VOL	TOTAL PAGES OF ITEMS PER YEAR	PAGES OF INDEXES PER VOL	PAGES OF INDEXES PER YEAR	TOTAL PAGES PUBLISHED
1985	28	37,500	72,504	110,004	220,004	2,267,590	2,196	4,348	1,953	3,851	4,149	8,199	3,322	6,498	14,697
	29	37,504	72,496	110,000			2,152		1,898		4,050		3,176		
1986	30	42,500	75,492	117,992	235,000	2,502,590	2,408	4,376	1,996	4,089	4,404	8,465	3,460	6,877	15,342
	31	37,500	79,508	117,008			1,968		2,093		4,061		3,417		
1987	32	42,601	79,685	122,286	250,000	2,752,590	2,402	4,922	2,126	4,341	4,528	9,263	3,720	7,721	16,984
	33	44,399	83,315	127,714			2,520		2,215		4,735		4,001		
1988	34	44,194	87,592	131,786	260,000	3,012,590	2,538	4,989	2,376	4,746	4,914	9,735	4,242	8,448	18,183
	35	42,806	85,408	128,214			2,451		2,370		4,821		4,206		
1989	36	44,735	86,407	131,142	261,000	3,273,590	2,439	4,912	2,171	4,305	4,610	9,217	4,361	8,743	17,960
	37	44,265	85,593	129,858			2,473		2,134		4,607		4,382		
1990	38	39,013	85,489	124,502	260,000	3,533,590	2,242	4,552	2,090	4,504	4,332	9,056	4,134	8,825	17,881
	39	39,987	95,511	135,498			2,310		2,414		4,724		4,691		
1991	40	40,146	90,119	130,265	260,000	3,793,590	2,331	4,611	2,306	4,621	4,637	9,232	4,514	9,056	18,288
	41	39,854	89,881	129,735			2,280		2,315		4,595		4,542		
1992	42	31,655	102,645	134,300	260,000	4,053,590	1,836	3,570	2,504	4,920	4,340	8,490	4,617	9,105	17,595
	43	29,345	96,355	125,700			1,734		2,416		4,150		4,488		
1993	44	35,555	96,370	131,925	260,649	4,314,239	2,119	4,135	2,441	4,891	4,560	9,026	4,822	9,539	18,565
	45	33,734	94,990	128,724			2,016		2,450		4,466		4,717		
1994^^	46^^	4,935	189,530	194,465	194,465	4,508,704	1,269	1,269	4,806	4,806	6,075	6,075	7,415	7,415	13,490

~ 1970–1986: Index pages counted in the Cumulative Index.
1987–1994: Index pages counted issue-by-issue.
* Product contents not categorized as Content Summaries and Meetings until 1985.
** Data not available.
^ Product name changes: 1965—*BioResearch Titles*
1967—*BioResearch Index*
1980—*BA/RRM*
^^ Due to an unexpected surplus of material, 1,935 Content Summary and 2,132 Meeting items were omitted from the printed *BA/RRM* and put only in the online database, *BIOSIS Previews*.

of recurring meetings while still responding to the appearance of critical new meeting literature.

Table 3 presents retrospective data about the fourteen largest meetings covered by BIOSIS in 1994. These data are presented according to the publication years of the meeting proceedings. Usually BIOSIS is able to put these items in the corresponding years of *BA/RRM,* but occasionally a meeting occurs so late in the year or the proceedings are received so late in the year that a few of these meetings have appeared in the subsequent year of *BA/RRM.* These data illustrate several key points about the biological literature in general and the meeting literature in particular. Although there are occasional exceptions, the general trend is for constant annual growth in the size of meetings (a parallel to the overall annual growth of the literature). The occasional hiatus in coverage of a specific meeting reflects the fact that meeting proceedings are often published in journal supplements that are not always considered parts of the regular journal subscriptions and can be extremely difficult to acquire. The International Conference on AIDS meeting has become one of the largest meetings in the BIOSIS database, showing how a rapidly emerging research field can quickly become a major numerical factor in the literature.

Factors Affecting Publication Size

The pattern of annual increases in the number of items in *BA* and *BA/RRM* should not be taken as a literal reflection of the year-by-year growth of the biological literature. It has been BIOSIS's challenge to respond over the years to the general push of the literature growth with stepwise increases in our coverage. Occasionally, sizeable corrections had to be taken, for example, the dramatic increase in items covered from 1984 to 1985 (refer to Tables 1 and 2). In contrast, the large increase in *BA* items in 1994 is an artifact of a decision to realign the materials constituting *BA* and *BA/RRM.* To maintain proper perspective about the 1994 increase, it must be compared with the parallel decrease in *BA/RRM* items that year. The objective of the realignment was to permit journals to be covered entirely in *BA* rather than being split across the two products. To accomplish this, we defined a new cite-only item type for *BA* to accommodate articles that lacked abstracts. We also moved full meeting papers published in special issues of journals from *BA/RRM* to *BA.* The big picture is the most reliable one. Figure 1 graphs selected data from Table 1 and Table 2 in five-year clusters to give a summary view of the growth of the BIOSIS database and probably best reflects the growth of the literature itself.

The great advance that *BA* represented over its two progenitors, *Abstracts of Bacteriology* and *Botanical Abstracts,* was that it provided for the regular publication of indexes to its abstracts. Naturally, as the number and complexity of indexes have grown over the years, the number of index pages in the print products has also increased, sometimes not proportionally to the number of text pages they accompany. Several factors have exercised opposing effects on the number of index pages in the print products over the years. Attempting to

TABLE 3
Retrospective Data on Number of Items in Fourteen Largest Meetings Covered by BIOSIS, 1994

Meeting Sponsor	Number of Items by Year of Meeting										
	1984	1985	1986	1987	1988	1989	1990	1991	1992	1993	1994
Society for Neuroscience^	4,694	5,144	6,178	6,712	7,751	8,152	7,821	9,371	9,354	11,026	10,394
Federation of American Societies for Experimental Biology (FASEB)^^	4,789	8,890	5,875	7,210	9,222	6,868	5,878	8,259	6,680	5,251	6,157
Assoc. for Research in Vision and Ophthalmology	*	*	1,757	2,080	2,282	2,636	2,985	3,137	*	*	4,483
Am Gastroenterological Assoc. and Am Assoc. for the Study of Liver Disease and the Gastroenterology Group	1,377	1,636	1,859	2,027	2,419	2,700	2,667	3,373	3,776	4,238	4,204
American Assoc. for Cancer Research	**	**	1,714	1,846	2,074	2,559	2,740	2,634	3,394	3,422	3,960
American Heart Association	1,861	1,951	2,053	2,213	2,590	2,699	3,070	2,975	3,451	3,563	3,617
American Society for Microbiology	1,848	2,339	2,522	2,468	2,494	2,923	2,620	2,592	3,171	3,118	3,536
International Conference on AIDS	***	***	***	***	***	5,269	2,874	3,323	4,570	5,135	3,336
American Society of Nephrology^^^	1,006	1,138	1,254	1,230	1,509	1,706	****	2,368	2,435	2,914	3,204
Biophysical Society	1,121	1,445	1,676	1,602	1,810	1,689	2,109	2,331	3,131	2,329	2,570
American Society for Cell Biology^^^^	1,665	1,871	2,113	1,915	4,937	1,922	2,873	2,803	2,141	2,649	2,834
American Society for Hematology	*	*	*	*	*	*	*	*	*	2,605	2,955
American Pediatric Society and Society for Pediatric Research (Joint Meeting)	1,881	1,862	1,962	1,995	2,207	2,225	2,159	2,256	2,173	2,304	2,382
American Society of Human Genetics	622	700	801	856	1,009	1,112	*	2,879	1,649	*	2,249

^ Both the 1993 and 1994 meetings appeared in 1994 BIOSIS indexes due to late receipt of the 1993 proceedings.

^^ In 1989–1994 (except 1991) the American Society for Biochemistry and Molecular Biology held and published its meeting separately from FASEB.

For 1989–1992, the biochemists/molecular biologists held joint meetings with other societies so that separate item counts are not available. The other separate meetings would add the following item counts had they been held with FASEB: 1993, 1,626 items; 1994, 1,488 items.

^^^ Both the 1991 and 1992 meetings appeared in 1992 BIOSIS indexes due to the timing of receipt of the 1991 proceedings.

^^^^ The 1988 data represent items from a joint meeting of the American Society for Cell Biology and the American Society for Biochemistry. It was held in January 1989 but given a publication date of 1988 by its sponsors.

* BIOSIS did not receive the journal supplements containing these proceedings in these years.

** Journal of publication not covered in these years.

*** The only nonserial meeting on this list; abstracts unavailable to BIOSIS until 1989.

**** Meeting changed its journal of publication this year; BIOSIS was unable to obtain a copy.

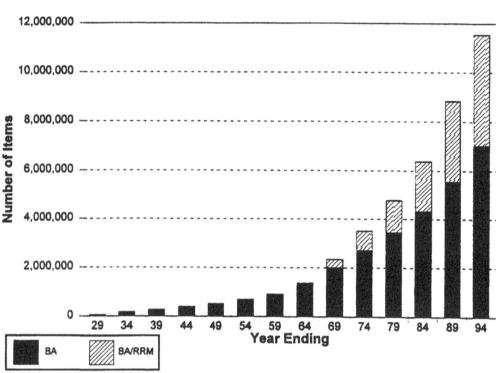

FIGURE 1
Cumulative Growth in BIOSIS Database, Five-Year Intervals, 1929–1994

Note: The initial interval is only thirty-seven months: December 1926 to December 1929.

establish their precise chronology and interrelationships would be extremely difficult. For example, changes in editorial policies have at times increased the number of index terms (e.g., the addition of molecular sequence indexing in 1989 and of document-type keywording in 1994) and at other times decreased the number of index terms (e.g., the changes in keywording practices in the early 1980s that capped certain classes of keywords such as drug affiliations and new genus-species names at a maximum of twenty of each kind per article). Other confounding factors in interpreting these data on pages of indexes (as given in Tables 1 and 2) are that the fonts used to print the indexes and the formats of the indexes have varied over time as we endeavored to improve readability and usability while controlling page printing costs. Finally, the type and number of indexes produced have varied over time.

An Author Index appeared in each issue from 1927 through 1937. From 1938 through 1953, the Author Index appeared only in the annual cumulated indexes. In 1954 it again began to appear in each issue as well as in the cumulations. It became computer-generated in 1957.

Cumulative subject indexes were issued annually for *BA* from its inception. They have evolved in both character and complexity as new technologies facilitated their preparation. A Geographical Index and a Geological Index to

Paleontological Material were begun with the annual cumulation of 1928 (previously, this information had been in the Subject Index) and remained virtually unchanged until 1959, when they were merged back into the Subject Index. The first computerized Subject Index was published with volume 34 in 1959.

In October 1961 the Subject Index changed from a manually prepared index to a computer-generated, permuted-title index called *B.A.S.I.C.* (for *Biological Abstracts Subjects in* Context). At the same time, it took a dramatic step forward by *appearing with the issue*, in addition to being cumulated later). Whereas BIOSIS had begun as an *abstracting* service, by 1961 it had grown into an abstracting *and indexing* service. The biological literature was growing very rapidly. Researchers' information needs were no longer being met by their scanning monthly or semimonthly abstracting journals and waiting for annual subject indexes to obtain targeted literature retrieval. For life-sciences researchers, the indexes had become as important as the abstracts in giving them access to the information they needed in an acceptable time frame.

In April 1964 the computer-arranged CROSS (for Computerized Rearrangement Of Subject Specialties) Index was introduced to provide the cross-referencing information, as an index, that had been included in the abstract sections prior to the introduction of *B.A.S.I.C.* In 1977 the CROSS Index was renamed the Concept Index; it was published through 1984 and then discontinued.

Taxonomic information appeared in the cumulative Systematic Index from 1927 through 1956. In the April 1963 issue, the Systematic Index became computer-generated and was introduced on an issue basis to meet the special needs of biologists for access to information organized from the perspective of large classes of organisms. Its name was changed to Biosystematic Index in 1965, and it underwent a major format change in 1978. In 1974, BIOSIS introduced the Generic Index in each issue, a specialized kind of subject index in which the entries are all genus names, genus-species pair names, or new subgenus names.

Vocabulary Control

In 1969, *BA-Previews* was initiated as the first nonprint product of BIOSIS; it was issued on magnetic tape and made available on a lease basis. In 1975 its name was changed to *BIOSIS Previews*, and it was made commercially available online through Lockheed Information Systems for computer retrieval of information on a royalty basis. It contains all the material from *BA* and *BA/RRM* (including its predecessors), 1969–present. In developing this massive database, which at the end of 1994 contained almost 9.5 million records, vocabulary control was an early critical issue. We developed an in-house authority file called the Master Vocabulary File (MVF), which contains the verified spellings of every term and organism name used in the print indexes (and thus in the online index fields).

Data from the early years of building the MVF are not per se a reflection of the growth of the biological literature. Two forces were at play. First, there was simply the mammoth task of capturing the preexisting vocabulary for the first time; second, there were the neologisms to record. By early 1975, the MVF contained almost 100,000 organism names and nearly 123,000 word entries. Over the next three years, the MVF continued to grow rapidly, most likely reflecting the fact that we still had not captured all the preexisting vocabulary. Since 1979, the growth in the number of new organism entries has been relatively stable (mainly in range of 28,000–38,000 new entries annually). The number of new term entries has been very variable each year, but the general trend has been for much greater growth in these entries than in the number of organism names (see Table 4 and Figure 2).

International Nature of Coverage

Prior to 1960, when the first separate listing of BIOSIS serial sources was published as *Biological Abstracts List of Serials*, records of BIOSIS serial sources appeared only as periodic listings in issues of *BA*, and numerical statistics about these listings were not maintained. Serials are a very dynamic type of publication: their titles change, merge, split, and cease in a constant flux. The editorial policies of journals change, affecting the journals' contents and often leading to changes in the relevance of these contents for BIOSIS products (and thus causing us to add them to or drop them from coverage). Since 1978, we have kept data on the number of archival titles in our serials list versus the active titles that we are monitoring for relevant items. Since 1971, we have kept records of the number of titles actually yielding items in any given year (a subset of the serials monitored). These data are given in Table 5.

The annual number of serials monitored and the number yielding items each year are a reflection both of BIOSIS's editorial policies as well as of the size of literature itself. Well into the 1980s, many marginal titles were maintained in active status that have subsequently been dropped from coverage after a realistic review of their service to the corporate mission. Many of them were extremely unreliable in publication frequency or were received very sporadically. Each year hundreds of excellent new serials vie for inclusion in BIOSIS's coverage. Because the total number of items in the database cannot grow at a proportional rate, we actively manage our serials list to serve best the information needs of the worldwide biological research community.

Although founded by American biologists, BIOSIS has always strived for and maintained a very international scope for its products. Nearly 6,400 serial titles published in 94 countries are currently monitored for relevant material by BIOSIS. These sources include primary research and review journals, conference proceedings, monographs, and books. The geographic origin of these sources is 50 percent from Europe and the Middle East, 31 percent from North America, 14 percent from Asia and Australia, 3 percent from Central and South America, and 2 percent from Africa (see Figure 3).

TABLE 4
BIOSIS Master Vocabulary File Counts, 1975–1994

DATE	NEW ORGANISM ENTRIES	TOTAL ORGANISM ENTRIES	NFW TERM ENTRIES	TOTAL TERM ENTRIES	TOTAL NEW ENTRIES	TOTAL ENTRIES TO DATE
03/75		99,843		122,884		222,726
03/76	76,737	176,580	24,547	147,431	101,285	324,011
12/77	90,151	266,731	44,735	192,166	134,886	458,897
12/78	51,404	318,135	23,815	215,981	75,219	534,116
10/79	38,729	356,864	20,993	236,974	59,722	593,838
10/80	44,596	401,460	24,688	261,662	69,284	663,122
10/81	20,446	421,906	18,471	280,133	38,917	702,039
12/82	41,458	463,364	29,123	309,256	70,581	772,620
12/83	42,169	505,533	26,998	336,254	69,167	841,787
12/84	36,856	542,389	56,058	392,312	92,914	934,701
12/85	44,306	586,695	95,685	487,997	139,991	1,074,692
12/86	35,397	622,092	77,789	565,786	113,186	1,187,878
12/87	37,249	659,341	93,397	659,183	130,646	1,318,524
12/88	37,300	696,641	77,962	737,145	115,262	1,433,786
12/89	32,727	729,368	84,797	821,942	117,524	1,551,310
12/90	34,924	764,292	71,622	893,564	106,546	1,657,856
12/91	34,327	798,619	71,817	965,381	106,144	1,764,000
12/92	32,652	831,271	74,842	1,040,223	107,494	1,871,494
12/93	31,068	862,339	82,508	1,122,731	113,576	1,985,070
12/94	28,847	891,186	109,447	1,232,178	138,294	2,123,364

Although the coverage of our database is strongly international, the statistics on the language distribution of items published in *BA* and *BA/RRM* show a steady growth in the proportion that are in English (see Table 6). These data are again only a reflection of the literature covered by BIOSIS and should not be construed as a parallel of what is happening in the literature except in a very broad sense. While more journals indeed have switched from foreign-language to English-language publication, BIOSIS's acquisition practices have also favored English-language source material during the past decade. We focus on journals with a broad international appeal, usually from major United States or European publishers, which are predominantly in English. The number of Russian-language and Eastern European–language articles has recently been lower simply due to the economic problems in those regions following their substantial political changes.

Subject Patterns in Coverage

Each entry in *BA* (both abstracts and, starting in 1994, cites for cite-only items) and each title in Content Summaries in *BA/RRM* are printed under one

FIGURE 2
Cumulative Growth of BIOSIS Master Vocabulary File, 1975–1994

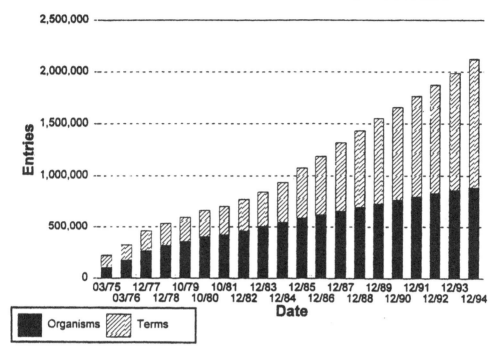

of about eighty-five section headers that corresponds to a main concept heading of the BIOSIS system of concept indexing. Assignment of an item to a main heading is based on the best judgment of the BIOSIS indexer as to the main topic of the item. It is possible to examine the shifts over time in the percentage of total items published under each heading in a given year. Table 7 presents such data for four time points over a thirty-year span. The headings have been grouped into some larger topic areas to facilitate examining them. Also, the headings are presented in each topic section in descending frequency according to their 1994 occurrences. It is obvious that the sort order for these headings would be quite different if 1964 frequencies were used to generate it.

Some of these shifts in subject frequencies in the database are well grounded in the worldwide research effort (such as the rise of "Genetics and Cytogenetics" to the top of the "General Biology and Multidisciplinary Fields" cluster as public and private funding for this specialty accelerated and the concomitant decline of "Aerospace and Underwater Biology" in this cluster after cutbacks in government funding for these subjects). Other shifts are driven by BIOSIS's editorial policies (which attempt to reflect the directions of the research community), such as the decline of the "General Biology" heading in this same cluster. Editorial policy has progressively restricted the appropriateness of this heading as an assignment header in favor of more specific headers.

TABLE 5
Biological Abstracts and *Biological Abstracts/RRM*: Serial Sources, 1960–1994

YEAR	TITLES YIELDING ITEMS^	ACTIVE TITLES^^	ARCHIVAL TITLES^^^	TOTAL TITLES
1960	**	**	**	5,000
1961	**	**	**	**
1962	**	**	**	5,200
1963	**	**	**	5,668
1964	**	**	**	5,968
1965	**	**	**	6,735
1966	**	**	**	6,876
1967	**	**	**	7,405
1968	**	**	**	7,444
1969	**	**	**	7,593
1970	**	**	**	7,663
1971	4,589	7,617	**	9,477
1972	5,224	7,661	**	10,447
1973	4,749	7,980	**	11,196
1974	4,309	8,129	**	11,974
1975	4,230	8,085	**	12,565
1976	4,140	8,312	**	13,300
1977	4,144	8,458	**	12,497
1978	3,972	8,580	4,290	12,870
1979	3,730	8,670	4,424	13,094
1980	3,765	8,934	4,568	13,502
1981	4,247	9,143	4,693	13,836
1982	4,090	9,430	4,810	14,240
1983	4,180	9,521	5,090	14,611
1984	3,543	9,549	5,312	14,861
1985	4,611	9,097	6,122	15,219
1986	5,148	9,242	6,401	15,643
1987	5,195	9,210	6,750	15,960
1988	5,233	9,379	6,998	16,377
1989	5,160	8,892	7,621	16,513
1990	5,133	8,585	7,977	16,562
1991	5,144	7,608	9,038	16,646
1992	4,998	6,956	9,951	16,907
1993	4,674	6,409	10,695	17,104
1994	4,829	6,395	10,935	17,330

* BIOSIS published listings of its serial sources under the following names:
   1960–1969: *Biological Abstracts List of Serials*
   1970–1977: *BIOSIS List of Serials*
   1978–1988: *Serial Sources for the BIOSIS Database*
   1989–1994: *Serial Sources for the BIOSIS Previews Database*
** Data not available.
^ These are a subset of "Active" titles.
^^ These titles were actively monitored for relevant items.
^^^ Includes serials that have ceased publication, changed title, or been superseded.

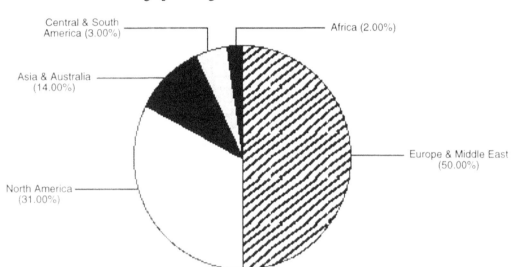

FIGURE 3
Geographic Origin of BIOSIS Serial Sources

Central & South America (3.00%)

Africa (2.00%)

Asia & Australia (14.00%)

Europe & Middle East (50.00%)

North America (31.00%)

Meeting coverage is the major component of *BA/RRM* and today makes up about 20 percent of *BIOSIS Previews* coverage. The large size of some of these meetings can significantly impact both the subject profile and the language frequency of the database. An example of how meeting coverage can affect subject coverage is provided by the first entry in Table 3. In the early 1980s we began covering the annual Society for Neuroscience meeting. This meeting has grown to approximately 11,000 items a year. If we decided to no longer cover this single meeting, the amount of neurology material in the database would drop dramatically and instantaneously. It is undoubtedly true that neuroscience is a now rapidly growing field in the life sciences; however, the size of this single meeting may have created an artifact in Table 7, where the "Nervous System" concept header narrowly outranked the "Neoplasms and Neoplastic Agents" header in the "Animal Physiology and Biomedicine" cluster. Due to receipt late in the year of the 1993 Society for Neuroscience meeting proceedings, its 11,026 items appeared in the 1994 *BA/RRM*, as did the 1994 Society for Neuroscience meeting much later in the product year. Without those additional items, the "Nervous System" concept header would probably be in second place in its cluster. Also, the meeting literature is generally more English-language than the journal-article literature, and increases in meeting coverage are virtually all English-language items, which contributes to the trends seen in Table 6 regarding the language distribution of items.

Since 1991 we have removed journals in peripheral areas of our coverage to make space for crucial new biologically oriented, basic-science research journals. For example, coverage indexable to psychiatry concept headings is lower in the past four years not because of changes in the literature but because we eliminated many psychology-related journals.

TABLE 6
Biological Abstracts and *Biological Abstracts/RRM*: Language Distribution
of Published Items, 1986–1994

Language of Items	Year of BIOSIS Coverage								
	1986	1987	1988	1989	1990	1991	1992	1993	1994
English	84.88%	84.75%	84.62%	85.05%	86.89%	86.75%	90.21%	90.11%	92.00%
Russian	4.01%	3.72%	3.84%	4.34%	3.41%	3.72%	2.07%	2.42%	1.79%
Japanese	2.35%	2.15%	2.28%	2.14%	2.06%	1.98%	1.84%	1.46%	1.30%
German	2.26%	2.36%	2.44%	2.20%	1.90%	2.10%	1.52%	1.45%	1.14%
French	1.99%	2.20%	1.92%	1.83%	1.56%	1.68%	1.33%	1.47%	1.05%
Chinese	0.46%	0.57%	0.57%	0.68%	0.75%	0.81%	0.69%	0.73%	0.77%
Spanish	1.13%	1.10%	1.08%	0.92%	0.86%	0.72%	0.62%	0.64%	0.48%
Italian	0.78%	0.78%	0.85%	0.67%	0.62%	0.58%	0.47%	0.39%	0.30%
Portuguese	0.45%	0.35%	0.34%	0.40%	0.32%	0.28%	0.25%	0.24%	0.29%
All Other	1.70%	2.01%	2.06%	1.76%	1.63%	1.40%	1.00%	1.10%	0.89%

Note: The same nine languages have held the top of the list in all years for which data are available, although some year-to-year shifts in rank have occurred among them.

The Zoological Record

Finally, we must mention the association between BIOSIS and the Zoological Society of London regarding the *Zoological Record (ZR)*, which the Zoological Society had founded in 1864. In 1980, BIOSIS reached an agreement with the Zoological Society of London to become joint publishers of *ZR*. BIOSIS assumed full production, distribution, and financial responsibility; the Zoological Society has an advisory role in editorial policy. At that time, publication of *ZR* was in serious arrears. BIOSIS undertook an ambitious program to bring publication up to date, which became a reality with volume 123 in 1987.

ZR is printed in more than twenty sections according to major phylogenetic classification divisions. Items that pertain to more than one section are printed as often as applicable (for example, an article with information about fish, birds, and mammals would appear in three sections) because each section can be purchased separately. This fact leads to a mismatch between the number of manuscripts indexed (source documents) and the number of citations published, which is always a larger number. The scope of *ZR* is quite narrow compared with that of *BA* and *BA/RRM* and also more "traditional" in nature, so that its research base (and hence its literature) grows much more slowly. These conditions are well reflected in Table 8, which presents publication data about the volumes of *ZR* that BIOSIS has produced.

Acknowledgments

The data presented here exist in many internal BIOSIS repositories. The author wishes to thank the following people for their generous help in researching or verifying data for Tables 1, 2, 3, 4, and 5: Joseph Bosik, Andrea DiDonato, Mary Jean Ehly, Joel Hammond, John Schnepp, Wanda Williams, and Janet Zimmerman.

TABLE 7
Subject Patterns of Biological Publication

Major Concept Heading	Year			
	1964	1974	1984	1994
Total Number of Items	107,103	140,024	360,000	553,452
	Percent of Total Items			
General Biology and Multidisciplinary Biological Fields	24.23	19.28	15.91	17.6
Genetics and Cytogenetics	1.48	2.43	4.49	4.92
Ecology (Environmental Biology)	4.14	3.82	3.17	3.80
Biochemistry	3.16	2.27	1.46	2.39
Cytology and Cytochemistry	1.51	0.91	0.95	1.12
Developmental Biology--Embryology	1.73	1.46	1.39	1.08
Food Technology (non-toxic studies)	1.47	1.12	0.68	0.89
Enzymes	1.66	1.83	0.95	0.86
Biophysics	0.65	1.43	0.51	0.55
General Biology	3.29	0.72	0.34	0.55
Behavioral Biology	0.95	1.39	0.80	0.44
Radiation Biology	2.60	0.71	0.53	0.39
Physical Anthropology: Ethnobiology	0.27	0.34	0.18	0.13
Methods, Materials and Apparatus, General	0.54	0.33	0.13	0.12
Mathematical Biology and Statistical Methods	0.14	0.07	0.03	0.11
Evolution	0.19	0.13	0.09	0.09
Social Biology (includes Human Ecology)	0.08	0.09	0.07	0.08
Aerospace and Underwater Biological Effects	0.37	0.20	0.12	0.05
Laboratory Animals	*	0.03	0.02	0.03
Animal Physiology and Biomedicine	33.97	38.46	51.01	52.16
Nervous System (excludes Sense Organs)	2.47	3.19	4.17	8.33
Neoplasms and Neoplastic Agents	4.42	5.54	7.80	8.25
Pharmacology	6.09	5.38	8.19	6.94
Cardiovascular System	3.60	2.81	5.21	4.94
Toxicology	0.32	3.12	4.02	3.19
Digestive System	1.99	1.10	1.73	2.28
Blood, Blood-Forming Organs and Body Fluids	1.52	1.97	2.08	2.2
Sense Organs, Associated Structures and Functions	0.66	1.12	1.21	2.08
Endocrine System	2.69	4.19	3.90	2.02
Urinary System and External Secretions	0.62	0.73	1.28	1.82
Psychiatry	0.64	2.65	2.83	1.70
Reproductive System	0.59	1.08	1.09	1.49
Bones, Joints, Fasciae, Connective and Adipose Tissue	0.52	0.87	1.16	1.46
Respiratory System	0.39	0.75	1.33	1.30
Metabolism	1.89	1.12	0.56	0.79
Nutrition	0.79	0.68	1.10	0.78
Muscle	0.49	0.61	0.94	0.76
Integumentary System	0.41	0.41	0.47	0.64
Dental and Oral Biology	0.29	0.41	0.83	0.37
Temperature: Its Measurement, Effects and Regulation	0.49	0.40	0.33	0.19
Gerontology	0.19	0.06	0.08	0.16
Physiology, General and Miscellaneous	1.05	0.20	0.23	0.14
Anatomy and Histology, General and Comparative	0.93	0.04	0.04	0.13
Pathology, General and Miscellaneous	0.63	0.11	0.28	0.12
Pediatrics	0.24	0.05	0.14	0.06
Circadian Rhythm and Other Periodic Cycles	0.05	0.07	0.01	0.02

TABLE 7 (continued)

	Year			
	1964	1974	1984	1994
Total Number of Items	107,103	140,024	360,000	553,452
Major Concept Heading	Percent of Total Items			
Microbiology, Immunology, Public Health, and Parasitology	**13.18**	**15.51**	**16.80**	**17.69**
Public Health	1.92	1.85	2.48	4.69
Immunology (Immunochemistry)	2.59	3.46	4.44	3.53
Medical and Clinical Microbiology (includes Veterinary)	2.07	2.83	2.55	3.48
Chemotherapy	1.12	1.19	1.50	1.52
Genetics of Bacteria and Viruses	0.28	0.97	1.07	1.06
Food and Industrial Microbiology	0.68	0.77	0.58	0.88
Physiology and Biochemistry of Bacteria	0.81	1.72	1.18	0.87
Parasitology (includes Ecto- and Endoparasites)	0.80	0.63	0.60	0.45
Virology	0.48	0.74	0.62	0.39
Allergy	0.59	0.21	0.55	0.26
Immunology, Parasitological	0.12	0.22	0.42	0.14
Bacteriology, General and Systematic	0.89	0.28	0.30	0.14
Soil Microbiology	0.26	0.23	0.21	0.11
Tissue Culture: Apparatus, Methods and Media	0.15	0.07	0.02	0.06
Microbiological Apparatus, Methods and Media	0.20	0.07	0.06	0 05
Disinfection, Disinfectants and Sterilization	*	0.07	0.10	0.04
Morphology and Cytology of Bacteria	0.22	0.14	0.11	0.03
Microorganisms, General (includes Protista)	*	0.06	0.01	0.01
Plant Sciences	**16.06**	**14.69**	**9.56**	**7.16**
Plant Physiology, Biochemistry and Biophysics	2.66	5.15	3.57	1.81
Phytopathology	2.65	2.24	1.45	1.11
Agronomy	3.96	1.63	1.16	1.06
Botany, General and Systematic	3.04	2.61	1.33	0.98
Horticulture	1.62	0.88	0.83	0.78
Soil Science	*	0.77	0.50	0.43
Pharmacognosy and Pharmaceutical Botany	0.41	0.57	0.11	0.32
Forestry and Forest Products	1.11	0.24	0.24	0.29
Pest Control, General (includes Plants and Animals); Pesticides; Herbicides	*	0.12	0.05	0.18
Palynology	*	0.17	0.08	0.07
Paleobotany	0.28	0.11	0.11	0.06
Morphology and Anatomy of Plants (includes Embryology)	0.30	0.17	0.08	0.04
Economic Botany	0.03	0.03	0.05	0.03
Animal Sciences	**12.53**	**12.06**	**6.71**	**5.22**
Zoology, General & Systematic (includes Chordata and Invertebrata)	5.67	5.76	2.71	1.71
Invertebrata, Comparative and Experimental Studies	1.73	3.45	2.02	1.40
Animal Production (includes Fur-Bearing Animals)	1.14	0.90	0.76	1.15
Economic Entomology	2.55	1.36	0.85	0.62
Poultry Production	0.41	0.28	0.23	0.22
Veterinary Science	0.92	0.06	0.03	0.06
Paleozoology	0.11	0.16	0.07	0.04
Paleobiology	0.00	0.09	0.04	0.02

* Heading not yet in use.

TABLE 8
Zoological Record: Publication Record, Volumes 115–130

VOL.*	COVERAGE YEAR	PRODTN. YEAR	MANUSCRIPTS INDEXED (Source Documents)	CITATIONS** (Items Published)	PAGES
115	1978	1981	51,840	57,180	6,887
116	1979	1982	56,074	62,285	7,250
117	1980	1982-83	60,392	66,346	7,613
118	1981	1983	58,820	68,836	8,193
119	1982	1984	61,635	72,247	8,965
120	1983	1985	64,218	75,140	9,371
121	1984	1986	61,910	72,685	9,197
122	1985	1986	62,287	72,396	9,599
123	1986	1987	67,281	78,787	10,618
124	1987	1988	69,923	82,176	11,055
125	1988/89^	1989	70,446	81,849	8,884
126	1989/90	1990	68,121	77,533	8,413
127	1990/91	1991	65,069	73,933	8,366
128	1991/92	1992	67,895	77,175	7,634
129	1992/93	1993	66,180	74,930	7,543
130	1993/94	1994	66,166	74,899	8,128

* Data for vols. 1–114 are not available; these volumes were not published under BIOSIS management.
** Citations are more numerous than manuscripts because citations are published in as many organism sections as apply, causing some to be published more than once.
^ Annual coverage policy was revised when production became current; volumes are now numbered to indicate the publication years that make up the bulk of each volume's content.

Reference

Steere, William Campbell. 1976. *Biological Abstracts/BIOSIS, The First Fifty Years*. New York: Plenum Press.

7

Secondary Publishing in Changing Times: Profile of Cambridge Scientific Abstracts

Angela Hitti

F lection also covers natural history files such as *Entomology Abstracts* and *Animal Behavior Abstracts*. Approximately 110,000 unique records with ab- rom the punched card to the Internet, since its founding in 1971 Cambridge Scientific Abstracts has been quick to use the latest technology to achieve its goal of providing access to the world's scientific literature in the biological sciences, environmental sciences, engineering, and related disciplines.

Cambridge Scientific has expanded significantly from the handful of physics and engineering abstracts journals it published in the early 1970s; several of these titles (*Computer & Information Systems Abstracts, Electronics & Communications Abstracts Journal, Solid State & Superconductivity Abstracts*) are now approaching thirty years of continuous publication. Through acquisition, Cambridge became the publisher of titles such as *Pollution Abstracts, Oceanic Abstracts, Conference Papers Index*, and *Mechanical Engineering Abstracts* (formerly *ISMEC*). In the early 1980s a further acquisition made Cambridge the home for some twenty life sciences journals (the Life Sciences Collection, formerly published in England), and also for the United Nations–sponsored *Aquatic Sciences and Fisheries Abstracts (ASFA)* series, which is celebrating its twenty-fifth anniversary in 1995. (See Table 1.)

The Life Sciences Collection—a portfolio of files on closely defined biological topics—is an indicator of research trends (See Table 2). Files such as *Oncogenes & Growth Factors Abstracts, Human Genome Abstracts*, and *Agricultural & Environmental Biotechnology Abstracts* were introduced to capture and disseminate published research in these booming areas. Specialized files include *Chemoreception Abstracts* and *Calcium & Calcified Tissue Abstracts*, as well as well-established publications in broader areas such as neuroscience, genetics, microbiology, virology, and immunology. The scope of the Life Sciences Col-

TABLE 1
Life Sciences/Aquatic Sciences/Pollution Databases Records Added per Year, 1982–1994

Year	Life Sciences	ASFA	Pollution
1994	108,033	36,109	11,000
1993	113,651	32,284	9,000
1992	108,273	33,425	9,000
1991	106,254	34,607	9,000
1990	117,239	34,481	9,000
1989	107,148	31,793	9,000
1988	98,811	23,764	9,000
1987	93,432	22,346	9,000
1986	97,632	23,040	9,000
1985	94,868	30,259	9,000
1984	95,522	33,705	9,000
1983	95,664	21,669	9,000
1982	67,675	21,155	9,000

stracts are added to the Life Sciences Collection database each year; they are drawn from more than 5,000 journals (87 percent of the database), conference proceedings, reports, patents, and monographs.

A partnership of leading research centers and international organizations led by the Food and Agriculture Organization of the United Nations, with Cambridge Scientific Abstracts as the publisher, has created the ASFA family of printed and electronic products. Through the contributions of ASFA partners worldwide, the database encompasses hard-to-find "gray" literature of limited circulation, as well as the traditional scientific journal coverage expected of the premier aquatic sciences abstracting/indexing service. Journal coverage is assigned to ASFA partners, generally on the basis of country or region of publication. More than 6,000 journals are on the ASFA monitoring list. Nonjournal records (conference papers, technical reports, monographs, etc.) make up 31 percent of the ASFA database. Papers published in languages other than English are 22 percent of this international information service.

The environmental sciences are featured in some of Cambridge's best-known

TABLE 2
Life Sciences Collection Subfiles, 1978–March 1995

Subfile Name	Number of Records
Agricultural & Environmental Biotechnology	4,591*
Amino Acids, Peptides & Proteins	133,990**
Animal Behavior	85,039
ASFA Marine Biotechnology	7,824
Biological Membranes	127,221**
Biotechnology Research	45,497**
Calcium & Calcified Tissue	52,834
Chemoreception	25,979
CSA Neurosciences	180,473
Ecology	190,984
Entomology	161,944
Genetics	219,246
Human Genome	18,836
Immunology	222,308
Medical & Pharmaceutical Biotechnology	4,886*
Microbiology A: Industrial & Applied	152,708
Microbiology B: Bacteriology	234,828
Microbiology C: Algology, Mycology, Protozoology	174,691
Nucleic Acids	150,971
Oncogenes & Growth Factors	14,875
Toxicology	144,802
Virology and AIDS	140,624

* From 1993, continues in part *Biotechnology Research Abstracts*.
** Updated through 1993.

publications, including *Pollution Abstracts, Ecology Abstracts,* and *Toxicology Abstracts.* This broad area of research has been expanded to include *Health & Safety Science Abstracts,* the multidisciplinary *Risk Abstracts,* and *EIS: Digests of Environmental Impact Statements,* a journal/database abstracting and indexing all environmental impact statements issued by the U.S. Environmental Protection Agency (450–500 per year). *Pollution Abstracts* began publication with the passage of the National Environmental Policy Act in 1970, and the database now includes 204,000 records.

8

Documenting the World's Sociological Literature: *Sociological Abstracts*

Miriam Chall and Terry M. Owen

The mission of *Sociological Abstracts* (*SA*) remains the same today as it was at its inception in 1953: to document the world's sociological literature, irrespective of the country of publication or language of the source document. Although *SA*'s coverage now includes journal articles, conference papers, dissertations, books, and book and other media reviews, between the years 1953 and 1965 coverage was limited to journal articles and books.

Because diversity is one of sociology's most notable features, the founding editors conceptualized *SA* as a service that would not only transcend linguistic and geographic boundaries but also cut across the various intellectual frames of reference that characterize the discipline, for example, empirical, philosophical, structural-functional, and symbolic interactionist, to name just a few. Moreover, they viewed the entire range of social science literature as the legitimate domain of sociologists.

The resulting editorial policy has as its basis the concept of inclusiveness: to abstract all articles (including research notes and reports) from journals and periodicals that have the term sociology in their titles or that are published by a sociological association or faculty. These constitute the "core" literature. A second tier of tangential sources from closely related disciplines, such as anthropology, education, economics, law, medicine, political science, and psychology, was also identified. Criteria for selection from these publications are contingent on the relevance of the subject matter and/or whether the author is identified as a sociologist.

For the first ten years of publication (1953–1962), the total number of abstracts published was 14,555. In *SA*'s second decade (1963–1972), the number of entries added to the file was 56,782 (an increase of 290.12 percent over the first ten years), and an additional document type—abstracts of conference papers—was included in the mix. (See Table 1.)

TABLE 1
Sociological Abstracts: Document Type and Number of Records Published, 1953–1994

Year	Vol.	Journal Article Abstracts	Book Abstracts	Conference Paper Abstracts	Reviews of Books & Other Media	Dissertation Citations	Total No. of Records
1953	1	609					609
1954	2	870	38				908
1955	3	914	54				968
1956	4	911	43				954
1957	5	888	129				1,017
1958	6	1,177	172				1,349
1959	7	1,418	258				1,676
1960	8	1,543	236				1,779
1961	9	2,047	275				2,322
1962	10	2,728	245				2,973
1963	11	3,652	175				3,827
1964	12	5,534	587				6,121
1965	13	3,585	719				4,304
1966	14	4,766	386				5,152
1967	15	5,164	314				5,478
1968	16	5,479	287	240			6,006
1969	17	5,320	152	565			6,037
1970	18	4,827	88	1,161			6,076
1971	19	5,500	179	866			6,545
1972	20	5,921	236	1,079			7,236
1973	21	5,517	4	1,084			6,605

TABLE 1 (continued)

Year	Vol.	Journal Article Abstracts	Book Abstracts	Conference Paper Abstracts	Reviews of Books & Other Media	Dissertation Citations	Total No. of Records
1974	22	5,220		2,064			7,284
1975	23	5,763		1,837			7,600
1976	24	5,955		1,335			7,290
1977	25	7,033		1,207			8,240
1978	26	6,713		2,679			9,392
1979	27	7,338		1,467			8,805
1980	28	7,406		989	5,725		14,120
1981	29	8,134	98	819	6,819		15,870
1982	30	7,454	94	1,721	6,814		16,083
1983	31	10,549	100	751	7,668		19,068
1984	32	10,797	131	760	7,243		18,931
1985	33	11,120	147	725	6,731		18,723
1986	34	10,192	170	1,847	5,443	485	18,137
1987	35	11,120	160	781	6,213	1,138	19,412
1988	36	11,566	150	823	7,679	1,011	21,229
1989	37	11,611	156	992	5,724	1,049	19,532
1990	38	11,626	143	2,777	7,293	1,071	22,910
1991	39	12,309	152	953	6,797	1,311	21,522
1992	40	12,820	150	1,032	6,820	1,135	21,957
1993	41	13,968	170	663	7,420	971	23,192
1994	42	15,986	175	3,893	7,851	1,477	29,382
TOTALS		273,050	6,573	35,110	102,240	9,648	426,621

The decision to add conference papers was met with a combination of enthusiasm and frustration on the part of *SA*'s users. On the one hand, conference paper abstracts represented the cutting edge of research and provided clues to newly emerging trends within the discipline. On the other hand, the problem of document supply, or lack thereof, complicated matters. Although conference participants were eager to disseminate their ideas to a broad international audience via the *SA* database, they were a bit reluctant to make their papers available prior to consideration by a primary publication. The document supply problem still haunts us, with only about 10 percent of the papers available directly from *SA*. However, many of the presentations do appear in the primary literature, albeit often a year or two later.

Between 1973 and 1982, an additional 101,298 records were added to the database (an increase of 78.4 percent over the previous decade). This surge can be explained in part by the inclusion of a new document type—book reviews (enhanced bibliographic entries of relevant reviews from the journals covered in *SA*)—that not only provided an overview of the most important books being published but allowed users to track who was reviewing whom in what journals, and the time lag between appearance of the book and appearance of the review. Another factor was the increase in the number of actual journals screened, from a meager 41 titles in 1953 to approximately 1,500 in 1982.

In the next twelve years (1983–1994), growth continued at an even greater pace. The number of entries more than doubled from the end of 1982 to 1994, reaching 270,080. Additional document types, including dissertation listings and a variety of media reviews, were added to the file during this period. The pool of relevant journals also expanded to approximately 2,300, with 40 percent of these published outside of North America. (See Tables 2 and 3.)

Beginning in the 1980s, sociology experienced stronger growth in both specialization and cleavages than at earlier times in its development. As new cadres developed, new journals were founded to reflect the specific interests of their constituents. Nowhere is this growth illustrated more dramatically than in the evolution of the *SA* classification scheme. The 19 categories in 1953 had more than doubled, to 46, by 1962. At present, after an additional thirty-three years of annual review and fine tuning, there are 94 categories subsumed under 29 major headings that reflect only the theoretical/methodological aspects of the field. An additional 44 categories correspond to the applied areas of social planning, policy, and development. (See Figures 1–4.)

To accommodate the vigorous developments within the field, it also became apparent that a review was needed of the vocabulary used to index the information *SA* published. The natural-language approach used since 1963 lacked both specificity and scope. A decision was made in 1984 to create an authoritative thesaurus of subject descriptors based on concepts found in the literature. In 1986 the first edition of *The Thesaurus of Sociological Indexing Terms* was published; it contained 3,563 main term descriptors. With its second revision in 1992, the number of main term descriptors increased by 6 percent, and many terms that had appeared in the earlier iterations were either retired or

FIGURE 1
Sociological Abstracts: **Classifications, 1953**

Classification Scheme 1953

01. General
02. General Sociology
03. Methodology
04. Social Structure
05. Formal Institutions
06. Group Dynamics & Intergroup Relations
07. Political Sociology
08. Social Control
09. Social Change
10. Communication
11. Sociology of Primitive Peoples
12. Demography & Ecology
13. Area Studies
14. Social Pathology
15. Applied Sociology
16. Marriage & the Family
17. Social Biology
18. Rural Sociology
19. Industrial Sociology

subsumed under other main terms. Ongoing review and revision of its classification system and indexing terminology allow *SA* to mirror the shifting paradigms within the discipline.

TABLE 2
Sociological Abstracts: Region of Entry Publication, 1953–1994

Year	North America	Central America & Caribbean	South America	Western Europe	Eastern Europe & CIS	Asia & Middle East	Australia & Melanesia	Africa
1953	512 (84.1%)			84 (13.8%)		13 (2.1%)		
1954	630 (72.4%)		6 (0.7%)	180 (20.7%)		44 (5.1%)		10 (1.1%)
1955	633 (69.3%)		19 (2.1%)	216 (23.6%)		41 (4.5%)		5 (0.5%)
1956	643 (70.6%)	8 (0.9%)	16 (1.8%)	203 (22.3%)		41 (4.5%)		
1957	597 (67.2%)	2 (0.2%)		236 (26.6%)	3 (0.3%)	49 (5.5%)		1 (0.1%)
1958	773 (65.7%)	9 (0.8%)	6 (0.5%)	323 (27.4%)	9 (0.8%)	47 (4.0%)	6 (0.5%)	4 (0.3%)
1959	961 (67.8%)	1 (0.1%)	12 (0.8%)	405 (28.6%)	18 (1.3%)	17 (1.2%)	4 (0.3%)	
1960	977 (63.3%)	16 (1.0%)	5 (0.3%)	385 (25.0%)	22 (1.4%)	138 (8.9%)		
1961	1,596 (78.0%)		5 (0.2%)	397 (19.4%)	23 (1.1%)	20 (1.0%)	7 (0.3%)	
1962	2,065 (75.7%)	7 (0.3%)	3 (0.1%)	510 (18.7%)	9 (0.3%)	134 (4.9%)		
1963	2,480 (67.9%)	13 (0.4%)	7 (0.2%)	759 (20.8%)	16 (0.4%)	369 (10.1%)	8 (0.2%)	
1964	3,588 (64.8%)	33 (0.6%)	107 (1.9%)	1,435 (25.9%)	82 (1.5%)	275 (5.0%)	9 (0.2%)	5 (0.1%)
1965	2,212 (61.7%)	9 (0.3%)	43 (1.2%)	983 (27.4%)	95 (2.6%)	210 (5.9%)	32 (0.9%)	1 (0.0%)
1966	2,718 (57.0%)	13 (0.3%)	74 (1.6%)	1,376 (28.9%)	199 (4.2%)	342 (7.2%)	39 (0.8%)	5 (0.1%)
1967	2,937 (56.9%)	18 (0.3%)	71 (1.4%)	1,796 (34.8%)	159 (3.1%)	177 (3.4%)	6 (0.1%)	
1968	2,849 (52.0%)	12 (0.2%)	105 (1.9%)	1,837 (33.5%)	312 (5.7%)	243 (4.4%)	119 (2.2%)	2 (0.0%)
1969	2,733 (51.4%)	27 (0.5%)	64 (1.2%)	1,664 (31.3%)	454 (8.5%)	345 (6.5%)	26 (0.5%)	7 (0.1%)
1970	2,542 (52.7%)	11 (0.2%)	33 (0.7%)	1,519 (31.5%)	416 (8.6%)	257 (5.3%)	35 (0.7%)	14 (0.3%)
1971	2,921 (53.1%)	37 (0.7%)	22 (0.4%)	1,602 (29.1%)	643 (11.7%)	224 (4.1%)	32 (0.6%)	19 (0.3%)
1972	3,086 (52.1%)	89 (1.5%)	76 (1.3%)	1,623 (27.4%)	862 (14.6%)	161 (2.7%)	16 (0.3%)	8 (0.1%)
1973	3,126 (56.7%)	46 (0.8%)	99 (1.8%)	1,628 (29.5%)	289 (5.2%)	263 (4.8%)	52 (0.9%)	14 (0.3%)

Region of Publication

TABLE 2 (continued)

Year	North America	Central America & Caribbean	South America	Western Europe	Eastern Europe & CIS	Asia & Middle East	Australia & Melanesia	Africa
1974	2,843 (54.5%)	23 (0.4%)	58 (1.1%)	1,296 (24.8%)	545 (10.4%)	356 (6.8%)	66 (1.3%)	33 (0.6%)
1975	3,098 (53.8%)	30 (0.5%)	50 (0.9%)	1,881 (32.6%)	389 (6.7%)	207 (3.6%)	104 (1.8%)	4 (0.1%)
1976	3,639 (61.1%)	44 (0.7%)	31 (0.5%)	1,561 (26.2%)	218 (3.7%)	294 (4.9%)	110 (1.8%)	58 (1.0%)
1977	4,025 (57.2%)	14 (0.2%)	19 (0.3%)	2,056 (29.2%)	408 (5.8%)	290 (4.1%)	93 (1.3%)	128 (1.8%)
1978	4,175 (62.2%)	22 (0.3%)	31 (0.5%)	1,925 (28.7%)	230 (3.4%)	178 (2.7%)	116 (1.7%)	36 (0.5%)
1979	4,340 (59.1%)	15 (0.2%)	25 (0.3%)	2,394 (32.6%)	326 (4.4%)	147 (2.0%)	60 (0.8%)	31 (0.4%)
1980	8,613 (59.6%)	70 (0.5%)	58 (0.4%)	4,384 (30.3%)	805 (5.6%)	319 (2.2%)	112 (0.8%)	86 (0.6%)
1981	9,285 (56.6%)	48 (0.3%)	66 (0.4%)	5,119 (31.2%)	1,303 (7.9%)	237 (1.4%)	215 (1.3%)	122 (0.7%)
1982	9,916 (63.2%)	5 (0.0%)	67 (0.4%)	4,621 (29.4%)	579 (3.7%)	245 (1.6%)	239 (1.5%)	26 (0.2%)
1983	9,972 (54.7%)	18 (0.1%)	49 (0.3%)	6,396 (35.1%)	1,030 (5.7%)	397 (2.2%)	154 (0.8%)	201 (1.1%)
1984	10,200 (56.5%)	16 (0.1%)	119 (0.7%)	6,148 (34.1%)	766 (4.2%)	357 (2.0%)	362 (2.0%)	72 (0.4%)
1985	9,500 (53.2%)	60 (0.3%)	115 (0.6%)	6,437 (36.1%)	906 (5.1%)	481 (2.7%)	256 (1.4%)	96 (0.5%)
1986	9,675 (60.0%)	60 (0.4%)	61 (0.4%)	5,198 (32.2%)	361 (2.2%)	525 (3.3%)	182 (1.1%)	58 (0.4%)
1987	10,438 (56.5%)	64 (0.3%)	93 (0.5%)	6,025 (32.6%)	777 (4.2%)	578 (3.1%)	381 (2.1%)	115 (0.6%)
1988	11,276 (55.7%)	28 (0.1%)	129 (0.6%)	7,120 (35.2%)	749 (3.7%)	531 (2.6%)	339 (1.7%)	84 (0.4%)
1989	10,930 (59.5%)	26 (0.1%)	109 (0.6%)	5,953 (32.4%)	639 (3.5%)	362 (1.9%)	253 (1.4%)	112 (0.6%)
1990	11,885 (59.5%)	22 (0.1%)	103 (0.5%)	6,563 (32.8%)	743 (3.7%)	290 (1.5%)	260 (1.3%)	124 (0.6%)
1991	11,976 (58.7%)	20 (0.1%)	134 (0.7%)	7,345 (36.0%)	326 (1.6%)	336 (1.6%)	216 (1.1%)	66 (0.3%)
1992	12,078 (58.1%)	33 (0.2%)	59 (0.3%)	7,414 (35.7%)	379 (1.8%)	382 (1.8%)	316 (1.5%)	114 (0.5%)
1993	12,216 (54.6%)	14 (0.1%)	110 (0.5%)	8,701 (38.9%)	371 (1.7%)	517 (2.3%)	233 (1.0%)	197 (0.9%)
1994	13,931 (55.0%)	38 (0.2%)	176 (0.7%)	9,106 (36.0%)	986 (3.9%)	634 (2.5%)	284 (1.1%)	159 (0.6%)

Region of Publication

TABLE 3
Sociological Abstracts: Language of Entry Publication, 1953–1994

Year	English	French	Spanish	German	Italian	Russian	Dutch	Others[a]
1953	569 (93.4%)	15 (2.5%)	11 (1.8%)	11 (1.8%)	3 (0.5%)			6 (0.7%)
1954	743 (85.4%)	9 (1.0%)	35 (4.0%)	62 (7.1%)	5 (0.6%)		10 (1.1%)	24 (2.6%)
1955	806 (88.2%)	24 (2.6%)	20 (2.2%)	34 (3.7%)	6 (0.7%)			29 (3.2%)
1956	766 (84.1%)	40 (4.5%)	25 (2.7%)	39 (4.3%)	1 (0.1%)		14 (1.5%)	32 (3.6%)
1957	747 (84.1%)	6 (0.7%)	2 (0.2%)	75 (8.4%)	25 (2.8%)	1 (0.1%)		26 (2.2%)
1958	954 (81.1%)	37 (3.1%)	21 (1.8%)	64 (5.4%)	15 (1.3%)	1 (0.1%)	59 (5.0%)	57 (4.0%)
1959	1,056 (74.5%)	81 (5.7%)	64 (4.5%)	93 (6.6%)	19 (1.3%)	5 (0.4%)	43 (3.0%)	52 (3.4%)
1960	1,221 (79.1%)	56 (3.6%)	49 (3.2%)	96 (6.2%)	2 (0.1%)	7 (0.5%)	60 (3.9%)	33 (1.6%)
1961	1,831 (89.4%)	34 (1.7%)	37 (1.8%)	72 (3.5%)	9 (0.4%)	13 (0.6%)	18 (0.9%)	
1962	2,398 (87.9%)	64 (2.3%)	34 (1.2%)	76 (2.8%)	35 (1.3%)	4 (0.1%)	46 (1.7%)	71 (2.6%)
1963	3,058 (79.9%)	314 (8.2%)	272 (7.1%)	53 (1.4%)	32 (0.8%)	5 (0.1%)	12 (0.3%)	81 (2.1%)
1964	4,619 (75.5%)	625 (10.2%)	304 (5.0%)	177 (3.0%)	208 (3.4%)	6 (0.1%)	48 (0.8%)	134 (2.2%)
1965	3,436 (79.8%)	296 (6.9%)	110 (2.6%)	118 (2.7%)	136 (3.2%)		47 (1.1%)	161 (3.7%)
1966	3,896 (75.6%)	391 (7.6%)	201 (3.9%)	81 (1.6%)	141 (2.7%)	47 (0.9%)	8 (0.2%)	387 (7.5%)
1967	3,643 (66.5%)	708 (12.9%)	221 (4.0%)	254 (4.6%)	203 (3.7%)	44 (0.8%)	31 (0.6%)	374 (6.8%)
1968	4,090 (68.1%)	629 (10.5%)	251 (4.2%)	66 (1.1%)	226 (3.8%)	61 (1.0%)	195 (3.3%)	488 (8.1%)
1969	4,212 (69.8%)	490 (8.1%)	238 (3.9%)	129 (2.1%)	152 (2.5%)	25 (0.4%)	149 (2.5%)	642 (10.6%)
1970	4,344 (71.5%)	561 (9.2%)	153 (2.5%)	126 (2.1%)	210 (3.5%)	213 (3.5%)	77 (1.3%)	392 (6.5%)
1971	4,658 (71.2%)	569 (8.7%)	161 (2.5%)	130 (2.0%)	164 (2.5%)	223 (3.4%)	31 (0.5%)	609 (9.3%)
1972	4,939 (68.3%)	630 (8.7%)	285 (3.9%)	165 (2.3%)	172 (2.4%)	251 (3.5%)	6 (0.1%)	788 (10.9%)
1973	4,227 (76.5%)	519 (9.4%)	200 (3.6%)	155 (2.8%)	169 (3.1%)		54 (1.0%)	202 (3.7%)

TABLE 3 (continued)

Year	English	French	Spanish	German	Italian	Russian	Dutch	Others*
				Language				
1974	3,888 (74.5%)	296 (5.7%)	156 (3.0%)	178 (3.4%)	96 (1.8%)	236 (4.5%)	15 (0.3%)	355 (6.8%)
1975	4,382 (76.0%)	440 (7.6%)	110 (1.9%)	136 (2.4%)	141 (2.5%)	199 (3.5%)	163 (2.8%)	192 (3.3%)
1976	4,749 (79.8%)	334 (5.6%)	223 (3.7%)	105 (1.8%)	136 (2.3%)		139 (2.3%)	269 (4.5%)
1977	6,914 (83.9%)	449 (5.5%)	88 (1.1%)	185 (2.2%)	178 (2.2%)	90 (1.1%)	90 (1.1%)	246 (3.0%)
1978	8,076 (86.0%)	491 (5.2%)	197 (2.1%)	174 (1.9%)	153 (1.6%)	53 (0.6%)	93 (1.0%)	155 (1.7%)
1979	7,301 (82.9%)	530 (6.0%)	230 (2.6%)	246 (2.8%)	127 (1.4%)	191 (2.2%)	89 (1.0%)	91 (1.0%)
1980	12,765 (82.7%)	888 (5.8%)	394 (2.6%)	303 (2.0%)	197 (1.3%)	211 (1.4%)	128 (0.8%)	550 (3.4%)
1981	13,431 (77.6%)	941 (5.4%)	417 (2.4%)	509 (2.9%)	266 (1.5%)	464 (2.7%)	275 (1.6%)	1,009 (5.8%)
1982	14,761 (84.3%)	1,045 (6.0%)	309 (1.8%)	285 (1.6%)	311 (1.8%)	160 (0.9%)	149 (0.9%)	494 (2.8%)
1983	14,452 (75.8%)	1,159 (6.1%)	317 (1.7%)	757 (4.0%)	709 (3.7%)	534 (2.8%)	482 (2.5%)	658 (3.5%)
1984	15,128 (79.9%)	1,133 (6.0%)	220 (1.2%)	722 (3.8%)	409 (2.2%)	430 (2.3%)	212 (1.1%)	677 (3.6%)
1985	14,637 (78.2%)	981 (5.2%)	407 (2.2%)	1,005 (5.4%)	330 (1.8%)	292 (1.6%)	409 (2.2%)	662 (3.5%)
1986	15,131 (83.4%)	1,020 (5.6%)	269 (1.5%)	719 (4.0%)	231 (1.3%)	173 (1.0%)	110 (0.6%)	484 (2.7%)
1987	15,687 (80.8%)	772 (4.0%)	339 (1.8%)	901 (4.6%)	313 (1.6%)	330 (1.7%)	503 (2.6%)	567 (2.9%)
1988	17,221 (81.1%)	751 (3.5%)	279 (1.3%)	1,161 (5.5%)	406 (1.9%)	271 (1.3%)	453 (2.1%)	687 (3.2%)
1989	16,378 (83.9%)	773 (4.0%)	303 (1.6%)	677 (3.5%)	382 (2.0%)	234 (1.2%)	281 (1.4%)	504 (2.6%)
1990	18,854 (82.3%)	1,304 (5.7%)	327 (1.4%)	984 (4.3%)	239 (1.0%)	279 (1.2%)	402 (1.8%)	521 (2.3%)
1991	17,932 (83.3%)	909 (4.2%)	312 (1.5%)	684 (3.2%)	336 (1.6%)	152 (0.7%)	267 (1.2%)	932 (4.3%)
1992	18,512 (84.3%)	881 (4.0%)	394 (1.8%)	801 (3.7%)	241 (1.1%)	83 (0.4%)	400 (1.8%)	645 (2.9%)
1993	18,992 (81.9%)	1,333 (5.6%)	424 (1.8%)	1,049 (4.5%)	342 (1.5%)	78 (0.3%)	254 (1.1%)	720 (3.1%)
1994	23,899 (81.3%)	1,468 (5.0%)	670 (2.3%)	1,034 (3.5%)	489 (1.7%)	348 (1.2%)	347 (1.2%)	1,127 (3.8%)

*Other languages include Afrikaans, Bulgarian, Chinese, Danish, Finnish, Hebrew, Hungarian, Japanese, Norwegian, Portuguese, Romanian, Serbo-Croatian, Slovak, and Swedish.

FIGURE 2
Sociological Abstracts: Classifications, 1962

01. Of General Interest
02. Of Professional Interest
03. Methodology (Social Science & Behavioral)
04. Research Technology
05. Statistical Methods
06. History & Present State of Sociology
07. Sociological Theories & Ideas
08. Social Structure (Organization)
09. Interaction Within (Small) Group Structure
10. Interaction Between (Large) Groups (Group Relations)
11. Interaction Between Societies, Nations, & States
12. Personality (& Culture)
13. Culture
14. Social Anthropology (& Ethnology)
15. Social Change & Economic Development
16. Rural Sociology (Village)
17. Sociology of Communities
18. Urban Sociology (Metropolis)
19. Social Stratification
20. Sociology of Occupations & Professions
21. Industrial Sociology
22. Leadership Studies
23. Military Sociology
24. Bureaucratic Structures

25. Political Sociology
26. Social Movements (& Revolutions)
27. Public Opinion (& Research)
28. Communication (Mass & Otherwise)
29. Collective Behavior
30. Sociology of Language & Literature
31. Sociology of the Arts (Creative & Performing)
32. Sociology of Education (& Teaching)
33. Sociology of Knowledge (& Ideology)
34. Sociology of Science (& Technology)
35. Sociology of Religion
36. Sociology of Law
37. Demography & Ecology
 *   Sociology of the Child (& Socialization)
 *   Sociology of Adolescence & Youth
38. Sociology of Sexual Behavior
39. Sociology of the Family
40. Sociology of Leisure
41. Social Gerontology
42. Social Biology
43. Sociology of Medicine
44. Social Psychiatry (Mental Health)
45. Social Disorganization (Criminology, Alcoholism, etc.)
46. Social Work & Welfare (or Applied Sociology)

FIGURE 3
Sociological Abstracts: Classifications (Theoretical/Methodological), 1994

Classification Scheme 1994

0100 methodology and research technology
  0103 methodology (conceptual & epistemological)
  0104 research methods/tools
  0105 statistical methods
  0161 models: mathematical & other
  0188 computer methods, media, & applications

0200 sociology: history and theory
  0202 of professional interest (teaching sociology)
  0206 history & present state of sociology
  0207 theories, ideas, & systems
  0267 macrosociology: analysis of whole societies
  0285 comparative & historical sociology

0300 social psychology
  0309 interaction within (small) groups (group processes, space use, leadership, coalitions, & teamwork)
  0312 personality & social roles (individual traits, social identity, adjustment, conformism, & deviance)
  0373 cognitive/interpretive sociologies, symbolic interactionism, & ethnomethodology
  0394 life cycle & biography

0400 group interactions
  0410 social group identity & intergroup relations (groups based on race & ethnicity, age, & sexual orientation)
  0491 refugees

0500 culture and social structure
  0513 culture (kinship, forms of social organization, social cohesion & integration, & social representations)
  0514 social anthropology

0600 complex organization
  0621 jobs, work organization, workplaces, & unions
  0623 military sociology
  0624 bureaucratic structure/organizational sociology
  0665 social network analysis
  0671 sociology of business & entrepreneurism
  0674 voluntary associations/philanthropy

0700 social change and economic development
  0715 social change & economic development
  0749 market structures & consumer behavior
  0770 capitalism/socialism - world systems

0800 mass phenomena
  0826 social movements
  0827 public opinion
  0828 communication
  0829 collective behavior
  0842 sociology of leisure/tourism
  0850 popular culture
  0868 transportation systems & behaviors
  0869 sociology of sports

0900 political sociology/interactions
  0911 interactions between societies, nations, & states
  0925 sociology of political systems, politics, & power
  0989 welfare state
  0995 nationalism

1000 social differentiation
  1019 social stratification/mobility
  1020 sociology of occupations & professions
  1022 generations/intergenerational relations

1100 rural sociology and agriculture
  1116 rural sociology (village, agriculture)

1200 urban sociology
  1218 urban sociology

FIGURE 3 (continued)

1300 sociology of language and the arts
  1330 sociology of language/sociolinguistics
  1331 sociology of art (creative & performing)
  1375 sociology of literature
1400 sociology of education
  1432 sociology of education
1500 sociology of religion
  1535 sociology of religion
1600 social control
  1636 sociology of law
  1653 police, penology, & correctional problems
1700 sociology of science
  1734 sociology of science
  1772 sociology of technology
1800 demography and human biology
  1837 demography (population studies)
  1844 human biology/sociobiology
  1864 genetic engineering/reproductive biotechnology
1900 the family and socialization
  1938 sociology of the child
  1939 adolescence & youth
  1940 sociology of sexual behavior
  1941 sociology of the family, marriage, & divorce
  1976 socialization
  1977 birth control (abortion, contraception, fertility, &
    childbearing)
  1978 sociology of death & dying
2000 sociology of health and medicine
  2045 sociology of medicine & health care
  2046 social psychiatry (mental health)
  2079 substance use/abuse & compulsive behaviors (drug abuse,
    addiction, alcoholism, gambling, eating disorders, etc.)
2100 social problems and social welfare
  2143 social gerontology
  2147 sociology of crime

  2148 social work & welfare services
  2151 juvenile delinquency
  2187 social service programs/delivery systems
  2190 victimology (rape, family violence, & child abuse)
  2192 sociological practice (clinical & applied)
2200 sociology of knowledge
  2233 sociology of knowledge
  2252 history of ideas
2300 community/regional development
  2317 sociology of communities & regions
2400 policy, planning, forecasting
  2454 planning & forecasting
  2460 social indicators
  2462 policy sciences
  2496 negotiation, dispute settlement
  2499 sociology of ethics & ethical decision making
2500 radical sociology
  2555 Marxist & radical sociologies
  2580 critical sociology
2600 environmental interactions
  2656 environmental interactions
  2681 disaster studies
  2682 social geography
  2697 famine, hunger, & malnutrition
2700 studies in poverty
  2757 studies in poverty
  2793 homelessness
2800 studies in violence
  2858 studies in violence
  2884 terrorism
  2898 genocide
2900 feminist/gender studies
  2959 feminist studies
  2983 sociology of gender & gender relations

FIGURE 4
Applied Areas of Social Planning, Policy, and Development, 1994

Classification Scheme 1994

6100 social welfare
  6110 welfare services
  6120 social case work/community organization
  6121 therapeutic interventions
  6122 crisis intervention, diversion programs, & residential treatment
  6123 informal support groups/networks
  6124 health care promotion/delivery systems
  6125 social security/insurance/pensions
  6126 acquired immune deficiency syndrome (AIDS)
  6127 social gerontology
  6128 women's health problems & services
  6129 addiction
  6130 private sector &/or public sector activities in social welfare
  6140 illness & health care
  6141 poverty & homelessness
  6142 mental & emotional problems
  6143 child abuse/neglect, family violence
  6144 marital & family problems
  6145 education, work, & occupations
  6146 crime & public safety
  6147 adolescence
  6148 problems of minorities
  6150 professional issues & perceptions in social welfare work
7200 social planning/policy
  7210 social policy & decision-making sciences
  7211 health policy
  7212 science/technology policy
  7213 communication/information policy
  7214 environmental policy/housing policy
  7215 education policy
  7220 evaluation research
  7225 social indicators
  7230 social policy implementation/administration
  7240 social planning & forecasting
  7250 development policy
8300 social development
  8309 social development/modernization
  8310 activism/action research/citizen participation
  8320 community development
  8340 public sector &/or private sector activities in social development
  8350 rural development
  8355 urban development
  8370 economic development/industrialization
  8375 education for social development
  8380 population dynamics in less-developed countries
  8381 health emergencies, disaster preparedness, relief efforts
  8390 women & development

9

Evolution and Revolution at *PAIS*: Technology and Concepts

Barbara M. Preschel

Background and History

Public Affairs Information Service, Inc. (PAIS), publishes bibliographic indexes with abstracts, to the literature of public and social policy. Its indexes are available in print, online, and on CD-ROM. It indexes, abstracts, and provides bibliographic access to journal articles; books; U.S. government documents on the federal, state and local level; government publications from governments outside the United States; reports; publications of international organizations; microfiche; and monographs from all over the world. It indexes publications originally published in any of six languages (English, French, German, Italian, Portuguese, and Spanish), although the language of the index headings and the abstracts in the data records is English.

PAIS was founded in 1914 by a group of librarians who felt the need for an index to the literature of public affairs. It continues today to be published and guided by librarians who are also trained as editors and indexers. However, both the subjects covered in the PAIS database and the methods of producing the database have changed over the years in response to changing world conditions and changing technology.

PAIS is Selective and Eclectic

PAIS subject coverage is very broad. It considers that a subject is a public policy or a social policy issue if it is a topic that is or might become the subject of legislation; if it is something people are talking about; if it is an issue in current debate.

Therefore, the subject matter of the materials indexed may range from real estate mortgage interest, to facilities for the disabled, educational curricula, hospital finance, the homeless, abortion, NAFTA, oil prices, agricultural price supports in the United States, civil rights in China, pornography, homosexuals in the military, medical malpractice, pollution, religion in the public schools, international trade, demography, public administration, terrorism, kidnaping by parents, savings and loans regulations, pensions, and so on. The level of emphasis of the topics covered in the database varies from year to year based on the level of emphasis of these topics in the journals, books, and government documents that are published.

It is probably safe to say that almost every topic related to public affairs is represented in the PAIS database. There is also a concerted effort to cover all points of view on a given topic. Publications from all parts of the political and social spectrum of opinion are indexed, including alternative press publications and many publications that are not indexed elsewhere. A well-defined selection policy guides the choice of type of publication.

PAIS covers non-technical publications, publications appropriate for the businessperson, legislator, college student, and intelligent layman. Publications are chosen for indexing because they are well written, informative, emphasize factual or statistical information, and contribute to the public debate. Business topics are extensively covered, as are materials that bear on public administration and legislation. In most subject areas, international comparisons and international relations are included. There is no attempt to cover every article in a particular journal or every item from a particular publisher.

PAIS adds between 18,000 and 20,000 items a year to its database, and currently, the machine-readable file contains almost 400,000 bibliographic records.

PAIS Indexes Material From Many Sources

About 70 percent of the journals and about 50 percent of the books indexed come to PAIS directly from the publisher. The rest are from the resources of the New York Public Library.

PAIS and the New York Public Library have a close relationship. PAIS is a separate, not-for-profit educational organization chartered by the Board of Regents of the State of New York, but the New York Public Library allows PAIS to examine (and index and abstract) incoming books and journals prior to cataloging, and in many cases, prior to purchase. Every morning, a PAIS editor goes to the library on 42nd Street and looks at all the publications that have come in that day. If it is something PAIS might want to index, the editor puts a yellow slip of paper in the journal or book, and the material is sent to PAIS for indexing. PAIS is very careful to index the items quickly, usually in twenty-four to forty-eight hours, so that normal processing at NYPL is not impeded.

The journals and books that PAIS receives directly from the publisher are chosen by PAIS editors because the subject matter covered is appropriate to the PAIS mission. Most usually, these publications have come to PAIS's attention through users' recommendations or through direct solicitation by the publisher.

PAIS prides itself on the completeness and the accuracy of its information. All indexing is done with the actual publication in hand. Each citation is complete and accurate. There are a number of quality controls and multiple proofreadings.

The listings in the PAIS indexes are viewed by most publishers as part of their marketing efforts. These listings alert potential users of the index to material in publications they may not know about. Many libraries will not subscribe to a journal unless it is indexed in one of the standard indexing services because they are aware that journals that are not indexed are likely to sit unused on the library's shelves.

Changes in Index Design and in Production Methods

Changes in Production Methods

In the beginning, in 1913–1914, the PAIS index was produced by collating citations sent to PAIS by librarians throughout the United States and mimeographing the resultant list. Within two years, the *PAIS Bulletin* became a print publication produced by linotype, although it was still organized and compiled by volunteers. By the 1930s, a professional editorial staff had been hired and indexing was done in-house. Later still, in the early 1970s, PAIS began to computerize the production of its index.

By the 1970s, the *PAIS Bulletin* had become a mainstay of libraries throughout the world. It was the premier index to English-language publications in the area of social and public policy. PAIS was apprehensive about the disruption a change from manual to automated production might cause.

Coincidentally, there had always been discussion of a need to index non-English language public-policy publications. It was decided that this was the time to develop this new publication, and to develop it as a computer-produced publication from the start. Thus, the *PAIS Foreign Language Index*, an index to social- and public-policy materials that had been originally published in French, German, Italian, Portuguese, and Spanish, was started. The lessons learned from the computerized production of this publication were utilized in the computerization of the production of the *PAIS Bulletin*.

Using a system developed by SADPO, later LIONS, the automation facility of the New York Public Library, the *PAIS Foreign Language Index* was first published in 1972, using material indexed 1968–1971. Starting in 1976, the successful database design and computer program used to produce the *Foreign Language Index* was then used to produce the *PAIS Bulletin*. It was a system in which data was input at the PAIS offices, and transmitted to a LIONS computer a number of streets distant. The LIONS computer then manipulated, exploded, and alphabetized the data, and produced tapes for photocomposition of pages.

By 1977, the growing market for electronic information made it possible for PAIS to go online as an electronic database on vendors such as DIALOG, BRS, and DataStar. Tapes produced at LIONS were also sent to the online vendors that provided access to the PAIS International database.

The database produced by LIONS was a compilation of the data from the two print publications, the *PAIS Bulletin* and the *PAIS Foreign Language Index*. The two publications used the same controlled vocabulary in indexing the materials cited, but as the years went on and each publication developed its own staff, indexing practices began to diverge. The most obvious manifestation of this was in the assignment of geographic terms in the index.

Starting in the late 1980s short abstracts began to be added to the data records for the items indexed, and the database began to be available on CD-ROM and on magnetic tape, as well as online and in print.

At the same time, advancing technology made it seem advantageous and practical to take physical production in-house. It was decided to undertake a zero-based redesign of the PAIS database and develop a new approach to the content of the database as well as to its production.

It was also decided to merge the two print publications into what is now *PAIS International in Print*, to match the electronic versions of the PAIS index. All PAIS publications, whether in print, online, on CD-ROM, or on magnetic tape, would thus have the same mix of English, French, German, Italian, Portuguese, and Spanish citations. This was done in response to the general internationalization of knowledge and of business that has become a part of our world.

After much investigation, Cuadra Associate's STAR System was chosen as the method for in-house production of both camera-ready pages and magnetic tape for online vendors, CD-ROM producers, and tape licensees. This conversion to in-house production has been very successful. It has saved PAIS time and money and the zero-based analysis of the content and the redesign of the database that was undertaken prior to conversion to in-house production has made the database more consistent, effective, efficient, and useful.

Changes in Index Design

As has been described above, the PAIS database in the late 1980s was a compilation of two machine-readable indexes that had been originally designed for print publication. The objective of the analysis and redesign of the content of the database that was undertaken in the 1980s was to turn this compilation from two somewhat disparate files into one relatively seamless database from which publications could be spun off in whatever format was required.

The first aspect that was analyzed was the actual terminology used in the index headings and the methods by which that terminology was applied by the indexers. An outside consultant, Dr. Jessica Milstead, was hired to look at the index headings, one by one, and in cooperation with the editors, to revise, consolidate, update, standardize, redefine, and redevelop the indexing vocabulary. This required looking at some 7,000 main headings, and more than

80,000 heading, subheading, sub-subheading variants. In many instances the index terminology was not changed; however, in many instances headings were dropped and/or new headings or new relationships among the headings were established.

The new index vocabulary was put into use as soon as the indexers could absorb it, and for new index headings that had a one-to-one relationship with headings previously used, global changes were done by computer to make the backfile congruent with the new indexing being done.

At the same time a new index design was instituted that put more emphasis on geographic access to the material in the database and standardized construction of heading/subheading/sub-subheading strings. The strength of the topical subject approach was maintained by slightly increasing the total number of index headings assigned to each data record.

Changes in Subject Coverage

PAIS does not have a core collection of journals that it indexes cover to cover. Editors review issues of approximately 1,600 journal titles per year and look at more than 8,000 books, as well as numerous reports, pamphlets, microfiche, and other types of publications. The journal titles reviewed change from year to year.

From the materials reviewed, approximately 18,000 to 19,000 items per year are chosen for indexing. This means that three or four articles might be indexed from a given issue of a journal, or one, or none. Whether a given journal article, government document, book, or microfiche is indexed depends on the subject covered in the item, the quality of the writing, whether or not a new point of view is being expressed, whether the item is factual, and the relative "importance" of the subject in the general climate of opinion.

One would expect that the number of items indexed that deal with a particular subject would vary from year to year based, at least in part, on the total number of items on this subject that were published. Thus a concept like "laundering of money" would be expected to have yielded no items in 1980 but a fair number of items in 1993–1994. A subject such as "child abuse," which was a hot topic of discussion in 1993–1994 and a less hot topic in 1980, would likewise be expected to yield more items in 1993–1994 than in 1980. Areas of the world, such as Somalia, that came into sudden prominence in 1993–1994 but were little written about in 1980 would presumably show the same pattern.

For the purposes of this paper, a search was made using words or phrases in the authorized vocabulary of the PAIS subject headings, of the number of times certain phrases or words were used to characterize the content of items in the PAIS database in 1980 and in 1993–1994. These two time periods were chosen because they represented a relatively wide time span and because the number of data records in the two time periods were roughly equal. A full text search of all the fields in the data records was not done, primarily because in

1980, PAIS data records did not have abstracts, and in 1993–1994, most PAIS data records have indicative abstracts. The addition of the terms in the abstracts would have skewed the results widely.

The subjects searched on were chosen at random. The items in the 1980 group were probably indexed at a slightly lower level (slightly fewer index entries) than those in the 1993–1994 group. This means that there were probably slightly fewer terms assigned to the 1980 group than to the 1993–1994 group, thus affecting the figures for number of times a given word was used to some degree.

It would be nice to say that the number of times a given subject was indexed in the PAIS index in a given year was indicative of the level of interest of that subject in the literature surveyed, but there are a number of reasons why that statement cannot be extrapolated from the tables below with confidence. The figures in the tables are indicative and do not represent a scientifically rigorous analysis. They are a simple tabulation of a random survey and should be understood as such.

Figure 1 shows words or phrases where the increase in incidence, 1980 to 1993–1994, was 50 percent or better. Certain topics, represented by words or phrases such as "acquired immune deficiency syndrome" "homeless" or "internet" could be expected to increase in the incidence with which they were subjects of the literature of public policy from 1980 to 1993–1994 because of an increase in emphasis on these topics in the literature. Other words, such as "gulf" or "Somalia" show an increase in incidence primarily because of historic events, in this case, wars. "Russia" is a term used more in 1993–1994 than in 1980 because the Union of Soviet Socialist Republics has changed its name to the Russian Federation in the interim.

On the other hand, certain other words or phrases could be expected to decrease in incidence from 1980 to 1993–1994 because of the reverse of the influences cited above. These are words like "coal" or "herbicides" or, of course, "soviet." See Figure 2.

There were also many cases in which the incidence of the words or phrases used to characterize a topic was just about equal in 1980 and in 1993–1994. Among these, of course, was "death" and "taxation," but also words like "disabled" or "Medicaid."

As new topics in the public debate develop and journals and books are written about them, PAIS attempts to cover these topics in its own selective and eclectic way. At any given time, PAIS tries to reflect the subjects that are in the current debate.

TABLE 1
Incidence of Words or Phrases in Subject Headings Used in PAIS International Database in 1980 and 1993–1994 That Showed a 50%+ Increase in Use

WORD OR PHRASE	NUMBER OF TIMES USED, 1972-1994	NUMBER OF TIMES USED, 1980*	NUMBER OF TIMES USED, 1993-1994**
abortion	723	40	96
acquired immune deficiency syndrome	881	0	183
aerospace	218	5	31
business	20,098	1,084	2,319
cancer	264	18	38
conservation	2,468	158	395
electronic information	93	1	20
environment	560	8	166
gangs	95	1	29
government	38,834	1,748	5,002
gulf	976	37	146
homeless	340	0	57
internet	29	0	29
intellectual property	332	3	55
medical or medicine	6,402	258	978
peacekeeping	270	1	166
pollution	3,314	125	484
Russia	1,117	1	799
Somalia	211	7	78
terrorism	1,240	38	107
women	5,743	291	710

* N = 25,433
** N = 24,553

TABLE 2
Incidence of Words or Phrases in Subject Headings in PAIS International Database
Showing Decreased Use, 1980 and 1993–1994

WORD OR PHRASE	NUMBER OF TIMES USED, 1972-1994	NUMBER OF TIMES USED, 1980*	NUMBER OF TIMES USED, 1993-1994
banking	9,828	637	564
coal	1,098	103	40
herbicides	69	11	5
hostages	177	47	11
marihuana	102	15	7
savings banks	501	38	17
soviet	10,105	604	211

* N = 25,403
** N = 24,553

10

The History and Scope of the American Economic Association's *EconLit* and the *Economic Literature Index*

Drucilla Ekwurzel

S hortly before the dawn of the Industrial Revolution, Adam Smith published his *Inquiry into the Nature and Causes of the Wealth of Nations* in 1776. This pioneering work is generally acknowledged as marking the point at which economics emerged as a separate, serious discipline of scientific inquiry. In a wide-ranging analysis, Smith discusses the familiar topics of labor productivity, economic growth, exchange, prices, wages, profits, capital, saving, investment, the economic development of Europe from ancient times to the eighteenth century, systems of political economy, taxation, public debts, and fiscal policy.

In the nineteenth-century atmosphere of growth in commerce and industry, the scholarly discipline of economics flourished in both Europe and the United States. One hundred years after the publication of *Wealth of Nations*, a group of economists founded the American Economic Association as a scholarly society. In 1911 the association established the *American Economic Review* as a journal for its members.

In the twentieth century, evidence of the importance of economics to business, citizens, and government is found in the burgeoning of scholarly articles by economists. In 1961 a committee of the American Economic Association began publication of the *Index of Economic Journals* in order to facilitate access to the literature of economics. The first volume of the *Index* contains a subject index and an author index to articles published in 88 journals over the years 1886–1924. Subsequently, *Index* volumes were expanded to include articles in conference volumes, collected essays, readings volumes, and the like, and the name was changed to the *Index of Economic Articles in Journals and Collective Volumes*.

In 1963 the *Journal of Economic Abstracts* began publication under the auspices of the association, and in 1966 this journal was included in members' subscriptions to the *American Economic Review*. The *Journal of Economic Abstracts* was replaced by the *Journal of Economic Literature* (*JEL*) in 1969. The quarterly issues of *JEL* included then, as they do today, survey articles on economic literature, book reviews, an annotated index of new books in economics, a contents listing and subject index of journal articles, and abstracts of articles from selected journals.

From almost the beginning, *JEL* made use of computer technology to achieve production efficiencies. Journal article records were entered one time into a fielded bibliographic database, which was used to create the *JEL* indexes. The *JEL* journal database was later augmented with collective-volume article records to produce the *Index*, beginning with the 1969 volume, which indexes 182 journals and 176 collective volumes.

The storage of the *JEL* bibliography on magnetic tapes made possible the mounting of the *Economic Literature Index* on the DIALOG Information Retrieval Service in 1981. At first the *Economic Literature Index* included only journal articles without abstracts, but in a few years it began to add collective-volume articles, beginning with the 1979 publication year, and abstracts for selected journals published in *JEL* 1984 and subsequent issues. By 1992 journal and abstract coverage in the online bibliography was expanded to include both journals and abstracts not indexed in *JEL*. More than 430 economics journals were indexed online in 1994.

In 1991 the association published its first CD-ROM bibliography in partnership with SilverPlatter™ Information. The new database, named *EconLit*, varies slightly in coverage dates of the collective-volume articles and abstracts from the coverage dates of the older *Economic Literature Index* because of media incompatibilities at the time. However, *EconLit* was also able to introduce dissertation records and abstracts of books from *JEL*, which were added to the DIALOG file at a later date. In 1994 the association began licensing Cambridge University Press *Abstracts of Working Papers in Economics* and including the records in the *EconLit* database. In that year also, *EconLit* began to include the full text of *JEL* book reviews. Table 1 shows the dates and numbers of records covered in *EconLit*, and Table 2 shows the total number of records for the different document types covered in both *EconLit* and the *Economic Literature Index*.

This year the association has increased the availability of *EconLit* by broadening its distribution through the Online Computer Library Center (OCLC) system. Over the next year the goal is to increase distribution options and make *EconLit* available in as many library systems as possible. *EconLit-AEA*, a shortened version of *EconLit* for association members only, covering the most recent fifteen years of records on a CD-ROM, was introduced in early 1995 at an affordable price for individuals.

More that two hundred years after the appearance of *Wealth of Nations*, the subject matter of economics differs in detail and emphasis, as well as in the

TABLE 1
EconLit: Records by Publication Year as of December 1994 Update[1]

YEAR	Journal Articles	Books	Collective Volume Articles	Working Papers	Dissertations	Book Reviews
1969	4,472	1				
1970	5,081					
1971	5,010					
1972	5,685					
1973	5,981					
1974	5,965			6		
1975	5,997	1		4		
1976	6,403	1		4		
1977	7,079	1		9		
1978	7,567			1		
1979	7,803	2		17		
1980	8,134			8		
1981	8,117	2		10		
1982	8,280	5		13		
1983	9,418	8		113		
1984	9,554	11	4,662	1,602		
1985	9,918	92	4,646	1,898		
1986	9,716	955	5,507	1,989	264	
1987	9,940	1,343	5,615	2,187	616	
1988	10,537	1,458	7,515	2,194	803	
1989	10,768	1,421	7,132	2,200	956	
1990	11,192	1,527	7,691	2,058	949	
1991	11,756	1,631	9,244	2,336	907	
1992	12,836	1,618	Note 2	2,152	929	
1993	12,481	1,518	"	1,298	1,074	77
1994	4,708	703		0	474	84

Notes: [1]Omits several pre–1969 and post–1994 documents, as well as a number of undated working papers.
[2]Scheduled to be added in 1995 and 1996 updates.

sophistication of its methods. However, the major categories of economic inquiry, as shown in Table 3, are not so very different from Smith's concerns in 1776. The subject categories shown in Table 3 are further subdivided into 650 classifications searchable in *EconLit* and the *Economic Literature Index* as either subject descriptor terms or numerical subject descriptors.

In addition to subject indexing, the online and CD-ROM bibliographies provide a geographic descriptor field for articles in journals and in collective volumes. Geographic descriptors may be countries, regions greater than countries, and economic groupings, such as OECD, LDCs, and so on. Those interested in country studies would do well to note the number of countries mentioned in the geographic descriptor field in one year of indexing on *EconLit* shown in Table 4.

A special "named person" field in the database identifies articles about contributors and contributions to the history of economic thought. Article records

TABLE 2
EconLit/Economic Literature Index: **Document Types as of December 1994 Update**

	EconLit		Economic Literature Index	
Document Type:	Number of Records:	Percent of Records:	Number of Records:	Percent of Records
Journal Articles	214,411	70%	214,411	70%
Collective Vol Art	52,012	17	70,753	23
Books	12,303	4	12,303	4
Book Reviews	161	0	0	
Working Papers	20,217	7	0	
Dissertations	6,983	2	6,983	2
Total	306,087		304,450	

TABLE 3
EconLit: **Main Subject Headings, 1995**

General Economics and Teaching

Methodology and History of Economic Thought

Mathematical and Quantitative Methods

Microeconomics

Macroeconomics and Monetary Economics

International Economics

Financial Economics

Public Economics

Health, Education, and Welfare

Labor and Demographic Economics

Law and Economics

Industrial Organization

Business Administration and Business Economics; Marketing; Accounting

Economic History

Economic Development, Technological Change, and Growth

Economic Systems

Agricultural and Natural Resource Economics

Urban, Rural, and Regional Economics

Other Special Topics

in recent years have contained an author's affiliation field. Working-paper records include not only an author's affiliation field but also an "available from" field. *EconLit* journal-article records may also include an availability field if requested by the publisher, and the records include ISSN numbers to aid in document delivery.

Information and its dissemination were as important to Adam Smith and economists two centuries ago as they are today. However, today's scholars benefit from tremendous advances in information technology as they grapple with contemporary problems of human welfare and the economic organization of society. As the twenty-first century approaches, the American Economic Association is committed to providing bibliographic information tools for economists and others interested in economic research.

TABLE 4
EconLit: Country and Country Groups Identified in Geographic Descriptor Field, 1991

Country		Country		Country		Country		Country	
Africa	317	Czechoslov.	31	Islamic Cntry.	1	Nicaragua	14	Spain	55
Albania	5	Denmark	46	Israel	44	Niger	48	Sri Lanka	10
lgeria	5	Domin. Rep.	7	Italy	179	Nigeria	42	St. Lucia	1
Angola	1	E. Asia	18	Ivory Coast	12	Norway	37	Sudan	7
Arab Cntrys.	44	E.&Cen. Eur.	141	Jamaica	42	OECD	118	Sweden	135
Argentina	85	E. Germany	15	Japan	457	OPEC	10	Switzerland	49
Asia	4	Ecuador	7	Jordan	13	Pacific Basin	2	Taiwan	42
Asia-Pacific	4	Egypt	24	Kenya	25	Pacific Rim	2	Tanzania	33
Australia	254	El Salvador	4	Kuwait	5	Pakistan	57	Thailand	27
Austria	74	Ethiopia	4	LDCs	346	Paraguay	2	Togo	2
Bangladesh	35	Europe & EEC	930	Latin Amer.	121	Peru	40	Trin.&Tobago	9
Barbados	5	Finland	65	Lesotho	3	Philippines	48	Tunisia	3
Belgium	36	France	177	Liberia	1	Poland	88	Turkey	34
Benin	3	Gambia	3	Libya	1	Portugal	17	U.K.	1032
Bolivia	9	Germany	380	MDCs	6	Prussia	3	U.S.	5164
Botswana	7	Ghana	25	Madagascar	5	Qatar	1	U.S.S.R.	324
Brazil	86	Global	101	Malawi	11	Romania	10	Uganda	8
Bulgaria	24	Greece	49	Malaysia	27	Russia	26	Ukraine	14
Burkina Faso	2	Grenada	1	Mali	1	Rwanda	1	Uruguay	10
Burundi	1	Guatemala	1	Malta	2	S. Africa	71	Venezuela	7
CMEA	52	Guinea	52	Mauritius	1	S. Asia	9	Vietnam	3
Cameroon	9	Guyana	2	Mediterranean	12	S. Korea	131	W. Germany	26
Canada	493	Haiti	5	Mexico	114	S.E. Asia	9	Yemen	1
Caribbean	24	Honduras	1	Middle East	9	Saudi Arabia	11	Yugoslavia	54
Central Amer.	13	Hong Kong	22	Morocco	6	Scandinavia	4	Zaire	4
Chad	1	Hungary	91	Mozambique	3	Select. Cntry.	8	Zambia	14
Chile	50	Iceland	2	N. America	18	Selected LDCs	6	Zimbabwe	9
China	138	India	182	Namibia	2	Senegal	10		
Colombia	19	Indonesia	80	Nepal	9	Serbia	1		
Costa Rica	7	Iran	6	Netherlands	96	Sierra Leone	2		
Cuba	3	Iraq	6	New Mexico	1	Singapore	26		
Cyprus	1	Ireland	53	New Zealand	36	Somalia	2		

Note: Includes 1991 updates for journal articles and working papers, and 1991 publication year for collective-volume articles.

11

INFO-SOUTH: Leading the Way on the Information Superhighway to Latin America and the Caribbean

Olivia A. Jackson

In the 1980s, a group of Latin American specialists in South Florida took a hard look at bibliographic databases and found no Latin American database that provided English-language abstracts based on English and non-English language articles. Although information on political, social, and economic conditions in Latin America was available, it was not being gathered systematically into a computerized bibliographic database. The extensive Middle East Database of Tel Aviv University's (TAU) Dayan Center was chosen as a model for a Latin American database at the University of Miami. TAU had an enviable record of identifying and incorporating a comprehensive base of bibliographic data about the events, social and political elements, and personalities likely to have an impact on the Middle East. Drawing on TAU's database experience, INFO-SOUTH, the Latin American Information System, was conceived November 16, 1987, with the support of a U.S. State Department grant.

Prior to the establishment of *INFO-SOUTH*, systematic access to information on Latin American commerce, economics, education, foreign trade, marketing, politics, and government was almost impossible. The major difficulty in establishing this type of English-language database was securing a wide variety of source materials published in several foreign languages on a regular basis. Many of these academic journals, periodicals, and newspapers are distributed only in the country of origin.

The *INFO-SOUTH* database was originally housed at the University of Miami's Graduate School of International Studies (GSIS). On June 1, 1993, *INFO-SOUTH* became a part of the University of Miami's North-South Center and, like the center, began receiving federal funding channeled through the United States Information Agency. A close relationship between the North-South Center and GSIS remains, providing *INFO-SOUTH* with a pool of multilingual, multicultural graduate students who work as part-time analysts writing the abstracts of articles that make up the database. In addition, adept, highly motivated, bilingual and multilingual full-time staff members edit and process the abstracts, ensuring their accuracy and readability.

Initially, *INFO-SOUTH* focused on political, economic, and social conditions in Latin America and the Caribbean. With the high demand for more business-related information, particularly on specific companies and industries, economic trends, and government policies affecting the business climate, the database's focus gradually shifted to encompass such issues in early 1994. By the end of 1994, 60 percent of each week's abstracts were drawn from business-related articles. In February 1995, the database's content was shifted more decidedly toward business issues, with a focus of 80 percent on business and 20 percent on sociopolitical and general economic news. This change in content has allowed *INFO-SOUTH* to meet increasing demands from its business clientele, while maintaining its high level of service to nonbusiness clients, such as academic institutions and government organizations.

INFO-SOUTH has grown at a phenomenal pace, from 1,662 records in its first year to 83,139 records by December 31, 1994 (see Table 1 and Figures 2,4, and 5). Also, Table 1 and Figure 1 show a dramatic increase in usage. The total number of annual log-ons to the database (including direct and indirect access via Dialog) has risen from 1,510 in the early stages to 26,684 as of the end of 1994. Of this total, 66 percent of the 1994 log-ons came from individuals accessing the database directly rather than through a secondary database provider. In fact, direct-access log-ons leaped from 1,510 in 1990 to 17,529 by 1994.

INFO-SOUTH is indexed by key terms (descriptors), with a thesaurus available on-line, allowing users to search the database by key terms or free-text. Other search capabilities include (1) limiting the search to language, to obtain articles based on language of publication; (2) author; (3) publication type (newspaper versus journal article); (4) title of article; (5) country of publication; and (6) publication date.

The database is still relatively young, but its base of 377 subscribers is expected to grow as additional subscribers, particularly from the business community find that knowledge truly is power.

Further, *INF0-SOUTH* monitors nearly 1,000 publications; 300 of these publications are obtained through *Current Contents*. The database is unique in that 100 of the publications it monitors are foreign-published, and 70 of those, many of which are newspapers, originate directly in Latin America and the Caribbean. Refer to Figure 3. In many cases, the newspapers, news magazines, and trade journals from the region have the highest circulation in their respective countries.

Further, to enhance the database's business-related information, in February 1994, *INFO-SOUTH* instituted its online *Directory Database of Key People, Businesses and Non-profit Organizations* in Latin America. *The Directory Database* is offered as a complimentary service with a subscription to the *INFO-SOUTH* database. Currently, *The Directory Database* contains a total of 17,076 records. As of December 31, 1994, people records numbered 6,668; business records totalled 6,924, many of which also include key contact data, addresses, and

TABLE 1
INFO-SOUTH Annual Activity, 1988–1994

INFO–SOUTH ANNUAL ACTIVITY
1988 thru 1994

Number of...	1988	1989	1990	1991	1992	1993	1994
Newspaper Articles Selected	4844	12172	16388	13902	11937	13181	10117
Journal Articles Selected	1955	4315	3236	2342	2622	3107	2403
Documents Catalogued	4268	13151	14471	12835	11725	10912	11008
Documents Abstracted & Indexed	6187	14953	14670	12584	12891	12588	13174
Search Requests Completed		75	90	208	332	213	192
Documents Requested		260	396	933	1407	1833	1487
Direct Access Logons (a)			1510	3381	2893	6681	17529
Dialog Logons (b)					3706	7205	9155
Documents Added to Database	2042	17036	14787	13270	11759	12040	13051
Total Records in Database	1662	17036	31469	44739	57685	70088	83139

(a) = The database's operations began in June 1988; online connection was initiated in 1989 once a sufficient number of abstracts were added to the database.

(b) = Entered into agreement with Dialog in August 1992.

FIGURE 1
Direct-Access and Dialog Log-ons, 1988–1994

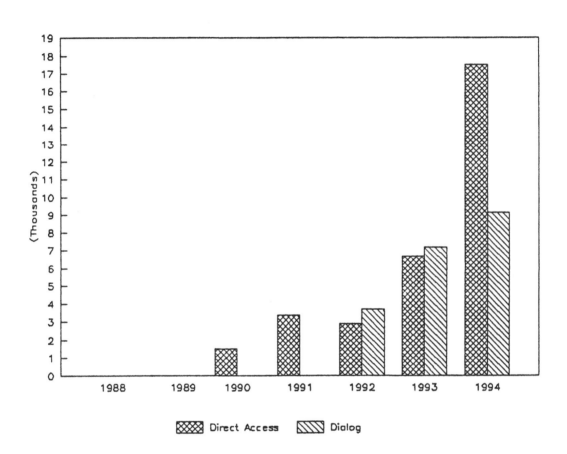

FIGURE 2
Documents Added to the Database, 1988–1994

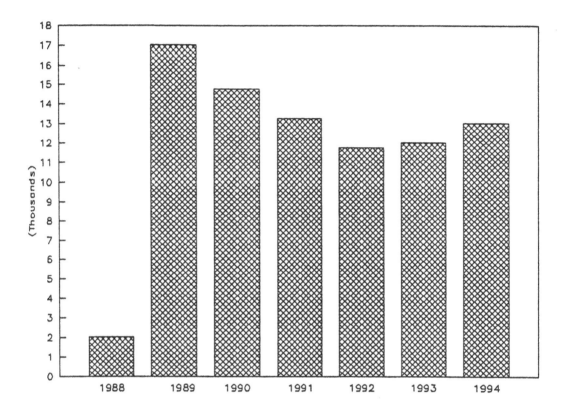

FIGURE 3
Newspaper and Journal Articles Selected, 1988–1994

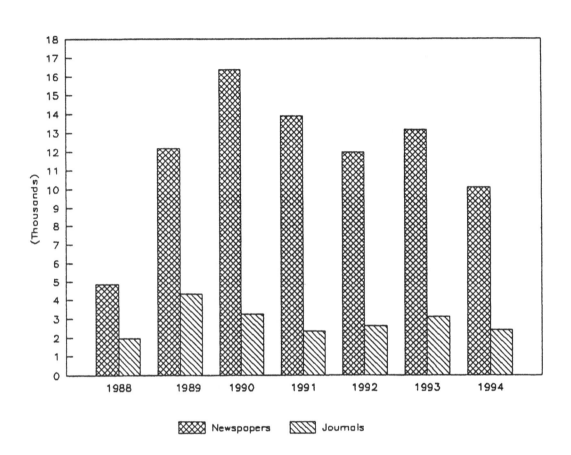

FIGURE 4
Total Records in the Database

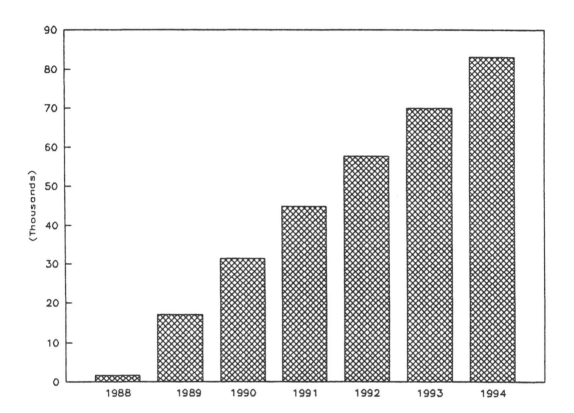

FIGURE 5
Documents Abstracted and Indexed, 1988–1994

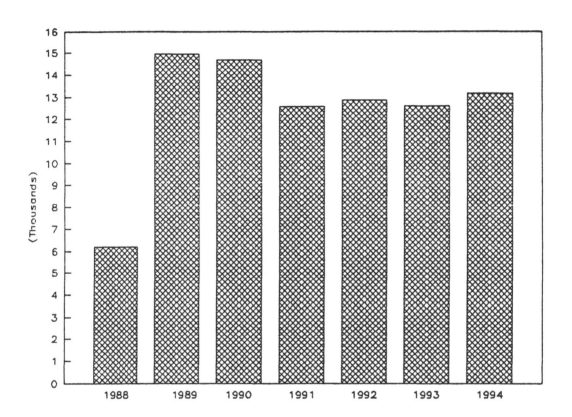

12

AgeLine Database on Middle Age and Aging: Reflecting Population Diversity

Margaret N. Eccles

A geLine is a specialized bibliographic database focusing on all aspects of the burgeoning older population in the United States and internationally. Grounded in the interdisciplinary field of social gerontology, it covers topics of interest to researchers, service planners, health professionals, policy makers, and older and middle-aged adults and their families. Journal articles, books, reports, and chapters are covered, reflecting the latest published writing from the perspectives of sociology, social work, economics, psychology, health, policy, and consumer issues. About half of the database focuses on health and health care in some manner, although clinical medicine is not covered. Gerontological dissertations are being added during 1995. Only English-language material is covered at present, although about 10 percent of the database focuses on aging outside the United States. Each reference includes a substantial abstract and subject keywords from the *Thesaurus of Aging Terminology* (latest edition 1994) .

Table 1 indicates the number of documents entered into *AgeLine* for each publication year from 1978 to 1994, with grouped figures for 1933–1965 and 1966–1977. The increase in total documents between 1983 and 1984 most likely reflects the shift in responsibility for the database from the federal Administration on Aging to the American Association of Retired Persons (AARP) in 1983. AARP supports a substantial gerontological collection in its Research Information Center, from which *AgeLine* is essentially built, with additional journal articles acquired from diverse sources. Total document numbers are somewhat subject to fluctuations in the center's acquisitions budget, as well as cataloging and abstracting/indexing staff resources (see, e.g., the temporary increase in 1991); yet the trend through the 1980s and early 1990s indicates a yearly increase in the number of aging-related publications covered of about 600 to 700 between 1980 and 1993. Our sense is that there has been a very modest in-

TABLE 1
AgeLine: Number and Type of Documents, by Publication Year, 1933–1994

PUBLICA-TION YEAR	NO. OF DOCUMENTS	JOURNAL ARTICLES	BOOKS, REPORTS, CHAPTERS
1933-65	93	22	71
1966-77	2511	605	1906
1978	1804	1016	788
1979	1831	981	850
1980	1623	1071	552
1981	1980	1066	914
1982	1922	1101	821
1983	1849	1075	774
1984	2194	1313	881
1985	2262	1473	789
1986	2472	1653	819
1987	2438	1681	757
1988	2481	1835	646
1989	2497	1765	732
1990	2587	1797	790
1991	2904	2052	852
1992	2662	1874	788
1993	2603	1829	774
1994	2018 (incomplete)	1692 (incomplete)	326 (incomplete)
TOTALS:	40,731	25,901 (64%)	14,830 (36%)

crease in journals focused on aging, but that nongerontological journals have substantially increased their coverage of aging, either on a continuous basis or through special issues.

Books, reports, and chapters constitute about 36 percent of the database. The 5 percent represented by chapters is the most vulnerable to fluctuation of resources, being cut back when resources are lean, although the yearly total has remained approximately the same over the long term. Reports are gathered from an extensive array of private and nonprofit corporate, academic, government, and program sources. The highest single year of report inclusion was 1981, reflecting documents from the White House Conference on Aging held that year. It remains to be seen what the yield will be from the same conference held in May 1995.

TABLE 2
AgeLine: Subject Analysis, by Keywords in *Thesaurus of Aging Terminology*

CLUSTER/AREA	TERMS USED	HITS
Demographics	Demography	467
	Population	206
	Population Aging	392
	TOTAL (terms combined using Boolean "or"):	891
Economics/Financial Planning	Financial*	83
	Income*	2808
	Economic*	1047
	TOTAL:	3503
Pension	Pension*	1667
	Employee Benefit Plans	509
	Retirement Planning	777
	Social Security	1284
	TOTAL:	3433
Older Workers	Workers	640
	Employment*	2078
	Employability	40
	Vocational*	76
	TOTAL:	2448
Employment	Employment*	2078
	Work*	874
	Occupations	121
	Labor*	695
	TOTAL:	2904
Caregiving	Caregivers	1684
	Caregiving Burden	597
	Dependent Parents	214
	Eldercare Programs	0
	Informal Support System	930
	TOTAL:	2450
Alzheimer's Disease	Alzheimer's Disease	1304
	Dementia	1004
	Presenile Dementia	14
	Senile Dementia	202
	Multi-infarct Dementia	11
	TOTAL:	2049

TABLE 2 (continued)

Health Care Services	Heath Service*	2918
	Preventive Health Services	264
	TOTAL:	3130
Housing/Retirement Communities	Housing*	1425
	Retirement Communities	357
	Retirement Housing	269
	TOTAL:	1809
Intergenerational Relationships	Intergenerational*	1138
	TOTAL:	1138
Long-Term Care	Long Term Care*	2865
	TOTAL:	2865
Health Assessment (Mental & Physical)	Physical Condition	530
	Health Status	884
	Health Examinations	100
	Physical Performance	62
	TOTAL:	1483
Middle Age	Middle Age	1468
	Age Differences	2505
	Menopause	434
	Age Stereotypes	110
	TOTAL:	3929
Nutrition and Exercise	Cooking	21
	Diets	181
	Eating Habits	189
	Food*	169
	Menu Planning	48
	Health	745
	Physical*	818
	Self Care	637
	Weight Control	31
	TOTAL:	2460
Psychology of Aging	Geropsychology	85
	Geriatric Psychology	187
	Psychological Aging	810
	Gerontology	592
	TOTAL:	1538

TABLE 2 (continued)

Public Policy and Legislation	Advocacy	717
	Government Agencies	188
	Policy Making	720
	Legal System	92
	Legislation	2608
	Lobbying	82
	TOTAL:	3837
Retirement/Retirement Planning	Retirement*	2876
	Money Management	460
	Pension Plans	979
	Security	17
	TOTAL:	3701
Services for Older Adults	Social Services	1247
	Supportive Services	1062
(Day Care, Supportive Services,	Day Care Services	445
Social Services)	Home Care Agencies	152
	Meal Programs	82
	Homemaker Services	224
	TOTAL:	2831
Social and Family Relationships	Social Interaction	879
	TOTAL:	879
Social Security	Social Security*	1473
	Post Retirement Work	296
	Disability Benefits	59
	Federal Aging Programs	61
	Pension Plans	979
	Retirement Income	851
	Aid to the Blind & Permanently	17
	Disabled	234
	Old Age Survivors*	
		3066
	TOTAL:	

TABLE 2 (continued)

Medicare/Medicaid	Medicare*	2174
	Federal Aging Programs	61
	Diagnosis Related Groups	239
	Health Care Financing	441
	Administration	154
	Supplemental Medical Insurance	1020
	Medicaid	46
	Asset Depletion	14
	Professional Standards Review Org.	28
	Peer Review Org.	
		2932
	TOTAL:	
Theories of Aging	Theories of Aging	200
	Aging	587
	Gerontology	592
	Models	1241
	Social Gerontology	417
	TOTAL:	2783

Other Document Types

DOCUMENT TYPE	NUMBER OF HITS
Bibliography	465
Consumer Guides	502
Personal Guides	848
Directory	404
Personal Account	551
Professional Guides	239

Number of records with Descriptor "Outside United States" _____4136_____.

*Indicates all keywords beginning with this term were searched, in addition to keyword itself (e.g., financial, financial assistance, financial institutions).

With the demographics of aging so dramatic here and abroad, and with the baby boomers poised to enter the realm of the 50 + generation, *AgeLine*'s subject coverage is shifting further down into middle age, with specific age category descriptors having been added in the 1994 *Thesaurus* for each decade and half-decade (i.e., age 50 + and age 55 +) from age 40 + upward to ages 85 +. In addition, all records were provided with the descriptor "Older Adults" or "Middle Aged" to aid in cross-database retrieval. In searching *AgeLine* alone, age-specific descriptors are not necessary because all database material is preselected for relevance to the middle-aged and older population and those interested in or working with these groups. Table 2 provides a brief subject analysis of *AgeLine* coverage as of December 1994 by certain major keyword clusters such as demographics, employment, caregiving, retirement, and public policy. An addendum to the table indicates how *AgeLine* sets off general or professional interest references from the predominant research literature by assigning subject keywords such as "Consumer Guides" (e.g., managing your money), "Personal Guides" (e.g., interaction with aging parents), "Professional Guides" (e.g., counseling manual), and "Personal Account" (e.g., second-career experiences).

The diversity of materials and potential audiences that fall within *AgeLine* 's scope is reflected in its source journals, which range from a core collection on gerontology and aging to such titles as *Consumer Reports, Forbes* and *Best Choices for Retirement Living*. The highest-yield journals include *The Gerontologist, The Journal(s) of Gerontology, Journal of the American Geriatrics Association, International Journal of Aging and Human Development, Research on Aging, Canadian Journal on Aging, Journal of Aging and Social Policy, Contemporary Long Term Care, American Journal of Alzheimer's Care and Related Disorders and Research, Medical Care, Journal of Gerontological Nursing*, and *Psychology and Aging*.

13

Statistics of *Historical Abstracts* and *America: History and Life* Databases

Peter Quimby

F igure 1 and Figure 2 display the present extent of the CD-ROM databases
for *HA* and *AHL*, respectively. Each currently contains thirteen annual
volumes of data, containing the same text as the print volumes. New volumes
are added as they appear, and preparations are under way to add previous
volumes also.

Each volume cites articles, books, and dissertations. Articles for coverage are
culled from more than 2,100 scholarly journals from around the world, and
bibliographical citations are published with an abstract. *HA* cites books as they
are reviewed in key historical journals; *AHL* cites reviews of books appearing
in major journals of American history. *AHL* also includes reviews of nonprint
historical products such as films, videos, and educational software. These are
included in the book reviews sections of the bars on Figure 2. Both titles cite
dissertations as they appear in *Dissertation Abstracts International*.

Article citations have held fairly steady in both *HA* and *AHL* in this period,
at about 8,000 to 9,000 in *AHL* and 18,000 to 19,000 in *HA*. Book reviews have
increased in *AHL* from about 4,000 to more than 5,000, as the number of titles
published each year has also increased. Book citations in *HA* are also up, to
about 3,200. Dissertations in *AHL* dropped slightly after the mid-1980s, reflecting the decline in graduate enrollment in history after the glut of doctorates in
the 1980s. Dissertations in *HA* have varied according to *Dissertation Abstracts
International* coverage, as it attempted to increase its international reach.

Historical scholarship has begun to become more international as historians
have taken advantage of the increasing ease of communication. In the United
States, the use of the Internet for e-mail communication and remote access to
information has increased greatly over the past couple of years. These developments in communication have begun to generate new media for historical

FIGURE 1
ABC-CLIO: *Historical Abstracts*

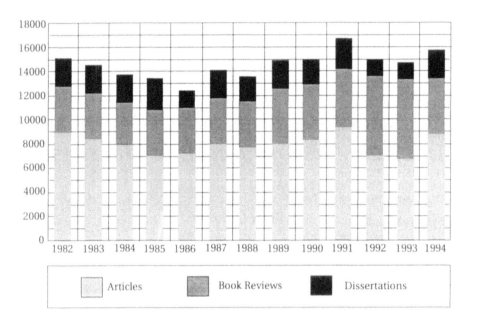

FIGURE 2
ABC-CLIO: *America: History and Life*

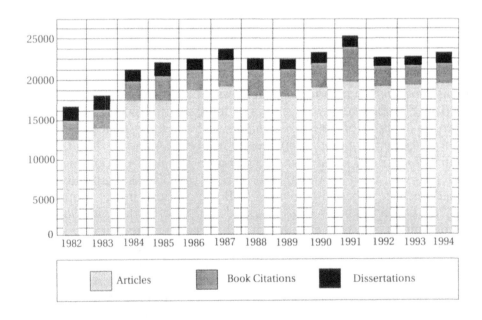

scholarship, such as online book reviews and even journals. Somewhat experimental so far, these will require new protocols of dissemination, usage, scholarly citation, and bibliographical coverage by *Historical Abstracts* and *America: History and Life*. Even history doesn't sit still.

14

Statistics of *RILM: Répertoire International de Littérature Musicale*

Adam P. J. O'Connor and Barbara Dobbs Mackenzie

E stablished in 1966 under the joint sponsorship of the International Musicological Society and the International Association of Music Libraries, Archives, and Documentation Centers, *RILM* was the pilot project of the interdisciplinary Bibliographic Center planned by the American Council of Learned Societies. In 1989 the International Council for Traditional Music added its sponsorship. *RILM*'s Commission Mixte, representatives of the three sponsoring societies, form a body of distinguished scholars and librarians.

The publication of *RILM Abstracts of Music Literature* is made possible by the efforts of approximately fifty national committees located in Europe, Asia, Africa, and North and South America. The committees are typically composed of musicologists and librarians, based at major universities, national libraries, and research institutes. Among the current host institutions are the British Library, the Russian State Library, the Bibliothèque National, the Bibliothèque Royal (Brussells), the Biblioteca Nacional (Rio de Janeiro), the National Library of Canada, the Gulbenkian Foundation (Lisbon), the Staatliches Institut für Musikforschung Prussischer Kultubesitz (Berlin), and the National Research Institute, Boroko, Papua New Guinea.

RILM's broad, international coverage and concise abstracts distinguish it from all other music reference sources. All scholarly works are included (articles, books, bibliographies, catalogues, dissertations, Festschriften, films and videos, iconographies, critical commentaries to complete works, ethnographic recordings, conference proceedings, reviews, etc.). Concert reviews, recording notes, pedagogical manuals, and the like are included if they are of scholarly interest. Areas of coverage encompass historical musicology, ethnomusicology, instruments and voice, librarianship, performance practice and notation, theory

TABLE 1
RILM Abstracts of Music Literature: **Abstracts per Volume, 1967–1992**

Year	No.	Year	No.	Year	No.
1967	2,532	1976	17,121	1985	7,639
1968	4,311	1977	6,042	1986	7,059
1969	5,106	1978	6,459	1987	9,844
1970	4,201	1979	5,916	1988	11,763
1971	4,639	1980	5,927	1989	12,950
1972	4,159	1981	6,641	1990	12,093
1973	4,504	1982	6,165	1991	12,802
1974	4,235	1983	6,654	1992	ca. 12,000
1975	4,701	1984	7,681		

and analysis, pedagogy, liturgy, dance, criticism, music therapy, and interdisciplinary studies on music and various other fields, including literature, dramatic arts, visual arts, acoustics, aesthetics, anthropology, sociology, linguistics and semiotics, mathematics, philosophy, physiology, psychology, and physics. The total number of records in the online database, covering 1969–1991, is about 2,200,000. The printed version, which begins in 1967, includes about 230,000. The number of records per volume has increased over the years from 2,532 records in volume 1(1967) to 12,802 records in volume 25 (1991). (See Table 1.) Lacunae from previous years were included in volume 10 (1976), increasing that volume to 17,121 records. All records are indexed by person and topic, and a thesaurus is available as a guide to headwords and indexing policies.

15

Trends in Courses Taught: Insights from CMG's College Faculty Database

John F. Hood

CMG's Course-Classification Scheme

C MG updates faculty name records and course assignments twice each year from class schedules and course catalogs collected from all 3,500 accredited U.S. colleges and universities. CMG's staff assigns each course in a given class schedule to one of CMG's 3,700 "standardized" courses that, in total, are intended to represent the curriculum offered in all colleges and universities in the United States. This compilation methodology has been used consistently since 1977 with incremental refinements.

The 3,700 CMG courses are not static or fixed; they are constantly changing. CMG keeps a record of every unassigned course, i.e., those appearing in a class schedule or catalog that a researcher is unable to assign to one of CMG's 3,700. The "unassigned" courses are periodically reviewed as candidates for new courses or potentially for the redefinition of or inclusion with existing CMG courses. In addition publishers are encouraged to inform CMG of courses they believe might represent new or emerging markets for their materials.

Courses are added when the same unassigned course appears at a number of different campuses and there is the reasonable expectation that the count of professors teaching the course will grow to about 100 or more. Courses are dropped or consolidated with others when they are no longer taught by meaningful numbers of faculty, say, about 25 or fewer. The number of courses has grown to its present size of 3,700 because more courses have been added than dropped over the twenty-year life of the database.

It is important to remember that the CMG database was not designed to provide trend information on courses taught but, rather, to provide the best available "snapshot" of who was teaching each course at the then-current time. Even though the compiling methodology has been consistent, courses are periodically rearranged or assigned to new disciplines or groups to make faculty names more accessible. Thus, the data shown below are best thought of as indicative rather than as absolute. In the following analysis, only major shifts in the database are considered to have the potential of identifying trends.

Organization of Courses

CMG organizes courses into disciplines, subdisciplines, interdisciplinary study areas, and other CMG-defined groups. For the most part this organization mirrors typical college and university structures. However, CMG also groups courses together for the convenience of the database users, publishers who are trying to find audiences for their books and materials. Thus, some CMG groups are not typical.

Disciplines are the typical academic disciplines, many of which offer an introductory-level course.

Subdisciplines are specialty areas within disciplines that represent the organization of the discipline in the largest universities. An example is Educational Administration as a subdiscipline of Education.

Interdisciplinary study areas are made up of courses offered by many different departments. Typically, there is no introductory course. The grouping of courses in interdisciplinary areas is more subjective than in the academic disciplines. An example of interdisciplinary studies is Women's Studies.

Other CMG-defined course groups include sets of courses that share an attribute that is independent of disciplines such as computer use or research methods.

Identification of Trends

Several ways of looking for course trends are possible.

1. The first is to examine the relative popularity of common introductory-level subjects as measured by the number of faculty teaching them (as a surrogate for the actual course enrollments).

2. The second is to look for significant changes in the number of courses offered in various disciplines and subdisciplines. This is an indication of change in the curriculum. Presumably, more established disciplines have more stable course sets.

3. The third is to review the growth or decline in the number of faculty teaching in various disciplines or subdisciplines. This is a strong indicator of the popularity of the discipline.

4. The fourth, and most subjective, is a selection from the courses added in the past few years. These are perhaps the best indicators of future directions.

1. Popularity of Introductory Courses

Below is a list of the twenty most popular introductory-level courses when judged by the number of faculty teaching them in the 1994-95 school year. Because many introductory courses are taught by teaching assistants (student instructors) who are not maintained on CMG's database, faculty counts in Table 1 understate the actual number of courses taught. The column on the far right shows how they would have ranked 10 years ago, in the 1984-85 school year.

2. Trends in Number of Courses by Discipline

The number of courses in each discipline, subdiscipline, interdisciplinary study area, or CMG-defined course group have generally been fairly stable over the past ten years. Table 2 shows the largest increases; Table 3, several areas that have experienced noticeable declines.

In recognition of the growth in Asian languages, CMG has broadened the number of courses in Chinese and added several Japanese-language courses in the past few years.

3. Trends in Faculty Count by Discipline Area

The following observations are based on the number of faculty teaching all the courses that are grouped by CMG into disciplines, subdisciplines, interdisciplinary areas, or CMG-defined course groups. This is a prime indicator of student demand for the subject area.

Computers. The impact of computer technology shows up more strongly than any other trend. "Computer Applications" is a CMG term for the group of courses dealing with the use of computers in the study of any particular subject. The common thread is the use of the computer. CMG began aggregating these courses in 1983, when 1,482 faculty members were teaching Computer Applications courses. By 1995, the Computer Applications faculty count had reached 18,985, an increase of almost 1,200 percent.

In contrast, as part of the Computer Science Discipline, CMG has been collecting computer-programming courses (in various programming languages) since 1981 with an initial faculty count of 4,447. Programming-languages faculty peaked in 1987 at 10,099 and has subsequently declined by 15 percent to 8,547.

Noteworthy increases in the number of faculty teaching in academic disciplines or subdisciplines, defined for this purpose as increases of 50 percent or more, are shown in Table 4, ranked by percentage of increase. Decreases are shown in Table 5.

TABLE 1
Most Popular Introductory Courses by Number of Faculty, 1984–85 and 1994–95

Rank 1994–95	Course	Number of Faculty 1994–95	Rank 1984–85
1	English Composition	21,267	1
2	Introduction to Psychology	8,328	3
3	Introduction to Literature	8,258	4
4	Accounting Principles	7,700	2
5	Principles of Economics	7,226	5
6	U.S. History Survey	7,085	6
7	Introduction to Sociology	5,985	7
8	General Chemistry (for majors)	5,888	11
9	Introduction to Computer Science	5,818	8
10	Speech	5,655	10
11	Introduction to Statistics	5,141	15
12	General Physics (for majors)	4,713	13
13	Principles of Management	4,617	12
14	Essential Physics (non-majors)	4,518	14
15	Elementary Spanish	4,513	16
16	General Chemistry (nonmajors)	4,428	9
17	General Biology (nonmajors)	4,227	*
18	Introduction to Philosophy	4,122	17
19	General Biology (for majors)	4,059	*
20	Principles of Marketing	3,894	18

* CMG did not differentiate between the two biology courses ten years ago, making rankings impossible to determine. Taking their places, Elementary French would have ranked eighteenth and Introduction to College Math would have ranked twentieth.

Comments

- Remedial Math and Remedial English

  Both of these subjects are taught by large numbers of faculty and have shown enormous growth in the past twenty years, but the pattern of growth is somewhat different. Between 1977 and 1985 Remedial Math grew by 101 percent and Remedial English by 81 percent. From 1985 to 1995, Remedial Math grew by another 56 percent and Remedial English gained a modest 6 percent.

- Education

  The faculty count in Education as a whole is down by 13 percent from 1977 to 1995. The decline is most evident in classroom-oriented topics such as Teaching Methods, Early & Elementary Education, and Secondary & Higher Education. Nevertheless, several Education subdisciplines appear as big gainers in Table 4: Educational Psychology, 178

TABLE 2
Increases (30 percent or more) in courses offered, 1984–85 to 1994–95

Courses	Number of Courses		Percentage Change
	1984–85	1994–95	
Discipline or Subdiscipline			
Oceanography	2	6	200
Computer Applications	7	16	129
World History	6	11	83
Sociology	54	93	72
Biochemistry	8	13	63
Speech	23	36	57
Criminal Justice	8	12	50
Agriculture	12	18	50
Music Theory	9	13	44
Chemical Engineering	13	18	38
Educational Administration	11	15	36
Higher Mathematics	11	15	36
Statistics	20	27	35
Zoology	23	31	35
Comparative Government	26	35	35
Finance	13	17	31
Management	46	60	30
Interdisciplinary Study Areas			
Ethics	6	11	83
Women's Studies	12	16	33
Paralegal Studies	19	25	32
Asian Studies	23	30	30

percent; Comparative Education, 149 percent; and Educational Administration, 84 percent.

- Women's Studies

  Another big increase in faculty activity is in Women's Studies. Being interdisciplinary, Women's Studies consists of courses found in other disciplines. The faculty count has increased steadily from 2,225 in 1977 to 7,143 in 1995, an increase of 221 percent.

- Psychology

  As a whole, the faculty count in Psychology has grown by 17 percent, from 22,270 in 1977 to 30,050 in 1995. The biggest growth has been in Social Psychology, 156 percent; Clinical Psychology, 106 percent; Psychological Measurement, 88 percent.

TABLE 3
Decreases in Courses Offered, Discipline or Subdiscipline, 1984–85 to 1994–95

Courses	Number of Courses		Percentage Change
	1984–85	1994–95	
Discipline or Subdiscipline			
Early & Elementary Education	21	18	(14)
Curriculum & Instruction	25	21	(16)
Secondary & Higher Education	26	20	(23)
Philosophy	52	40	(23)
Developmental Psychology	15	11	(27)

- Mathematics

   The growth in Statistics, 63 percent, appears to be related to the need to apply statistical methods in many other disciplines—Business, Computer Science, Economics, Psychological Measurements, and others.

4. Current New-Course Trends

Below is a selection of the new courses CMG has added since 1992. The courses were chosen and grouped because they reinforce the trends appearing above or they have the potential to signal new directions. The actual course titles provide further insights into the nature of the changes occurring. The discipline or subdiscipline in which the course is classified follows in parentheses.

Women's Studies

- Women in Antiquity (Classics)
- Women in Crime & Justice (Criminal Justice)
- Women and the Media (Mass Communications)
- Women in Music (Music)
- Women's Health (Health, Phys. Ed, & Recreation)
- Biology of Women (Biology)
- Women & the Law (Political Science)
- Women & the Economy (Economics)
- Women in European History (History)

New courses, cont'd

Law, Ethics, & Paralegal Studies

TABLE 4
Increases (50 Percent or More) in Faculty Teaching, 1976–1977 to 1994–95

Courses	Number of Faculty		Percentage Change
	1976–77	1994–95	
Discipline or Subdiscipline			
Remedial/Developmental Math	6,479	20,354	214
Educational Psychology	4,817	13,384	178
Allied Health	4,264	11,734	175
Industrial Engineering	1,592	4,364	174
Social Psychology	4,783	12,242	156
Aerospace Engineering	459	1,145	149
Comparative Education	489	1,219	149
Clinical Psychology	5,564	11,476	106
Business Math	3,067	6,244	104
Oceanography	1,867	3,552	90
Psychological Measurements	3,281	6,173	88
Comparative Religion	3,209	5,956	86
Educational Administration	1,676	3,086	84
Remedial/Developmental English	7,809	12,700	81
Dance	2,567	4,648	81
Technology	6,993	12,640	81
Finance	3,635	6,534	80
Guidance & Counseling in Education	3,426	6,093	78
Metallurgy & Materials Science	1,122	1,914	71
Economic Policy (base year 1985)	2,494	4,225	69
Art History	4,502	7,500	67
Cinema	2,048	3,398	66
Social Work	3,855	6,393	66
Social Problems	5,518	9,053	64
Statistics	11,010	17,955	63
Architecture	2,954	4,783	62
Health & Safety	5,891	9,456	61
Econometrics	1,432	2,247	57
Biochemistry	2,265	3,491	54
Evolution & Genetics	2,864	4,328	51
Calculus	10,705	16,197	51
Interdisciplinary Study Areas			
Women's Studies	2,225	7,143	221
Ethics (base year 1981)	4,131	7,594	83
Latin American Studies	2,081	3,638	75
Environmental Sciences	6,641	10,920	64
Asian Studies	2,810	4,548	62
Paralegal Studies(base year 1981)	8,242	12,745	55
Human Sexuality	1,939	2,890	49
Middle East Studies	1,936	2,769	43
American Studies (base year 1979)	23,716	33,639	42
American Ethnic Studies (base year 1983)	6,154	8,372	36
African-American Studies	4,057	5,218	29

TABLE 5
Decreases in Faculty Teaching, 1976–1977 to 1994–95

Courses	Number of Faculty		Percentage Change
	1976–77	1994–95	
Discipline or Subdiscipline			
French	6,437	5,150	20
German	4,497	3,265	27
English Language Methods (in Education, base year 1985)	10,431	6,769	35
Classics	3,961	2,247	43
Interdisciplinary Study Areas			
Energy (base year 1985)	6,301	5,170	18
Urban Studies	5,843	4,660	22

- Legal & Ethical Issues in Counseling (Education)
- Environmental Ethics & Law (Environmental Science; Philosophy)
- Computer Applications Law (Law)
- Sports & the Law (Health, Phys. Ed, & Recreation)
- Sports Ethics (Health, Phys. Ed, & Recreation)
- Women & the Law (Political Science)
- Law & Ethics in Psychology (Psychology)
- Administrative Law (Political Science)

Technology driven

- Computers in Agriculture (Agriculture)
- Computers in Architecture (Architecture)
- Image Processing (Computer Science)
- Computer Vision (Computer Science)
- Video Art (Art)
- Electronic Music (Music)
- Computer Applications Law (Law)
- Remote Sensing (Geography)
- Video Production (Mass Communications)

Criminal Justice, Conflict

- Social Conflict (Sociology)

- Family Violence (Sociology)
- White Collar Crime (Sociology)
- Victimology (Criminal Justice)
- Women in Crime & Justice (Criminal Justice)
- Conflict Management (Communications)
- Psychology of Aggression (Psychology)

Environmental

- Environmental Ethics & Law (Environmental Science; Philosophy)
- Economics of Natural Resources (Economics)
- Environmental Toxicology (Environmental Sciences)
- Conservation Biology (Biology)
- Environmental Anthropology (Anthropology)
- Environmental History (Environmental Sciences; History)
- Environmental Sociology (Sociology)

Multicultural/International

- Minorities & Mass Media (Mass Communications)
- Cross-Cultural Counseling for Minorities (Education)
- Native American Religions (Religion)
- Sociolinguistics (Anthropology)
- Food & Culture (Anthropology)
- Peoples & Culture of the Caribbean (Anthropology)
- Anthropology of Education (Anthropology)
- Geography of Developing Nations (Geography)
- Third World History (History)
- Human Behavior in Social Environment (Sociology)
- Social Work of Ethnic/Minority Groups (Sociology)
- Colonial Latin America (History)
- Medical Geography (Geography)
- Economics of Latin America (Economics)
- Economics of Asia (Economics)

16

Statistical Analysis of the TULSA Database, 1965–1994

Rafael E. Ubico, John A. Bailey, and Pamela J. Weaver

T he University of Tulsa has provided information products and services to the petroleum exploration and production industry since 1961. The *Petroleum Abstracts* bulletin was introduced in January, 1961 and has been published continuously ever since.

During 1964 we developed the *Exploration and Production Thesaurus* to support the indexing operations that in 1965 started the development of what is now known as the TULSA database. That database now covers thirty years of material and contains over 550,000 entries. TULSA first became available, online, in 1975.

Before discussing the statistical tables, we would make the following general statements:

- We cover both technical literature and patents, worldwide.

- We cover patent families. The first patent instance that we acquire is fully indexed and becomes the primary entry in the database. Subsequent instances that we acquire are given minimal indexing and are carried as related items.

- Similar treatment is given to republication of literature items. The first article received (e.g., a conference proceeding) is fully indexed; subsequent instances (e.g., publication in a professional journal) are carried with minimal indexing as related literature items.

- Our subject coverage is heavily influenced by our customers through our industry advisory council.

- Our coverage statistics will occasionally be influenced by the availability of material, particularly foreign patents.

- The industry we serve has experienced several economic cycles since 1965, including a boom period during the late 1970s and early 1980s and the recent, severe economic downturn.

Patents by Country of Publication

Table 1 presents the numbers of patents that we have abstracted by country of publication for the years 1965 through 1994. The only discernible trend in this table is the entry of patents from the former Soviet Union in 1993. This reflects an increased interest by our customers in technology from this area and our current agreement with Derwent Publications as a source of Soviet English-language patent abstracts.

Abstracts by Language

In Table 2, "Abstracts by Language," there are two notable trends. Our coverage of Chinese materials increased dramatically beginning in 1982, reflecting a subscription relationship that we had established a few years earlier. This both increased our interest in Chinese abstracts and eased the availability of these materials. Of course, the opening of China to outside petroleum exploration helped to maintain our customers' interest in Chinese technology.

A second trend concerns our coverage of Russian materials. From a significant coverage early in our history, the amount of Russian-language abstracts declined in the late 1970s and early 1980s reflecting the (then) common opinion that the Soviet Union would never be opened to outside petroleum activities. The significant increase in coverage in 1993 and 1994 reflects the increased interest in this part of the world and the fact that we now have a reliable source of patent abstracts.

Abstracts by Document Type

Table 3 shows the number of abstracts listed by document type for the years 1984 through 1994 (the years for which reliable data are available). Document type refers to the document-type field that is searchable in the TULSA database. The meaning of those types, as listed in the table, should be evident with the exception of the following:

- Meeting Paper Abstract. These are items selected from conference proceedings for which the text of the papers are not available.

- Meeting Paper Text. Items selected from conference proceedings for which full text is available. We established this type in 1981.

Only one trend is notable from this table: the decline in the number of items from government reports. We decided that the availability of this material from other sources made it less important for us to cover it so comprehensively.

Patent Country (PC)	1965	1966	1967	1968	1969	1970	1971	1972	1973	1974	1975	1976	1977	1978
Australia (AU)	58	27	14	26	5	63	14	42	36	50	72	67	62	57
Germany (DE)	134	185	180	174	143	92	81	58	82	65	58	98	191	224
France (FR)	278	329	307	405	433	491	436	378	185	589	410	29	660	472
Canada (CA)	479	311	202	210	174	237	250	198	147	198	273	177	78	84
Europe (EP)														
United States (US)	1567	1405	1633	1563	1512	1553	1571	1351	1354	1239	1327	1256	1219	1512
Great Britain (GB)	180	161	167	259	215	312	243	167	283	189	270	267	209	125
World (WO)														
South Africa (ZA)	27	33	25	35	59	4	87	48	59	39	49	52	52	47
Netherlands (NL)														

Patent Country (PC)	1979	1980	1981	1982	1983	1984	1985	1986	1987	1988	1989	1990	1991	1992	1993	1994
Australia (AU)	36	41	133	180	195	121	223	147	191	161	208	142	162	176	152	104
Germany (DE)	0	100	492	216	256	224	357	198	200	61	115	92	112	65		
France (FR)	102	122	1144	518	390	149	140	352	307	121	175	145	152	155	164	96
Canada (CA)	137	186	520	850	751	669	564	535	549	470	602	415	699	606	711	499
Europe (EP)				68	81	337	555	477	524	464	552	481	516	509	428	405
United States (US)	973	955	1664	1900	1340	1479	2026	1474	1807	1483	1579	1539	1381	1617	1230	1375
Great Britain (GB)	247	682	1200	883	731	469	545	412	484	354	346	358	331	323	261	250
World (WO)				13	9	18	98	94	92	89	114	92	141	327	327	241
South Africa (ZA)	54	33	112	129	94	39	55	30	50	38	29	19	26	6		
Netherlands (NL)			196	219	131	55	25									
Russian (RU)															890	
Soviet (SU)															401	1712

TABLE 2a

Abstracts by Language (1965–1978)

Language (LA)	1965	1966	1967	1968	1969	1970	1971	1972	1973	1974	1975	1976	1977	1978
Chinese	6	4	0	0	0	0	1	4	1	1	9	2	4	3
English	9412	9811	11153	10318	11138	11946	12631	10055	11506	11638	13308	11603	11318	12136
French	626	884	874	1015	1046	1362	1145	987	672	1363	1061	446	.1307	861
German	531	627	750	589	666	451	535	388	466	478	441	396	559	559
Russian	1381	1390	1540	1310	1738	1560	1617	732	1030	1199	878	553	614	562
Spanish	406	255	571	500	605	428	371	570	495	251	190	168	278	275
Other	310	886	631	546	648	500	624	376	650	459	417	370	351	360

TABLE 2b

Abstracts by Language (1979–1994)

Language (LA)	1979	1980	1981	1982	1983	1984	1985	1986	1987	1988	1989	1990	1991	1992	1993	1994
Chinese	21	14	37	92	127	264	182	147	134	294	228	124	304	343	413	636
English	12157	14789	17731	17938	17436	18159	19791	15497	18047	19791	20177	18422	20374	22586	20937	20474
French	518	727	1556	1045	870	654	655	719	746	661	591	605	557	523	555	370
German	318	529	784	589	582	580	630	339	366	280	288	276	340	290	168	149
Russian	231	594	240	386	544	381	633	247	351	600	487	442	381	340	1076	2157
Spanish	225	217	420	262	120	143	154	64	35	70	124	56	54	57	67	61
Other	366	378	446	393	359	267	270	94	147	140	179	138	95	151	249	183

TABLE 3
Abstracts by Document Type, 1984–1994

Document Type (DT)	1984	1985	1986	1987	1988	1989	1990	1991	1992	1993	1994
Book (B)	418	553	719	719	1030	475	295	536	705	362	548
Government Report (GR)	1154	1837	514	514	779	825	723	596	905	779	382
Map (M)	5	13	32	32	55	0	38	43	48	20	19
Meeting Paper Abstract	3158	4024	2852	2852	4669	5125	4759	4914	5751	5368	5783
Meeting Paper Text (AT)	4482	4595	3614	3614	5634	5633	4660	5647	6473	6458	6444
News (N)	100	64	136	136	41	23	50	45	39	49	60
Patent (P)	3504	4723	3721	3721	3241	3720	3283	3467	3693	4122	4893
Thesis (T)	355	300	273	273	316	462	363	371	472	629	516
Journal Article	7167	6304	5247	7965	6071	5811	5891	6073	6236	5678	5385

Coverage by Category

Table 4, Abstracts by *Petroleum Abstracts* category code, reflects more than any of the tables the trends in the technical interests of our customers. Every abstract that we publish is assigned to one of these thirteen categories, defining the primary technical thrust of the abstract. We can identify major trends in three of the categories.

In 1975 we established a separate category for abstracts pertaining to environmental issues, Ecology. Although showing some fluctuation from year to year, the number of abstracts in this category has remained at a fairly high level. In contrast, the number of abstracts published in the Alternate Fuels category peaked in the early 1980s, reflecting the decline in our subscribers' interest in alternate energy sources that occurred because of the slump in world petroleum prices.

Finally, because many of our subscribing companies were getting involved in nonpetroleum minerals in the mid 1970s, we established the Mineral Commodities category in 1977. Again, the number of abstracts published in this category peaked and then declined sharply as the oil companies refocused on petroleum operations in the later years.

Country of Publisher

We complete this presentation with Table 5, "Abstracts by Country of Publisher." Due to lack of earlier data, this table goes back only to 1988. There are no identifiable trends exposed in the table except for a possible decline in the proportion of material originating as U.S. publications.

TABLE 4a
Abstracts by Petroleum Abstracts Category Code (1961–1978)

Category Codes (CC)	1961	1962	1963	1964	1965	1966	1967	1968	1969	1970	1971	1972	1973	1974	1975	1976	1977	1978
Geology	2247	2393	2670	2704	2592	2900	3401	3136	3342	3285	3956	3020	3263	3421	3461	3069	2814	2827
Geochemistry	992	804	968	913	622	753	912	704	611	689	879	461	615	686	739	558	540	537
Geophysics	1672	1710	1736	1681	1998	2411	2246	1583	1594	1702	1817	1060	991	1116	1305	1031	988	1071
Drilling (Wells)	1255	1333	1303	1153	1284	1392	1518	1429	1772	1846	1610	1200	1535	1649	1772	1355	1356	1224
Well Logging	400	353	432	395	401	388	439	456	586	457	403	371	308	351	298	248	294	223
Well Completion	658	733	788	618	683	657	808	792	865	812	941	738	873	723	721	600	517	495
Production	758	583	685	557	671	703	868	927	857	1022	1039	956	1062	1039	998	666	681	726
Reservoir	839	952	1235	1002	981	993	1056	856	912	990	1089	854	1000	921	878	908	876	739
Pipelining				398	983	941	1290	1315	1576	1712	1852	1058	1347	1486	1683	1296	1597	1502
Ecology															270	495	649	473
Alternate Fuels															317	873	854	1057
Supplemental Technol	1667	1955	2207	1695	1447	1161	1118	1348	1838	1730	1336	1034	1910	2279	2171	910	1004	966
Mineral Commodities																	247	853
Related Patents			119	890	1100	1558	1863	1732	1888	2000	2002	2360	1916	1718	1691	1529	1776	1566
Related Literature																	238	397
Category Code Total	10488	10816	12143	12006	12762	13857	15519	14278	15841	16245	16924	13112	14820	15389	16304	13538	14431	14656

TABLE 4b
Abstracts by *Petroleum Abstracts* Category Code (1979–1994)

Category Codes (CC)	1979	1980	1981	1982	1983	1984	1985	1986	1987	1988	1989	1990	1991	1992	1993	1994
Geology	3141	3212	3340	3729	4187	5579	5718	4289	5051	7163	6977	6063	6212	6884	6202	6250
Geochemistry	613	616	666	604	629	736	1059	854	1188	1468	1715	1521	1809	1592	1500	1722
Geophysics	881	1074	1038	1320	1855	1743	2064	1682	2141	2907	2712	2661	2939	3895	2955	2898
Drilling (Wells)	975	1145	1830	1596	1293	1389	1778	1327	1505	1255	1199	1164	1392	1325	1616	1949
Well Logging	221	291	314	460	406	467	388	513	774	643	660	592	767	712	840	986
Well Completion	414	601	719	734	741	750	884	716	1209	1094	1148	1156	1446	1343	1565	1922
Production	633	1259	1608	1046	1010	1122	1333	1088	1699	1308	1352	1384	1361	1463	1707	1694
Reservoir	667	1019	1369	1580	1299	1181	1465	1187	1737	1892	2039	1816	1940	2372	2180	2201
Pipelining	1175	1887	2548	1740	1752	1336	1430	1030	1150	1247	1134	1299	1073	1118	1414	1510
Ecology	415	574	1560	871	836	579	593	244	371	492	465	504	945	1329	1500	1303
Alternate Fuels	1096	1056	1571	783	848	1013	1008	653	552	614	589	349	476	552	185	197
Supplemental Technol	919	1239	1358	1317	1649	1255	1126	876	1388	1433	1858	1411	1151	1545	1754	1343
Mineral Commodities	916	1256	1221	1737	1283	1107	1288	957	1061	320	226	142	181	192	47	55
Related Patents	1135	1367	1495	2113	1464	1295	1644	1080								
Related Literature	635	652	525	1076	786	791	635	612								
Oil & Gas Fields Bibl.					1387	3195										
Category Code Total	13836	17248	21162	20706	20038	20343	22413	17108	19826	21836	22074	20062	21692	24322	23465	24030

TABLE 5
Abstracts by Country of Publisher, 1988–1994

Country of Publisher	1988	1989	1990	1991	1992	1993	1994
Australia	277	372	262	306	257	321	175
Belgium	25	13	40	8	0	14	0
Brazil	6	52	23	30	17	29	9
Canada	647	1018	767	263	868	924	711
China	202	247	83	263	156	185	587
Czechoslovakia	6	8	12	9	1	1	9
France	555	529	436	452	414	473	279
Germany	785	975	842	888	865	605	622
Hungary	18	33	13	14	37	4	
India					19	44	14
Iraq			12	0	0		
Israel	3	8	1	39	0	12	7
Italy	78	97	43	39	50	32	28
JAPAN	56	36	48	30	50	41	61
Kuwait	2	7	4	0	1	2	1
Malaysia				13	38	13	16
Mexico	13	13	5	23	14	6	7
Netherlands	698	541	736	678	881	614	549
New Zealand	26	17	16	27	12	24	7
Norway	68	74	34	29	72	15	13
Poland	59	42	48	15	23	28	33
Romania	6	15	18	18			
South Africa	38	29	19	26	6		
Sweden	12	23	18	3	6	7	6
Switzerland	143	163	142	193	282	336	272
Taiwan							15
UAE						18	6
United Kingdom	1172	981	1139	1349	1881	937	3387
United States	8267	8619	8148	8962	7850	5475	6719
Uruguay	0	19	21	3	5	2	0
USSR	595	486	442	380	336	216	217
Venezuela	4	4	5	0	3	3	7

17

A Brief History of the
Abstract Bulletin of the Institute of Paper Science and Technology

Rosanna M. Bechtel

Background

T he Institute of Paper Chemistry (IPC), now the Institute of Paper Science and Technology (IPST), was founded in 1929 to promote the development of the U.S. pulp and paper industry. It is a nonprofit organization funded mainly by contributions from member companies, who in turn receive benefits such as free publications and preferential access to the online database.

One of IPST's main purposes is to provide research services for the pulp and paper industry and the federal government. In addition, as an accredited graduate school affiliated with the Georgia Institute of Technology, it grants M.S. degrees and Ph.D.'s in pulp and paper technology, and many of the leaders of the industry today are IPST graduates. The third component is the Information Services Division (ISD), which includes the William Haselton Library and the American Museum of Papermaking, as well as the Abstracting Department, which is responsible for the production of the abstract bulletins, the online database, and other ISD publications.

The monthly publication now called the *Abstract Bulletin of the Institute of Paper Science and Technology* (*ABIPST*) was first produced in 1930 as the *Bulletin of the Institute of Paper Chemistry: Library Notes*, a title it retained until volume 29. Written almost singlehandedly by the chief librarian, with only occasional contributions of abstracts from research staff, it functioned as both an abstract bulletin and a library accessions list.

The first full-time abstractor was hired in 1953, and three more had been added by the end of 1956. In 1958, the title of the publication was changed to *Abstract Bulletin of the Institute of Paper Chemistry*, and library accessions were handled separately. In the mid-1960s, the staff was increased by two more abstractors and a second clerk, and in 1969 the PAPERCHEM database, the online version of the bulletin, was created. During this period, the abstracting staff received editorial, typesetting, and eventually keywording and computer support from other departments. The number of abstractors remained constant until IPC moved from Appleton, Wisconsin, to Atlanta, Georgia, in 1989. When the Institute subsequently became IPST, *ABIPST* was rechristened as well.

The present in-house staff consists of an editor, five abstractor/keyworders, one clerk, and two typesetters, with considerable support from ISD and IPST computer personnel. There are also fourteen freelancers, several of them former in-house abstractors still residing in Appleton. In addition to *ABIPST* and its annual indexes, the Abstracting Department produces the *Graphic Arts Bulletin of the Institute of Paper Science and Technology* (*GABIPST*), published until January 1992 by the Rochester Institute of Technology as *Graphic Arts Literature Abstracts*. The issues in the present volume of *GABIPST* contain an average of 700 abstracts, with only minimal overlap with *ABIPST*. The abstracting staff also produces a series of monthly *Paper Technology Updates* (*PTUs*) that focus on topics of particular interest to the pulp and paper industry, including recycling, bleaching, and the environment. The number of abstracts varies from issue to issue to keep the information as up-to-date as possible. ISD also maintains the *Thesaurus of Pulp and Paper Terms*, which contains a controlled vocabulary of more than 22,000 keywords used for online searching of the PAPERCHEM database; the third edition was published in 1990. *PaperSearch*, a CD-ROM containing the past five years of data from PAPERCHEM, is another ISD product that recently entered the market.

Coverage

The earliest *Library Notes* contained author indexes and rudimentary subject indexes whose content varied from issue to issue, although even in the beginning it reflected the library's mandate, which was to establish the most complete collection of literature on pulp, paper, and related topics in the world. In 1930 this amounted to some 90 journals and an increasing number of books and conference proceedings. In 1946 the library began to acquire U.S. and Canadian patents. Russian patents were added in 1959, French and British patents two years later, and German patents in volume 34 (1963). Japanese patents, which represent a large proportion of those now covered, were first abstracted in 1976. Present library holdings include almost 30,000 monographs, 7,000 translations, 218,000 patents from all countries with significant pulp and paper industries (including Scandinavia), and more than 700 journals. These are essentially the materials covered by *ABIPST* and PAPERCHEM.

Table 1 shows the number of *ABIPST* abstracts produced each year since 1930, with separate figures for patent and nonpatent literature, which includes journal articles, books, and conference proceedings. Increases in abstract numbers are due mainly to the increasing amount of literature published in areas of interest to the industry, which, thanks to advances in computer technology, ISD is able to cover with essentially the same number of in-house abstractors it employed in the 1960s.

In Table 2, the abstracts from volume 64 of *ABIPST* are divided into patent and nonpatent literature; the former are grouped by country and the latter by type of document.

Table 3 ranks the first 50 of the 754 sources of nonpatent abstracts in volume 64 by frequency.

The subjects covered in *ABIPST* are grouped into these broad categories: analysis, testing, and quality control; biology and biochemistry; carbohydrates; cellulose and cellulose derivatives; cellulosic textiles; chemicals (raw materials and additives); chemistry, physics, and mathematics; economics, research, and miscellaneous; engineering and process control; fiber webs and nonwoven fabrics; fibers; films, foils, and laminates; finishing and converting; gluding, labeling, sealing, and taping; graphic arts (now restricted to subjects directly related to paper); hemicellulose, holocellulose, and pectin; lignin and lignin derivatives; machinery, equipment, and maintenance; mill construction and operation; molding and molded articles; packaging, wrapping, and materials handling; packaging materials; bags and pouches; boxes and cartons; paper and board; paper and board machines; paper and board manufacture; paper and board specialties; paper and board treatment; particle board and related structural products; pulp; pulp manufacture; pulp treatment; pulpwood; spent liquors and by-products; water and power; wood; wood extractives and silvichemicals; wood waste, bark, and agricultural residues; and woodlands and forestry.

When ISD began producing *GABIPST* in 1992, the library greatly expanded its coverage of journals dealing with the graphic arts and printing, including areas such as design and copy preparation, manufacturing operations, composition and imagesetting, prepress and prepatory operations, printing and reproduction processes, postpress operations, related R&D, and the handling of materials such as film, plates, inks, and blankets in addition to paper.

The *PTUs* are intended to provide easy access to topics that span a range of the subjects normally covered in *ABIPST* and *GABIPST*. For example, a typical *PTU* on the environment can contain abstracts that would appear in *ABIPST* under spent liquors and by-products or woodlands and forestry and in *GABIPST* under manufacturing operations or inks.

Languages

Originally, *Library Notes* covered only documents in English and German. With the hiring of several abstractors from Eastern Europe during the 1950s, coverage was extended to the Slavic languages, the Romance languages, and other Germanic languages such as Swedish. Almost all documents in foreign languages are now abstracted by freelancers, including one in China and one in Japan.

TABLE 1
Publication Record, 1930–1994, *Abstract Bulletin of the Institute of Paper Chemistry/Institute of Paper Science and Technology*

Vol.	Year[1]	Patent Abstracts	Other Abstracts[2]	Total Abstracts	Vol.	Year[1]	Patent Abstracts	Other Abstracts[2]	Total Abstracts
1	1930–1931		554	554	34	1963–1964	4880	4603	9483
2	1931–1932		853	853	35	1964–1965	4800	3809	8609
3	1932–1933		985	985	36	1965–1966	4900	4420	9320
4	1933–1934		1240*[3]	1240*	37	1966–1967	4947	4575	9522
5	1934–1935		1408*	1408*	38[6]	1967–1968	4649	5104	9753
6	1935–1936		1944*	1944*	39[7]	1968–1969	4907	5393	10,300
7	1936–1937		1780*	1780*	40[8]	1969–1970	5020	5659	10,679
8	1937–1938		2016*	2016*	41	1970–1971	4370	6669	11,039
9	1938–1939		2348*	2348*	42	1971–1972	4710	7290	12,000
10	1939–1940		1920*	1920*	43	1972–1973	5138	7312	12,450
11	1940–1941		1876*	1876*	44	1973–1974	5012	7608	12,620
12	1941–1942		1712*	1712*	45	1974–1975	4883	7787	12,670
13	1942–1943		1984*	1984*	46	1975–1976	5137	6953	12,090
14	1943–1944		1740*	1740*	47	1976–1977	5567	6773	12,340
15	1944–1945		1960*	1960*	48	1977–1978	4524	7166	11,690
16	1945–1946		2332*	2332*	49	1978–1979	3714	6726	10,440
17[4]	1946–1947	360*	2620*	2980*	50	1979–1980	4662	6348	11,010
18	1947–1948	530*	3905*	4435*	51	1980–1981	4815	6855	11,670
19	1948–1949	735*	3770*	4505*	52	1981–1982	4974	8006	12,980
20	1949–1950	1120*	3540*	4660*	53	1982–1983	3614	8866	12,480
21	1950–1951	1155*	3365*	4520*	54	1983–1984	3958	8862	12,820
22	1951–1952	1365*	3505*	4870*	55	1984–1985	4361	8359	12,720
23	1952–1953	1155*	3590*	4745*	56	1985–1986	4827	8563	13,390
24	1953–1954	1365*	3845*	5210*	57	1986–1987	6279	8671	14,950
25	1954–1955	1155*	3945*	5090*	58	1987–1988	5661	8629	14,290
26	1955–1956	1575*	3755*	5330*	59[9]	1988–1989	4681	7119	11,800
27	1956–1957	2570*	4940*	7510*	60	1989–1990	4512	6436	10,948
28[5]	1957–1958	3360	3971	7331	61	1990–1991	5800	6980	12,780
29	1958–1959	2990	4665	7665	62	1991–1992	3921	10,379	14,300
30	1959–1960	3570	4506	8076	63	1992–1993	4755	9545	14,300
31	1960–1961	3270	5641	8911	64	1993–1994	5473	9927	15,400
32	1961–1962	3680	6587	10,267	65[10]	1994–1995	6225	11,834	18,059
33	1962–1963	4910	6668	11,578					

[1] IPST's publication year parallels its fiscal year, which runs from July through June.
[2] Includes journal articles, books, conference proceedings, reports, and other monographs.
[3] Numbers followed by asterisks are approximations based on total pages times the average number of abstracts per page.
[4] Volume 17 was the first to cover patents.
[5] Volume 28 was the first to number abstracts.
[6] Volume 38 contains the first data available in PAPERCHEM.
[7] With Volume 39, the number of issues in each volume was reduced from twelve to eleven to allow in-house staff time to process the annual indexes.
[8] Volume 40 was the first to be produced online; the two preceding volumes were added to PAPERCHEM later.
[9] Volume 59 was produced before, during, and after the move to Atlanta, when the Institute of Paper Chemistry became the Institute of Paper Science and Technology.
[10] Volume 65 is the first to be produced on the present computer system. The numbers given represent the first through the eleventh of what will again be twelve annual issues.

TABLE 2
**Percentages of Abstracts in Volume 64 of *ABIPST* by Patent Country of Origin and
Document Type**

5512 PATENTS	(35.79%)			
		1895	Japan	34.36%
		1832	U.S.A.	33.36%
		1180	Germany	21.41%
		410	Canada	7.44%
		182	France	3.30%
		7	Russia	0.13%
		3	Europe	0.05%
		2	Sweden	0.04%
		1	Norway	0.02%
		39	Translations	0.71%
9888NON-PATENTS	(64.21%)			
		6072	Journal Articles	61.41%
		2082	Conference Papers	21.01%
		711	Title only	7.19%
		171	Books & Pamphlets	1.73%
		379	Secondary	3.83%
		164	Translations	1.66%
		290	Dissertations	2.93%
		19	Bibliographies	0.19%

In volume 64 of *ABIPST*, 64.81 percent of the documents abstracted were written in English, and 35.19 percent in foreign languages. Table 4 shows the distribution of these documents by language.

Hardware and Software

Like many publications of its type, *ABIPST* has passed through all the stages of technology characteristic of the Information Age. Abstract bulletins that went into production before 1950 often shared a similar problem: even after computers were introduced, the resulting online databases were designed to support the production of the printed product and their own potential as a product was not immediately recognized. The 1994 incarnation of PAPERCHEM is the first version of the database deliberately designed to facilitate both *ABIPST* production and complex online searching.

From 1930 to 1967, all the abstracts were written on manual or, later, electric typewriters and typeset by hand. Indices were compiled manually for each issue and volume from information stored on index cards, which were also used as authority files.

In 1967 the first electronic typesetting system was installed, although its ability to sort even the simplest of data was extremely limited. Also, clerks still copied the abstracts into the system from typewritten manuscripts, thus introducing entirely new errors. The installation of an IBM mainframe a year later

TABLE 3
Sources of Nonpatent Abstracts, Volume 64 of *ABIPST*, Ranked by Frequency

Count	Publication Name	Rank
1749	TAPPI Press	1
280	Tappi Journal	2
262	Papeterie	3
241	CTAPI	4
205	Paper (London)	5
146	Papier Carton et Cellulose	6
133	1994 TAPPI Engineering Conference	7
131	Pulp and Paper Canada	8
129	CPPA Standards	9
124	PaperAge	10
123	Canadian Journal of Forest Research	11
121	Japan Tappi Journal	12
118	Pulp and Paper	13
116	1994 TAPPI Pulping Conference	14
113	Wochenblatt fur Papierfabrikation	15
108	1994 TAPPI Environmental Conference	16
107	Pulp and Paper International	17
105	Packaging Week	18
94	Svensk Papperstidning	19
83	Papier	20
79	Journal of Applied Polymet Science	21
79	Proceedings of the European Pulp and Paper Week	21
71	Holzforschung	23
69	China Pulp and Paper	25
69	Pacific Paper Expo Technical Conference	25
69	1994 TAPPI Polymers Laminations Coating Conference	25
68	1994 TAPPI Papermakers Conference	27
65	PIMA Journal	28
63	Journal of the Japan Wood Research Society	29
63	Paper, Film, & Foil Converter	29
61	Paperi ja Puu	31
61	Proceedings of the Pan-Pacific Pulp and Paper Technology Conference	31
60	International Paper and Board Industry	33
60	Nordic Pulp and Paper Research Journal	33
59	Paper Focus	35
58	Pulp and Paper Week	36
56	Appita Journal	37
55	Folding Carton Industry	38
55	Forest Ecology and Management	38
54	Cellulose Chemistry & Technology	40
53	TAPPI Alkaline Papermaking Anthology	41
53	Paper Europe	41
52	Boxboard Containers	43
50	American Papermaker	44

led the abstracting staff to experiment with the development of suitable key-words, which formed the basis of what is now the *Thesaurus of Pulp and Paper Terms*. Volume 40, begun in 1969, was the first that could be searched online,

TABLE 4
Languages of Documents Abstracted in Volume 64 of *ABIPST*

A. 499 Slavic	3.24%		
		359	Russian
		46	Polish
		35	Czech
		25	Slovakian
		22	Bulgarian
		9	Slovenian
		2	Croatian
		1	Belorussian
B. 1701 Germanic	11.05%		
		1615	German
		56	Swedish
		23	Norwegian
		7	Hungarian
C. 2176 Oriental	14.13%		
		2022	Japanese
		144	Chinese
		10	Korean
D. 1136 Romance	7.38%		
		797	French
		241	Spanish
		42	Portuguese
		39	Italian
		17	Romanian
E. 17 Miscellaneous	0.11%		
		17	Finnish

Note: Because a few items appear in more than one language, the total number of abstracts listed for the volume is slightly less than the sum of the figures for individual languages.

although volumes 38 and 39 were added when PAPERCHEM was made available on DIALOG.

The abstractors were not able to write abstracts online until volume 56 (1985), when a network of UNISYS B20 microcomputers was installed and eventually linked to a UNISYS tape drive and mainframe. However, editors still demanded paper copies, and clerks still had to input these corrections as well as manuscripts from freelancers. It was not until after the move to Atlanta that the editorial staff was weaned from hard copy and freelancers began submitting their work on floppy disks.

The present system, which went into operation in July 1994, uses the STAR database framework from Cuadra Associates. STAR runs on Solaris 2.3 (Unix) on a Sun SPARCserver 1000 with 64 megabytes of memory and 6 gigabytes of disk storage. The new version of PAPERCHEM is available from both DIALOG and STN, where it is updated weekly, and on the CD-ROM *PaperSearch*.

18

Growth of the Computing Literature as Reflected in the *Computing Information Directory*, 1981–1995

Darlene M. Hildebrandt and Mark D. Crotteau

*C*omputer Science Resources: A Guide to the Professional Literature first appeared in 1981. It was published by Knowledge Industry Publications, Inc., for the American Society for Information Science and designed to be a road map to a new and burgeoning literature.

In 1985 a new publisher took over and the title changed to *Computing Information Directory* (CID). At that time six important decisions were made. First, *CID* would be an annual publication so it could document the frequent changes in the literature. Second, it would be a road map with enriched road signs for the professional who needed quick access to computing information. It was also apparent that timeliness was critical, so a third decision was made to get the work to market in the shortest possible time—one month from the date of the last entry. Fourth, *CID* would try to provide access to readily available information in the popular literature and point to expensive loose-leaf and comprehensive services for more in-depth needs. Making *CID* a tool that could be easily used by new information professionals was an important fifth decision. The brief introduction to each chapter provides some background and helps put a particular *type* of literature in its appropriate context. The seasoned professional can skip the introductions and rely solely on the body of the chapter for important sources. Sixth, it was determined that *CID* would provide original information when it could not point to other significant bibliographic or reference sources.

Although the seventeen chapters in *CID* have remained relatively stable for twelve editions, the coverage in each chapter has gradually evolved, taking into account new computer-related technologies, the developing relationship between computer science and electrical engineering (known as *computer engineering*), user input, and the availability of other published resources.[1]

This article focuses on chapter 1 of *CID*, "Computer Journals." The word *journals* is used by *CID* to include, academic journals, trade magazines, newspapers, newsletters, research journals, and other serial-type computer-related publications issued on an irregular or regular basis. Serial-type publications are also found in other chapters in *CID* when they serve a particular role (e.g., an indexing and abstracting services or review resources) or cover a particular area of the literature (e.g., literature on hardware or software). Most of the serial-type publications appearing in the latter example represent comprehensive loose-leaf services that are published with a base-volume that is updated on an irregular or regular basis. The number of titles cited in the first edition of *CID* (1981) and the most recent edition (1995) has grown considerably, yet this represents a conservative number of published titles (see Table 1).

Of the 3,839 active and ceased English-language journal and magazine titles listed in chapter 1 of *CID*, less than 10 percent were published between 1872 and 1972. The other approximately 90 percent have been published in the past twenty-three years.[2] Some of the very early titles were represented by publications started by the Institution of Electrical Engineers in London, which was founded in 1871, the Association for Computing Machinery, founded in 1947, and the Institute of Electrical and Electronics Engineers, founded in 1963.

Other milestones such as the launching of artificial intelligence, IBM's introduction of the electronic calculator, and the development of programming languages all have played a part in developing the literature from 1947 to 1970. After 1971 and the introduction of the microprocessor, computer-based technology seemed to grow as it never had before. Various microprocessor chips, such as the Motorola 6800 and Zilog Z80, debuted. Hardware needed software to make it sell, and another revolution began. Bill Gates (founder of Microsoft) and Paul Allen developed a version of the BASIC language for microcomputers, and Ashton Tate created the popular database program called dBASE. Everything that influenced the marketplace added to the literature. Professionals soon complained about overload and their inability to keep up with the myriad of products and services being introduced. Successful technologies such as microcomputers, word processing, desktop publishing, networking, and computer graphics each created a body of literature that announced, researched, compared, reviewed, studied, promoted, indexed, and abstracted information about various products and technologies (see Table 2).

The market penetration of the microcomputer into U.S. households[3] contributed to a literature that more than doubled the overall literature between 1977 and 1986. Because expertise was limited early on, the general public needed information on what to buy and how to use it, (see Figure 1). It was also during this same period that a significant number of titles ceased (see Figure 2).[4] Some of the reasons for a sharp increase in the number of ceased titles could be:

1. The demise of the small publisher and inability of home-brew titles to compete with larger publishers.

2. The buyout and/or merger of competitive titles.

TABLE 1
Computing Information Directory Coverage of Computer Journals, Indexing
and Abstracting Services, and Review Resources: 1981 and 1955
(includes current and ceased titles)

Chapter	1981	1995
	(1st edition)	(12th edition)
I-Computer Journals[3]	380	3,839[b,c]
V-Indexing & Abstracting Services[4]	25	70[d]
VII-Review Resources[4]	0[a]	28[e]

[a] A chapter on review resources not published in the 1981 edition.
[b] Includes active titles (2,632) with beginning dates, active titles for which no beginning date could be found (118), ceased titles with ending dates (1.002), and ceased titles with no ending date (87).
[c] Serial titles listed in chap. 5, Indexing and Abstracting Services (70), and chap. 7, Review Resources (28), are not included in this count.
[d] Does not include 25 indexing and abstracting services that ceased in or before 1990.
[e] Does not include 30 review titles that ceased in or before 1990.

3. The demise of publications covering outdated technologies.

4. Titles with poor response were quickly dropped or merged with existing successful titles; very few titles, however, were actually announced but never published (see Table 3).

5. Some titles were first made available at no charge as a marketing incentive. Later, subscribers were offered an opportunity to renew for a fee. Strong titles survived and weaker ones ceased.

6. Authors focused on the most prestigious titles or opted to publish with their professional societies.

7. Profiteering and price gouging by a few publishers severely impacted the ability of libraries to purchase materials; higher costs mean less purchasing power for the same dollar.

8. Inflation lowers the purchasing power of the dollar.

9. One of the most, if not the most significant reason for the demise of journal titles can be tied to severe budget cuts. These cuts began in the early 1980s and have continued. Academic science libraries see few or

TABLE 2
Computing Milestones and Growth of Computing Literature as Reflected in
Computing Information Directory

IEE (London) founded	Association for Computing Machinery founded	Numerous languages first compiled: ALGOL 58, APL, BASIC, COBOL, LISP, PL/1, GPSS, etc.	Bubble memory developed (A.H. Bobeck/Bell Laboratories)
Punched card tabulating machine (Herman Hollerith)	Artificial intelligence launched (Alan Turing)		First medical diagnostic program created (J. Lederberg/Stanford University)
Turing machine developed (Alan Turing)	604 calculator introduced (IBM)	Digital Equipment Corp. (DEC) and Control Data Corp. (CDC) founded	Intel Corp. founded (Gordon Moore and Robert Noyce)
Hewlett-Packard Co. founded	First chess playing machine (Claude Shannon/MIT)	First fully transistorized super-computer built (Seymour Cray)	PASCAL compiler written (Nicklaus Wirth)
First automatic digital computer (Atanasoff and Berry/Iowa State College)	Microprogramming concept introduced (Maurice V. Wilkes)	First integrated circuit (Jack Kilby/Texas Instruments)	Intel introduces the first microprocessor (Intel 4004)
Mark I relay-based computer (Howard H. Aiken)	First computer manual written (Fred Gruenberger)	First computer science department established (Purdue)	Cray Research Founded (Seymour Cray)
ENIAC computer dedicated (University of Pennsylvania)	IBM 701 the first electronic stored program computer (Remington Rand)	IBM ships first second computer	Prime Computer corporation is founded
	First magnetic tape device (IBM)	First minicomputer developed (PDP-1/DEC)	Intel introduces the 8080 8-bit micro-processor that would be used in numerous personal computers
	The first first generation computer shipped (IBM)	Removable disks debut	Zilog, developer of microprocsessor chips is formed
	Programming language FORTRAN compiled	IBM ships first third generation computer	Several popular computing titles are published. *(People's Computer Company Newsletter; Creative Computing; Popular Electronics; ACM Transaction series; and Byte)*
	IBM 704 uses the first operating system (Gene Amdahl/IBM)	First Ph.D. in computer science granted (Richard L. Wexelblat/ University of Pennsylvania)	
		First hand-held solid-state calculator (TI)	
1872–1946 (76 years)	1947–1956 (10 years)	1957–1966 (10 years)	1967–1976 (10 years)
Started: 27 titles Ceased: None	Started: 29 titles Ceased: None	Started: 100 titles Ceased: None	Started: 313 titles Ceased: 14

no alternatives to cancellations if they are to keep within budgets that are under constant assault from reductions, inflation, and even in some cases, publisher greed.

Each of the above reasons has played a part in the shaping of the computing literature and in particular the journal literature. But the last three items listed have done much to decimate research libraries with large holdings in science, technology, and medicine. *CID* has been one of the few titles that has kept the same subscription fee for the past five years. As costs continue to spiral upward, the computing literature will wax and wane as computer-based tech-

TABLE 2 (continued)

Apple Computer is founded	IBM begins selling personal computers	PS/2 personal computers introduced (IBM)	RISC-based 6000 family of high-end workstations introduced (IBM)
Apple introduces the Apple II First 32-bit supermini-computer introduced (VAX 11/780/DEC)	First portable computer introduced (Osborne I/Osborne Computer)	First Sun RISC-based workstation released	Windows ver 3.0 released (Microsoft)
First ComputerLand franchise opens as Computer Shack	Sun Microsystems founded Microsoft licenses MS-DOS to microcomputer manufacturers	Macintosh II and Macintosh SE introduced (Apple Computer) Systems Applications Architecture introduced (IBM)	Most hardware vendors have a line of Notebook PCs Most hardware vendors have a line of Notebook
First digital speech synthesis toy introduced (Speak-and-Spell/Texas Instruments)	Adobe PostScript developed ICON programming language developed (Ralph E. Griswold/ University of Arizona)	PageMaker introduced (Aldus) First AI microprocessor chip available (Texas Instruments)	General-purpose pen computers introduced
COMDEX holds its first show			Windows for Workgroups available (Microsoft)
Ada programming language compiled		Cray Y-MP supercomputer released (Cray Research)	NetWare 4.0 networking software released (Novell)
CompuServe goes online		Portable Macintosh (Apple Computer)	Microsoft reveals Windows NT
First electronic spreadsheet software demonstrated (VisiCalc)		First pocket sized MS-DOS compatible computer announced (Poqet)	Pentium-based systems become available to personal computer consumers
Wordstar, word processing program released		GridPad (recognized hand-writing input (Grid)	Virtual Reality developed
VIC-20 home computer debuts		80486-based personal computers are introduced	Multimedia workstations available for the home market
			Internet popularized

1977–1986 (10 years)	1987–1995 (1st Qtr) (8 years, 3 months)
Started: 1,206 Ceased: 398	Started: 937 Ceased: 590

nologies flow into the marketplace replacing older and outdated technologies. The Review Resources (see Table 4) and Indexing and Abstracting Services (see Table 5) will also reflect changes in the computing literature. As all these changes occur, *CID* will be there to announce the birth of new titles and also memorialize those titles that could no longer compete and have quietly been laid to rest.

Notes

1. *CID's* seventeen chapters consist of (1) Computer Journals; (2) University Computing Center Newsletters; (3) Books, Biblios, and Special Issues; (4) Dictionaries and Glossaries; (5) Indexing and Abstracting Services; (6) Software Resources; (7) Review Resources; (8) Hardware Resources; (9) Directories, Ency-

TABLE 3
Announced but Never-Published Computer-Related Titles Tracked by *Computing Information Directory*

1985	-KnowSys Report. (Compusophic System). -Micro/Online. (Micro/Online).
1989	-Document Management: the Journal of Records Automation and Image Processing. (Frost & Sullivan). -Music, Computers, and Software. (?).
1990	-CrossExaminer. (Pinnacle).
1992	-Biomedical Optics. (Springer-Verlag). -Journal of Technology in Mathematics. (Academic). ISSN: 1055-789X[a]
1993	-Applied Data and Knowledge Engineering (Springer-Verlag). ISSN: 0942-251X
1984	-Computer Communications Newsletter. (Sten-O-Press). -PC Digest Newsletter (MV Publishing, Inc.). -QSR Bulletin. (Was to review newly published statistical packages.)
1986	-QL Owner. (Europe House).
1987	-Memory and Microcomputers (Gordon and Breach). ISSN: 0733-2394.
1989	-Japanese Journal of Ergonomics/Human Factors. (VSP). ISSN: 0920-5050 -Journal of Software Engineering. (Frost & Sullivan). -Software Maintenance: Research and Practice. (Wiley). ISSN: 1040-550X.
1991	-Complexity: An International Journal of Complex and Adaptive Systems. (Pergamon). ISSN: 0964-1815
1994	-Journal of Electronic Material Applications. (Technomic). ISSN: 0968-2783.

[a]Although *Journal of Technology in Mathematics* was never published by Academic Press, it is listed in OCLC's FirstSearch online database. The 1994 *The Serials Directory* published by EBSCO (entry 3382) lists this title as ceased with an unknown ending date.

[b]*Software Maintenance: Research and Practice* is another title that vaporized. Although it is not listed in either the 1994 *Serials Directory* published by EBSCO or in Bowker's *Ulrichs International Periodicals Directory, 1994–95*, it is listed with a beginning date of v.1, no: 1: September 1989 in OCLC's FirstSearch online database.

clopedias, and Handbooks; (10) IEEE; (11) ACM SIG Proceedings; (12) Tutorials; (13) Career and Salary Trends Bibliography; (14) Expansion to the Library of Congress Classification Schedule; (15) Research Marketing Companies (including citations to tables and figures including marketing research and trends; (16) Publisher's Addresses; (17) Master Subject Index (all citations are listed by subject).

2. Of the 2,750 active titles listed in chapter 1, beginning dates could not be verified for 118 titles.
3. According to the 1993 *Computer Industry Almanac*, approximately 10,500 microcomputers were shipped to consumers in the United States in 1975. That number grew to an estimated 4,750,000 in 1985 and to more than 7,050,000 in 1990. Link Resources (1994) estimates that multimedia PCs will penetrate approximately 20 percent of U.S. households in 1995.
4. In *CID*, a title is determined to have ceased when its volume and numbering cease. If the volume and

TABLE 4
Computer-Related Review Services by Dates of Coverage as Published in the
Computing Information Directory

Beginning Date	Title	Beginning Date	Title
1940	–Mathematical Reviews –Computing Reviews –Computer Review	1983	–Computer Book Review –Data Base Product Reports... to 1993 –Microcomputer Review...to 1991

1973	–Data Entry Awareness
	  Reports...to 1993
	–Computer Terminals Review...
	  to 1991
	–Computer Peripherals Review...
	  to 1991
			–Business Computer Digest &
			  Software Review...to 1987
			–Business Systems Product
			  Update...to 1987
			–Business Systems Update...
			  to 1987
			–Computer Classified Blue

1975	–Packaged Software Reports...
	  to 1993?
			book...to 1987
			–Digest of Software Reviews:
			  Education...to 1987

1978	–Telecommunications Product
	  Review
	–Officemation Product Reports...
	  to 1993
			–EPIE & Consumers Union Micro-
			  Hardware...to 1985/86
			–Infoworld Report Card...to 1983
			–Micro-Hardware/Micro-
			  Courseware Pro/files & Evalua-

1979	–Library Computer Systems... to Dec 1993		tions –Microindex Journal...to 1984 –Software Reports
1981	–School Microware Reviews...to 1983	1984	–Software Digest Ratings Report –TESS

1982	–COMPendium...to 1983
	–Educational Micro Review...
	  to 1986
	–LAMP...to 1984
	–Micro Courseware Pro/files...
	  to 1987
	–Computer Bookbase...to 1984
			–Communications Product
			  Reports...to 1993
			–Computer Software/Hardware
			  Index...to 1987
			–Current Index of Computer
			  Literature...to 1985

Note: Includes review of books, journals, hardware, and software.
Source: Colville, WA: *Computing Information Directory, 1995.* Copyright 1995, D.M. Hildebrandt.
Reprinted with permission.

numbering continue after to a name change or merger, then a *see* reference is made from the former
title to the newest title. In cases where there are multiple name changes, each former title refers to the
most recent title. In the note position of the newest title is a history of all the changes. Titles with name
changes or mergers are counted only once.

TABLE 4 (continued)

Beginning Date	Title	Beginning Date	Title
1984 Cont'd	–Infoworld in Review...to 1985 –Micro Software Evaluations –MicroReviews...to 1988 –PC Products...to 1986	1988 Cont'd	–Executive Business Tools –Science and Technology Annual Reference Review
1985	–Software Reviews on File –Microalerts...to 1988	1989	–Law Office Technology Review –CE Computing Review...to 1994 –Computer & Office Products Evaluation...to 1990
1986	–Artificial Intelligence Review –Bits & Bytes Review –Computer Industry Digest...to 1987 –Maeventec Software Review –Micro Software Reports...to 1986/8 –PC Review...to 1988	1990	–LAN Reporter...to 1993 –PC Review (London) –Law Office Software: Attorney's Guide to Selection –PC Review
1987	–Neural Network Review...to 1991 –MacGuide...to 1989 –PCr²...to 1989	1991	–Digital Signal Processing –Software-CD...to 1993
		1993	–Directory of Educational Software for Nursing
1988	–Software Digest Macintosh Ratings Report...to 1992	1994	–M-CAD Buyer's Guide –PDM Buyer's Guide –Superconductivity Review

Note: Includes review of books, journals, hardware, and software.
Source: Colville, WA: *Computing Information Directory, 1995.* Copyright 1995, D.M. Hildebrandt. Reprinted with permission.

TABLE 5
Computer-Related Indexing & Abstracting Services by Dates of Coverage as
Reflected in *Computing Information Directory*

Beginning Date	Title	Beginning Date	Title
1895	–U.S. Supt. of Documents, Monthly Catalog	1970	–Index to U.S. Government Periodicals...1987
1921	–Imaging Abstracts	1971	–Index to IEEE Periodicals (1971–1973 serials only)
1946	–Selected Rand Abstracts		
1951	–Cumulative Index to Entire IEEE Group –Transactions / Journals...to 1971	1972	–Computers, Control & Information Theory
		1973	–Index to IEEE Publications
1955	–Data Processing Digest	1974	–Human Factors Society, Computer Systems Technical Group, Bulletin
1957	–Computer Abstracts		
1960	–ACM Guide to Computing Literature –ACM Collected Algorithms –IFIP Bibliography...to 1985 –International Computer Bibliography...to 1970 –Solid State and Superconductivity Abstracts	1975	–Periodical Guide for Computerists...to 1982 –Computer Science: Dissertation Bibliography...to 1980
		1976	–Computerworld Editorial Index...to 1991
		1977	–Personal Computer News...to October 1977
1961	–New Literature on Automation...to 1983	1978	–Computer Business –Precis...to 1984?
1962	–Computer and Information Systems Abstracts –Microelectronics and Reliability	1979	–Computer Industry Update
1963	–Current Papers on Computers & Control	1980	–Computer Literature Index –Microcomputer Abstracts
1964	–Computer Applications...to 1973	1981	–Micro...Publications-in-Review...to July 1982 –China Science & Technology Abstracts, Series 3...to 1987 –Electrical Engineering & Computer Science –Index to Proceedings of the IEEE...to 1987
1966	–Computer & Control Abstracts –Electrical & Electronics Abstracts		
1967	–Electronics and Communications Abstracts		
1968	–Bibliography of Computers and Data Processing...to 1979 –Ergonomics Abstracts	1982	–DataCom Reader Service...January 1994 –Government Computer News Index...to 1985

Source: Colville, WA: *Computing Information Directory, 1995.* Copyright 1995, D.M. Hildebrandt. Reprinted with permission.

TABLE 5 (continued)

Beginning Date	Title	Beginning Date	Title
1982 Cont'd	–LAMP...to 1984 –Softindex	1987 Cont'd	–Key Abstracts: Measurements in Physics –Key Abstracts: Optoelectronics –Key Abstracts: Power Systems & Applications –Key Abstracts: Robotics & Control –Key Abstracts: Semiconductor Devices –Key Abstracts: Software Engineering –Key Abstracts: Telecommunications –PCr^2...to 1989 –Synopsis...to 1988? –Turing Institute Abstracts in Artificial Intelligence...to 1994
1983	–Microindex Journal...to 1984 –Computer Contents...to 1989 –Infoscan...to 1984 –IT Focus...to 1988 –Micro Software Report...to 1984–85 –Robotics Abstracts...to 1992 –Telecommunications Alert		
1984	–Artificial Intelligence Abstracts...to August 1992 –CAD/CAM Abstracts...to August 1992 –CAD/CAM Abstracts Annual... to 1992? –Printer Reviews: 1984 to 1992 –Microcomputer Industry Update –Current Index of Computer Literature...to 1985	1988	–Key Abstracts: Microwave Technology –Key Abstracts: High-temperature superconductors –Key Abstracts: Machine Vision –Key Abstracts: Microelectronics & Printed Circuits
1985	–Computer Industry Forecasts –Data Sources Computer Industry Digest...to 1986	1989	–Computer-aided Process Control Abstracts...to 1991 –Key Abstracts: Business Automation –RECAP: PC...to 1990
1986	–Computer Abstracts on Microfiche...to 1992 –Computer Information Review –Japan Computer Technology and Applications Abstracts...to 1987	1990	–Abstracts in Human-computer Interaction...to 1993 –Deadline (Began: 1988. Abstracts from 1990)...to 1994 –Information Management & Technology Abstracts
1987	–Computer Executive News Briefing...to 1988 –Key Abstracts: Advanced Materials –Key Abstracts: Antennas & Propagation –Key Abstracts: Artificial Intelligence –Key Abstracts: Computer Communications & Storage –Key Abstracts: Computing in Electronics & Power –Key Abstracts: Electronic Circuits –Key Abstracts: Electronic Instrumentation –Key Abstracts: Human-computer interaction	1991	–Computer Industry Update Japan...to 1992 –Key Abstracts: Factory Automation –PC Computer Review...to 1992
		1992	–Key Abstracts: Human-computer Interaction –Key Abstracts: Neural Networks
		1993	–HILITES...to 1993 –Artificial Intelligence Database of Abstracts (CD-ROM)

FIGURE 1
Growth of Computer-Related Journals Reflected in *Computing Information Directory* by
Date of First Issue Published, 1872–1995 (First Quarter)

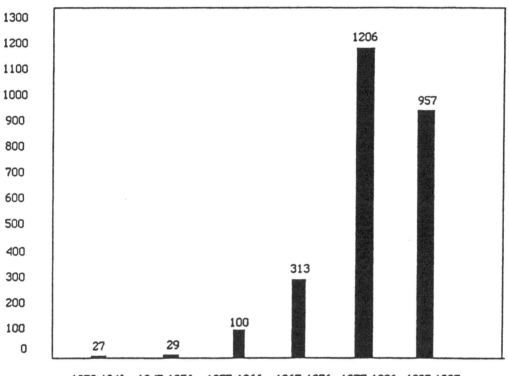

FIGURE 2
Ceased Computer-Related Journals Reflected in *Computing Information Directory* by
Date of Last Issue Published, 1872–1995 (First Quarter)

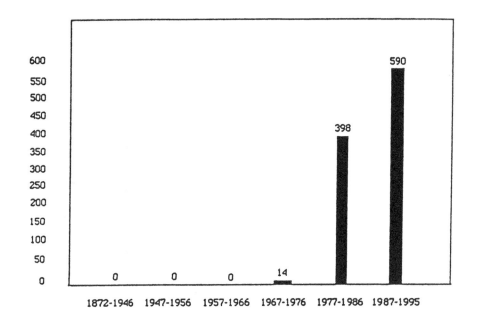

19

Library of Congress Cataloging in Publication Program

Glen Zimmerman

The purpose of the Cataloging in Publication (CIP) Program is to prepare prepublication cataloging records for those books most likely to be widely acquired by the nation's libraries. These records (CIP data) are printed in the book and greatly facilitate cataloging activities for libraries. They are also distributed prior to the books' publication in machine-readable form via the MARC (MAchine Readable Cataloging) tapes, alerting libraries, and other bibliographic services around the world to forthcoming titles; therefore, the CIP data are also used for acquisitions purposes.

The CIP Program began in 1971 as a special project, funded in part by grants from the Council on Library Resources, Inc., and the National Endowment for the Humanities. It is now fully supported by Library of Congress appropriations and is administered by the Cataloging in Publication Division.

Publishers participating in this program submit a manuscript or galley of a forthcoming title to the CIP Division. This prepublication information is forwarded to the cataloging divisions, where it proceeds through various cataloging stages, including descriptive cataloging, subject analysis, and the assignment of full Library of Congress and Dewey decimal classification numbers. At the end of the cataloging process, the record is forwarded to the CIP Division, where the publisher's copy is prepared and sent to the publisher to be printed on the copyright page of the book. Meanwhile, the MARC version of the record is distributed to the library community, worldwide, where it appears in a variety of publications, bibliographic vendor services, and national and regional bibliographic networks. The CIP Program is a partnership formed among the Library of Congress, publishers, and the library and information communities.

TABLE 1
Growth of the CIP Program, 1971/1972–1994

Fiscal Year	CIP Data Provided to Publishers	Number of Publishers in Program
1994	50,961	3,400*
1993	48,772	3,200*
1992	47,690	3,100*
1991	45,987	**
1990	45,673	**
1980	28,609	**
1971/1972	6,400	(1972) 198
		(1971) 27

* Estimate
** Data not available

20

The National Technical Information Service (NTIS) Bibliographic Database

Mona F. Smith

NTIS Mission

The National Technical Information Service (NTIS) provides access to the results of both U.S. and foreign government–sponsored research and development (R&D), engineering, and business-related activities. Throughout its years of operation, the NTIS mission has been to improve the transfer of technology from the government to the private sector and improve competitiveness of U.S. business and industry in a global economy.

History

In 1945, President Truman established the Publications Board (PB) to review all scientific and technical research documents produced during World War II. The purpose of the Publications Board was to determine what could be made available to U.S. industry and the general public. In 1950, Public Law 81-776 directed the Department of Commerce to operate a national clearinghouse to collect and distribute scientific and technical information. In 1970, this clearinghouse was reestablished as the National Technical Information Service.

In 1992 passage of the American Technology Preeminence Act (ATPA) mandated government agencies to submit all federally produced or financed scientific, technical, and engineering information to NTIS in a timely manner. Until the passage of ATPA, all items were submitted to NTIS voluntarily by government agencies, sometimes unevenly and irregularly. The ATPA will play a key role in building a more comprehensive and centralized collection of current government information.

TABLE 1
Titles in NTIS Collection

Dates	Items in Collection	Items in Database
Cumulative– FY 1974	834,111	388,263
1975	63,670	63,670
1976	58,146	58,146
Transition Quarter	15,482	15,482
1977	80,993	80,993
1978	74,927	74,927
1979	67,692	67,692
1980	77,335	77,335
1981	78,223	78,223
1982	82,683	82,683
1983	79,471	79,471
1984	71,587	71,587
1985	70,211	70,211
1986	69,760	69,760
1987	62,906	62,906
1988	68,096	68,096
1989	61,307	61,307
TOTAL	1,976,976	1,208,683

The NTIS Bibliographic Database online covers 1964 to the present. Printed or microform indexes provide access to the titles that predate the online database.

Acquisition and Evaluation

One of the major advantages of the NTIS database is that it combines unclassified input from the Department of Defense, Department of Energy, and NASA with that of other government agencies, such as the Environmental Protection Agency, National Institute of Science and Technology, Department of Interior, National Science Foundation, Department of Agriculture, Department of Health and Human Services, and others within one database. The major contributors to the database come from the combined input of NASA, Defense, and Energy. This material is supplied to NTIS in machine-readable form on magnetic tapes and is essentially merged into the database. The PB-collection documents are processed by NTIS. Other sources for these titles include hundreds of federal

TABLE 2
NTIS Information Sources: Annual Input of Federal Agency–Sponsored R&D by
Major Contributors, 1988 and 1994

Organization	1988	1994
Agency for Int'l Development	—	223
Agriculture Dept.	775	680
Commerce Dept.	2,200	1,405
Defense Dept.	13,100	14,845
Energy Dept.	12,100	22,473
Health & Human Services	1,600	1,520
Labor Dept.	50	—
Interior Dept.	1,000	720
Transportation Dept.	800	750
Environmental Protection Agency	1,900	2,540
NASA	4,800	13,370
Nat'l Science Foundation	700	460
Nuclear Regulatory Commission	400	330
Fach Informations-zentrum (FIZ)	—	2,020
Canada Institute for Scientific & Technical Information	—	3,940

agencies, numerous state and local governments, federal contractors, academic institutions, foreign governments, international organizations, and private sector organizations. Because the U.S. government funds more than half of the research and engineering activities in the United States, the NTIS Bibliographic Database contains information on such diverse topics as environmental sciences, computer sciences, telecommunications, health care, physical sciences, international trade and marketing, regulations, research administration, business, and education.

Major Traits of the Collection

- Very diverse collection based on a wide range of U.S. and foreign government sources.

- Approximately 2.5 million titles are available for searching. Each year 70,000–80,000 titles are added to the database.

- Primarily a collection of unclassified reports and computer products rather than journal articles in the open literature.

TABLE 3
NTIS Subject Coverage, 1988 and 1994

Subject area	1988	1994	Ten year average
Administration & management	2,640	4%	2,150
Aeronautics & aerodynamics	2,530	3	2,030
Agriculture & food	1,840	3	1,690
Astronomy & astrophysics	2,020	3	790
Behavior & society	1,920	5	3,340
Biomedical & human factors	940	2	870
Building industry	1,120	2	1,220
Business & Econ.	1,610	4	1,490
Chemistry	6,060	9	6,310
Civil Engineering	1,520	2	1,780
Combustion, engines & propellants	1,620	3	1,340
Communication	1,260	3	1,210
Computers & Information theory	3,350	6	2,710
Detection & countermeasures	760	2	760
Electrotechnology	2,520	5	2,060
Energy	6,780	9	8,590
Environment	5,880	16	6,780
Health care	1,300	2	2,130
Library & info. Science	3,160	9	1,960
Manufacturing & industrial eng.	3,370	5	3,100
Materials Science	3,960	8	3,930
Mathematical Sci.	1,680	2	1,480
Medicine & biology	6,060	11	6,260
Natural resources & earth sciences	4,140	9	4,160
Nuclear science & technology	6,600	11	7,390
Ocean technology & engineering	1,850	3	1,810
Physics	9,990	16	7,810
Space technology	2,020	5	1,020
Transportation	1,640	3	1,990
Urban & regional technology & development	1,310	3	1,870

- Twenty-five percent of all new titles come from foreign sources through various international exchange agreements.

- Covers state-of-the-art technology, and practical and applied research.

- Provides current information not readily available from any other source.

TABLE 4
NTIS Top Ten Non-U.S. Contributors, 1994

Country of Origin	Number of Citations
Canada	4,631
Germany	3,021
Netherlands	1,886
Japan	1,796
France	1,230
United Kingdom	1,195
International Agencies	1,094
*U.S.S.R.	838
Sweden	786
Finland	546

*These documents from the former Soviet Union were published prior to the breakup into the Commonwealth of Independent States.

Types of Documents	1994
Reprints from Journal Articles	3,604
Government-owned Inventions	
Patents	1,035
Patent Applications	439
Computer Products	451
Technical Reports	
Conference Proceedings	
Theses	
Bibliographies	
Published Searches	
CD-ROM	
Videotapes	

Processing

NTIS provides information management to agencies whose documents or magnetic tapes are submitted. NTIS creates a bibliographic record for each item, lists each item in its online database and maintains the item in its archives.

Products

NTIS provides current awareness, government inventions available for licensing, a directory of Japanese technical resources, and software catalogs. A major high point of NTIS services is its document delivery service. Most documents noted in the bibliographic database are available from the agency.

NTIS Preview Database via FedWorld

NTIS receives an average of 7,000 Scientific and Technical Information (STEI) and business-related information products each month. NTIS is making the bibliographic citations of items it has acquired within the most recent thirty days available to the public via FedWorld. Anyone may access FedWorld with a computer and a modem. To connect by modem: Set parity to none, data bits to 8, and stop bit to 1. Set terminal emulation to ANSI. Set duplex to full. Then set communication software to dial FedWorld at 703-321-FEDW (3339); via Internet: Telnet to fedworld.gov; For File Transfer Protocol (FTP) services, connect to ftp.fedworld.gov; For World Wide Web (WWW) access, point web browser to http://www.fedworld.gov.

21

Calculators and Crystal Balls: Predicting Journal Subscription Prices

Ronald E. Akie

Background

The purchase of journal subscriptions by libraries is an atypical institutional acquisition. Not only must subscriptions be paid for in full before the product is received, but libraries must make decisions on what to purchase before they know what the actual price is going to be. As a result, libraries have come to depend upon projections for journal subscription prices in order to prepare their budgets. Generally, serials vendors—the industry intermediary between publishers and libraries—have provided price projections as a service to their clients.

In the past decade, a convergence of factors has heightened the importance of these projections to libraries. First and foremost, library budgets have come under pressure from the combined effects of inflation, reduced federal and state funding, and increased costs for both print and electronic acquisitions. Enough has been written about this issue in the library literature; suffice it to say that in recent years libraries have faced their most strenuous belt-tightening of the postwar era. While the first wave of tighter budgets generally affected book purchasing, sustained pressures have led institutions to cancel journal subscriptions.

At the same time, libraries have increasingly turned to alternate sources to meet their patrons' needs, and newer technologies have facilitated this shift. Libraries' use of interlibrary lending, commercial document delivery services, and CD-ROM databases has grown, to the detriment of journal subscriptions.

All of these factors have resulted in increased cancellations of journal subscriptions. In order to cover their costs with a decreased number of units,

TABLE 1
Five-Year History of Price Increases (%)

	1991	1992	1993	1994	1995
North American Titles:	12.0	11.3	10.3	9.0	9.8
European Titles:	25.6	−0.2	24.5	1.5	9.6
Typical overall collection:	16.2	9.2	17.0	5.7	9.7

publishers have had to increase prices more rapidly than in the past to make up for their lost revenue.

A volatile U.S. dollar has caused prices for European journals—the core of many research collections—to increase as much as 25 percent in some years (1991 and 1993) and hardly at all in others (1992 and 1994), as shown in Table 1.

The data on actual price increases is based on Faxon's database of 120,000 journal titles. In order to determine actual price increases for each year, we consider both the percentage increase for each title and the number of orders for each title to obtain a weighted average. A title that increases 20 percent and has only one order counts far less than a title that increases 12 percent and has 5,000 orders. This method ensures that we obtain data that reflect the materials libraries are actually purchasing, rather than what is simply available for purchase.

Because we try to look at the broadest range possible, the database analyzed is more extensive than that used for the U. S. Periodical Price Index sponsored by the Library Materials Price Index Committee (LMPIC) of the Association for Library Collections and Technical Services (ALCTS) of the American Library Association, for which Faxon has maintained the core database. That study tracks a smaller subset of approximately 4,000 titles in accordance with the ANSI Z39.20-1983 standard for computing price indexes.

Faxon's client base is composed of large academic and public libraries, college libraries, Fortune 1000 corporations, medical institutions, and government agencies. Our price studies therefore tend to focus on scientific, technical and medical (STM) journals. While social sciences, humanities and other disciplines are represented, as are consumer magazines and newspapers, their overall impact is smaller. Our price projections are therefore best suited to organizations with strong STM collections.

Faxon traditionally begins to receive inquiries from clients on journal prices one year in advance. In other words, in January of 1995, clients began asking for projections for 1996 subscription prices. Most U.S. academic institutions must prepare and submit their budgets between January and June and complete their selection lists by October. Publishers generally set prices for the following year between June and September. The methodology explained below focuses on projecting prices for the U.S. market, but the same principle would apply for other markets as well.

Price Projection Methodology

At Faxon, we have developed a price projection methodology that has resulted in accurate projections over the past decade. While the core methodology remains essentially the same each year, its application varies according to the particular circumstances of the publishing environment in a given year. Projecting prices is more than a mathematical exercise; it requires an understanding of economic principles, knowledge of the current state of the publishing industry, and an intuitive sense of pricing behavior within the serials industry. Judgment must be applied to the pure numbers.

To prepare a price projection, we begin by examining three main components of journal cost: general economic inflation, publisher-related cost factors, and currency exchange values.

General Inflation

Like any business, publishers are subject to overall inflationary cost increases. Inflation drives up wages and other routine operating expenses and will therefore tend to increase subscription prices.

We estimate expected overall inflation for the coming year in each country that is a major source of journals for our clients. We identify countries where publishers incur the majority of their publishing costs. In the case of a multinational publisher with publishing activity in several countries, we look at each publishing program separately. Typically, we consider the United States, Canada, the United Kingdom, Germany, The Netherlands, France, and Switzerland in detail and other regions more generally. Fortunately, no dearth of estimates exists. Numerous business publications, economic consulting groups, financial service companies, and government agencies produce country-by-country inflation estimates. We routinely monitor a number of different sources, comparing both the numbers and their underlying assumptions. A solid grounding in basic economic concepts and theory is essential for this work, as is up-to-date knowledge of global financial conditions and trends.

Once an inflationary factor has been determined for each country, the job is not complete, because the publisher does not automatically pass along the full amount of inflation as part of the subscription price. As in any business, management must decide how much of its cost increases can be offset by cost-saving measures, determine whether a lower level of margin is acceptable to shareholders, and, finally, consider the price elasticity of its product to gauge how much of the inflationary increase to pass along as part of the price. The predictor, therefore, also needs a thorough understanding of the current dynamics of the publishing industry in order to assess how much of the general inflation the publishers in each country will choose to pass along.

Publishing Factors

While general inflation affects every business, publishers also have a unique set of cost elements that can affect subscription price more directly. Some of the more important factors include:

- Manuscript submissions/page increases. Journal editors often receive an increasing number of manuscripts each year. Even with more selective publication criteria, the pressure to increase the number of articles published is strong, particularly in rapidly evolving scientific disciplines. The result is an increase in both labor and production costs for the publisher. In some cases, publishers split journals or spin off new titles, which can mask actual price increases. While we ask publishers to estimate this factor, it is usually difficult to project a year in advance.

- Paper. The cost of paper is a significant component of publishers' cost of goods. Sudden increases in the cost of paper will drive up publishers' costs. Our projections focus on print journals and do not provide reliable measures for other media such as CD-ROM or online journals, where pricing policies and patterns still vary widely by publisher.

- Postage. Postage is another significant cost for publishers. Increases in postal rates directly affect the cost of each unit sold.

- Market shifts. Publishers' overall cost structures are also affected by shifting conditions in the marketplace. In recent years, tighter budgets as well as increased use of electronic information formats, shared resources, and document delivery services have led libraries to cancel more subscriptions than in the past. With fewer units across which to spread their costs, publishers must sometimes resort to increasing their subscription prices to cover their fixed costs.

For each of the factors described above, the predictor must first make a determination of what the overall affect will be on publishers, country by country, and then estimate how much of the impact the publisher will choose to pass along to the buyer. We try to forecast the actual price that a typical client will pay, which is the publisher's list price inclusive of shipping and handling. We do not include any service charge of our own in the projection because such charges vary according to each client's collection and service needs.

The result of determining a general inflationary factor and assessing the impact of publishing factors is the **Base Price Increase** by country. This is the amount that we expect publishers in each country, on average, to increase their prices in their own currencies. The formula thus far would look as follows:

TABLE 2
Base Price Increase Formula

for each country:
> **General inflation impact**
+   **Publishing factor impact**
> > (Page increase impact + Paper impact
> > + Postage impact + Market impact)
> > ────────────────────────────
=   **Base price increase**

Currency Exchange Effects

Because journal publishing has become a global market, we must address the differences in currency values between suppliers and purchasers in addition to the Base Price Increase. A German library purchasing a German-published subscription will experience only the base price increase because the purchaser and supplier are dealing in the same currency. When a U.S. library purchases the same journal, however, it must convert U.S. dollars to pay the publisher in German marks. (In practice, the serials vendor typically handles the mechanics of the currency exchange for the library and publisher.)

Many publishers, particularly smaller ones, simply set prices in their own currencies. Libraries pay based on the market exchange rate in effect at the time the publisher receives the order (these figures are published daily in a variety of sources, including the *Wall Street Journal*). We refer to this as a **Floating Exchange Rate**. Different libraries in the same country can pay different prices depending upon the exchange rate on the day their order is processed. Wide daily swings in exchange rates can dramatically affect price in this model. Projecting prices for publishers who use a Floating Exchange Rate is difficult because we must estimate one average rate over the period when most libraries order (September through November).

To illustrate, let us assume that the exchange rate at time of purchase is 1.50 German marks to 1.0 U.S. dollar. If the German journal is priced at 100 German marks, the U.S. library will pay 100 divided by 1.50, or 66.67 dollars. If the exchange rate moved to 1.40 marks per dollar, the library would pay 100 divided by 1.40, or 71.43 dollars, an increase of 7 percent. Table 3 illustrates how much currencies can move over several years.

Larger publishers have tried to temper the effects of currency fluctuations on the market either by setting a fixed exchange rate or by setting their prices in multiple currencies. In the first case, a publisher might set a price of 100 German marks and fix the exchange rate at 1.45 for a six-month period. This means that any U.S., library that purchases the journal in that period will pay $68.97 (100 divided by 1.45), regardless of what the actual exchange rate is on the day of purchase. We refer to this as a **Fixed Exchange Rate**. Generally, publishers will set a fixed exchange rate between June and August.

In the last several years, many larger publishers have moved from this model

TABLE 3
Key Foreign Exchange Rates
In cents per unit of foreign currency.

A. 1960–1995 at Midyear.

	1960	1965	1970	1975	1980	1985	1990	1995
French Franc	20	20	18	24	25	11	19	20
German DeutschMark	24	25	28	40	57	34	64	71
Dutch Guilder	26	28	28	39	52	31	57	64
Swiss Franc	23	23	23	38	62	42	77	86
British Pound	280	279	239	218	238	138	190	159

B. 1994–1995 Fluctuations.

	Dec.	Jan.	Feb.	Mar.	Apr.	May	June	July	Aug.	Sept.	Nov.
French Franc	19	19	19	20	21	20	20	21	20	20	20
German DeutschMark	64	65	67	71	72	71	71	72	69	68	71
Dutch Guilder	57	58	60	63	65	63	64	64	62	61	63
Swiss Franc	75	78	78	85	88	85	86	86	83	84	87
British Pound	156	157	157	160	161	159	159	160	157	156	158

Source: Federal Reserve Bulletin

to setting prices directly in U.S. dollars in an attempt to provide even more stability in the marketplace. A publisher in this case might set prices of 100 German marks and $69.00 U.S., eliminating any currency conversion factor.

To arrive at the dollar price in this model, publishers generally try to predict exchange values for the entire forthcoming year and average them, while also considering the general U.S., market conditions. This provides a stable price for the market and a stable revenue projection for their own financial projections. Here again, publishers may choose to absorb some of a currency increase themselves rather than pass it along to the clients.

Estimating this figure is more than just a mathematical exercise; we must consult with publishers throughout the year and then attempt to predict their behavior in this regard to develop our projections. We must predict what the relative values of the currencies will be at particular points in time, again consulting government statistics, financial advisers, and other sources as well as our own estimates. This is perhaps the most difficult and uncertain piece of the formula. Predicting the future relative value of world currencies is not a task that can be done quickly or without risk. Global politics, natural disasters, and financial speculation can move currency markets substantially without any warning. We saw this with 1992 journal prices, for example, when the U.S.

dollar suddenly shot up in value following the Gulf War in 1991. To achieve reliable projections consistently, the predictor must monitor currency markets and global politics throughout the entire year.

For each country, we arrive at a weighted total price increase by multiplying the proportion of floating, fixed and U.S. dollar prices by the estimated percentage increase for each to reach an average currency impact. We now add this data to our formula:

TABLE 4
Total Price Increase Formula

for each country:

	General inflation impact
+	Publishing factor impact
	(Page increase impact + Paper impact + Postage impact + Market impact)
=	Base price increase

+	Currency impact
	(weighted average of floating, fixed and U.S. dollar-priced)
=	Total price increase

The Consolidated Projection

Once this exercise has been completed for each country, it is time to consolidate the data into an overall projection. Many libraries find detailed country-by-country projections unwieldy and prefer a more consolidated projection to apply to their budgets. We have traditionally provided a projection for North American-published titles (U.S. and Canadian) and for European-published titles, with additional detail available for those who desire it. Recently, we have split out UK-published titles separately from the rest of the European group because the UK has chosen not to tie the pound to the continental European currencies. While the German mark, French franc, Swiss franc, and Dutch guilder move more or less as a related group, the pound moves independently.

We base our consolidated projection on an overall average client mix of titles by country to reflect our typical client's collection. Let us assume as shown in Table 5, an overall average collection based on budget dollars for a 1996 subscription year.

We develop a Continental European average price increase by means of a weighted average of the individual country increases (see Table 6).

A final weighted averaging provides a consolidated projection for a typical overall library collection (see Table 7).

A typical library collection would therefore experience an 11.3 percent overall price increase based on this sample data. A client whose collection is mark-

TABLE 5
Sample Journal Collection—1996

Country of publication	Portion of budget dollars
North America	60%
Continental Europe	25
(Netherlands, Germany,	
France, Switzerland)	
UK	10
Other	5
Total	**100%**

TABLE 6
Sample Weighted Average for Continental European Journals—1996

Country of Publication	Portion of European group		Increase		Weighted Increase
Netherlands	50%	x	15%	=	7.5%
Germany	20	x	17	=	3.4
France	20	x	12	=	2.4
Switzerland	10	x	14	=	1.4
Total					**14.7%**

TABLE 7
Weighted Price Projection for Sample Library Collection—1996

Country of Publication	Portion of European group		Increase		Weighted Increase
North American	60%	x	10.0%	=	6.0%
Continental European	25	x	14.7	=	3.7
UK	10	x	11.2	=	1.1
Other	5	x	11.0	=	0.5
Total					**11.3%**

edly different can perform a customized weighted average using this same base data.

Conclusion

Over the past five years, Faxon's overall projections for journal prices have fallen within 1 percent of the actual increases, as shown in Table 8.

Journal price projections are helpful for library planning and budgeting purposes and can be highly accurate, allowing libraries to determine their future costs before actual prices are set. The price projection methodology in use at Faxon has evolved over the years with input from numerous staff members,

TABLE 8
Five-Year History of Faxon Projections versus Actual Price Increases (%)

	1991	1992	1993	1994	1995
North American Titles:					
Projection:	9.5	10.0	9.5	10.0	9.9
Actual:	12.0	11.3	10.3	9.0	9.8
European Titles:					
Projection:	20.5	3.5	25.0	1.8	10.4
Actual:	25.6	-0.2	24.5	1.5	9.6
Typical overall collection:					
Projection:	17.0	9.0	18.0	6.2	10.5
Actual:	16.2	9.2	17.0	5.7	9.7

clients, and publishers. While the basic calculations have remained unchanged, the methodology's application and the interpretation of various factors have evolved as the publishing environment and library market have changed over the past decade. For example, the increase in journal cancellations in the past three years caused us to begin considering cancellations as a separate factor that had not previously been isolated. Now, in our discussions with publishers, we routinely ask what they expect the direct effect of cancellations on prices to be.

Over the years, various parties have argued for a restructuring of the journal industry pricing model, but as yet no viable alternative has been developed. Libraries will continue to depend for some time upon price projections to develop their budgets, and changes in the publishing industry and subscription market will continue to influence the application of the base methodology for developing price projections. In this unusual market, the methodology described has attempted to apply a consistent economic model, illustrating that while the future cannot be known with certainty, past behavior and general economic indicators can provide reliable benchmarks.

22

Monitoring the Health of North America's Small and Mid-Sized Book Publishers Since 1980

John Huenefeld

The management consultants of The Huenefeld Company coach modest-sized book publishers on the application of effective small-group dynamics to their operations. In 1980, they were persuaded by several of their clients to use the readership of their biweekly publishing management newsletter, *The Huenefeld Report*, to generate performance evaluation guidelines and planning ratios specifically appropriate to their constituency—under-$30-million (annual sales) U. S. and Canadian publishers. Every year since, subscribers to this newsletter have received a four-page questionnaire (currently 41 questions with numerous sub-parts), with the understanding that only those who answer *all of the questions* will receive the extensive report of results—broken down and averaged by 19 different types and sizes of publishing programs (both commercial and not-for-profit . . . serving trade, textbook, direct response, and nontraditional markets). Enclosure within regular issues of the newsletter is the only method used to circulate the questionnaire.

Each year, about 200 publishers (it has ranged from 163 to 268) decide that the feedback is worth the time required to complete and return this rather exhaustive questionnaire. The questionnaire is anonymous, and respondents are promised that their entries will be destroyed soon after the individual bits of data are entered into Huenefeld's computer. Participants are instructed to include self-addressed envelopes for their copies of the eventual report. (Data is collected from January through March—and the report is disseminated to all participants early each May.)

Four percent of the publishers submitting 1994 data were Canadian, the other 96 percent from the U.S.A. Their average 1994 sales volume was $3,434,349—with 14 percent (primarily "start-ups" and "self-publishers") below the $300,000 sales level the Huenefeld consultants consider a normal "break-even" point. Not-for-profit publishing programs (which in most of the last fourteen years have reported higher operating margins than the for-profits) accounted for 38 percent of the responses.

The survey averages hard numbers on annual sales volume, returns, expenses and margins. Participants are asked to rank the importance (to them) of a comprehensive list of marketing tactics, and to provide a very detailed breakdown of their budgetary allocation of resources between all major publishing functions.

The survey also probes levels of new-title acquisition and inventory investment, print quantities, pricing formulas, average and maximum discounts given middlemen, author royalty terms, average units-of-sale, year-end levels of receivables and payables, average age of receivables, bad debt and inventory write-off percentages, subsidiary rights and export revenue levels, and specific salaries paid the people performing each of eighteen basic publishing jobs.

Subscribers frequently tell the Huenefeld consultants that—because of its longevity and comprehensive nature—they use this survey report as a point-of-departure for their annual budget deliberations and salary adjustments. But the consultants are persistent in warning that the data is anonymously submitted and unverified, and should thus be treated as reasonable approximation rather than certainty.

An overview of the fifteen years of resulting averages indicates that North America's small and mid-sized publishing houses are indeed alive and well as they approach the twenty-first Century. While 1990–94 average annual sales were $2.7 million, compared to a 1980–89 average of $1.5 million, the consultants believe this is more reflective of normal growth in a consistent constituency (67 percent of the *Report* subscribers renew each year) than of any shift in the nature of their constituency. Cumulative growth rates applied to the 1980s sales volume suggest that the $3.4 million 1994 average volume is more-or-less on target.

Comparing the decade of the 1980s, then, with the first half of the 1990s and—assuming (as the spectrum of responses suggests) that the Huenefeld constituency is typical of North America's small and mid-sized publishers (though it makes no pretense of seriously incorporating unstaffed "self-publishing" operations) —the survey yields this overview of the health of under-$30-million publishers:

	1980–89	1990–94
Annual sales volume growth	11.2%	9.1%
Annual operating margin	7.4%	11.6%
% of sales from new titles	35.6%	34.2%
% reporting a deficit	31.1%	25.8%
Employees @ $100,000 sales	1.2	0.9
New titles @ $100,000 sales	1.5	1.1
Salary+benefits paid top manager	$57,851	$70,912

In its generalized reporting of survey results to its total readership (who get only a few highlights unless they've actually submitted data), *The Huenefeld Report* has attempted to trace the course of perceived industry trends. Thus it tracked the use of computers from 47.4 percent in 1981 to near-unanimity by the end of the decade (when it quit asking the question), and the steady increase of telephone orders from 22.9 percent in 1987 to 38.2 percent in 1994.

Today, as small publishers struggle to get their books into major trade outlets reluctant to deal directly with them (without intervening distributors, whose commissions cut heavily into the publishers' margins), the survey is carefully tracking publishers' willingness to pay the 55 percent + discounts required by most distributors. Since most (78.9 percent) of their constituents pay author royalties based on net receipts rather than list prices, the Huenefeld consultants have also been concerned with the possible impact of high distributor discounts on authors' remuneration. To date, the data indicate:

	1980–89	1990–93	1994
Average over-all discount given	33.3%	34.5%	34.4%
Average highest discount given	48.5%	49.8%	50.2%
Author royalties on net receipts	10.9%	10.6%	10.7%

Though the modest trend toward paying higher discounts is obvious, the *Huenefeld Report* survey suggests a significant number of small publishers are attempting to escape it by turning to alternate retail channels other than the conventional book trade. The percentage achieving at least 35 percent of their sales volume from retailers other than bookstores has edged up steadily, from 17.6 percent in 1991 to 22.5 percent in 1994.

But perhaps most dramatic among the survey's discoveries has been the special aptness of very small publishing houses at desktop page-generation. In 1991, when *The Huenefeld Report* began measuring total average costs of getting raw manuscripts ready for the press (including copy-editing and other internal payroll) with desktop publishing software, the survey found that per-page costs increased steadily with the size of the publishing house—from $13.62 at the break-even level to $44.81 among the largest subscribers. This relationship between size of publisher and per-page pre-press costs has prevailed each year since. From follow-up discussion with a number of their clients, the consultants conclude that "the more people you have to convince of—and convert to—a new technology, the less effective you tend to be at absorbing that technology."

The *Huenefeld Report* subscriber questionnaire has evolved, from year to year, as publishers' concerns have changed. In addition to tracking alternate-media trends (*Huenefeld Report* subscribers got 8.3 percent of their 1994 sales from information packages other than books), special emphasis will be placed —in the years just ahead—on the impact of very-short-run "computer-to-press" printing technology on the strategies and fortunes of small and mid-sized publishers. The hope is that the short-run unit-cost protection promised by this emerging print-on-demand technology will enable publishers to introduce and test significantly more new titles each year—without expanding their risky investments in inventory.

23

National Federation of Abstracting and Information Services Member Data Services

Richard T. Kaser

For the first 30 years that NFAIS collected the numbers in the following table the data were often seen to reflect the exponential growth in the scientific literature that occurred in the aftermath of World War II. Growth rates in the 1960s were astonishingly high. During the five years between 1962 and 1967, for example, the number of abstracts published by NFAIS members grew 67% from 1.13 million a year to 1.88 million—or about 10% a year, compounded. This tremendous growth was facilitated by the increased use of automation by NFAIS members and motivated in part by the Cold War and the arms race. In the 1970s and 1980s growth rates continued to be higher than 5% a year—or approximately 30% every five years, reflecting the dramatic growth in scientific knowledge during this period. Since 1992, however, the data would seem to indicate a leveling off in the growth rate to about 2% to 3% a year.*

In 1993, NFAIS members collectively referenced a total of 9.9 million journal articles, books, and other documents in their databases. In 1994, this number increased about 3% to 10.2 million. Of course, some organizations grew faster than others, with some posting gains in the double digits. In other cases, some members published fewer references in 1994 than in the prior year. There are a variety of reasons for these annual fluctuations, which also existed in the earlier years, the largest factors no doubt being budget constraints along with constantly evolving editorial policies.

As the large number of footnotes to these numbers imply, it is very difficult to gather consistent data for the wide range of members who belong to NFAIS.

---

* Though the summary figures reflect an overall increase in coverage of 18% between 1992 and 1993, this is primarily due to a doubling of volume at Information Access Company. The growth rate for all other members between 1991 and 1992 averaged 2%.

The table presents the annual production data for every fifth year from 1957 to 1992, plus data for 1993, 1994 and an estimate for 1995. There is also a column of information that shows the total number of records that are currently held in the entire database of each member who has elected to participate in this survey. (Some NFAIS members do not produce databases.) All told, NFAIS member databases now contain more than 157 million records!

TABLE 1
Growth in Abstracting/Indexing of Scientific Literature, 1957–1995

1957	1962	1967	1972	1977	1982	1987
--	--	--	--	--	--	2,716
--	--	--	9,300	11,200	9,400	21,700
--	12,048	33,116	35,794	41,633	38,267	44,377
--	--	--	29,507	21,435	26,531	34,148
--	--	--	837	7,200	7,200	7,200
9,074	8,776	14,840	24,316	26,980	36,890	43,692
--	--	--	--	7,669	9,200	10,000
40,060	100,858	193,108	240,006	250,148	315,024	506,020
--	--	--	--	--	23,075	6,945
102,525	175,138	269,293	379,048	478,225	557,447	578,597
21,000	23,897	65,777	49,603	45,740	47,359	43,616
--	--	1,327	3,618	4,721	5,995	8,800
--	--	--	600	1,110	2,110	2,400
--	--	--	--	217,957	255,116	235,045
26,797	38,120	51,670	83,653	95,000	179,300	220,000
--	--	--	--	--	196,000	239,000
--	--	--	--	6,143	9,792	24,086
982	1,110	1,863	933	1,344	2,624	1,501
--	--	--	--	64,195	403,463	575,221
--	--	--	--	--	--	--
148,883	251,274	367,300	470,184	545,099	372,055	495,548
16,452	39,272	71,032	132,394	135,184	187,054	246,313
115,367	182,771	360,056	432,842	715,146	952,344	1,079,561
--	--	--	5,473	14,305	19,000	24,200
--	--	--	--	--	--	1,059
--	--	25,534	46,534	44,371	39,817	43,393
--	11,386	107,260	81,810	96,293	76,000	79,496
98,409	94,968	102,198	124,592	144,389	150,405	108,842
--	--	--	--	--	--	--
104,517	150,000	165,000	221,000	259,980	282,180	317,435
--	--	--	--	--	23,600	21,000
477	1,124	2,007	1,308	2,705	5,120	6,732
1,015	2,957	9,460	14,064	13,800	24,294	27,620
25,000	27,000	28,000	28,000	54,000	83,000	630,000
--	10,816	15,519	13,112	14,431	20,705	19,826
--	--	--	--	--	--	560,914
710,558	1,131,515	1,884,360	2,428,528	3,320,403	4,360,367	6,267,003

TABLE 1 (continued)

1992	1993	1994	Cum. 1994✦	Est. 1995	MEMBERSHIP
3,313	2,653	1,952	39,900	3,000	American Association of Retired Persons
21,949	23,924	46,037	306,087	26,000	American Economic Association[1]
46,278	46,550	52,550	2,004,113	63,000	American Institute of Aeronautics and Astronautics[2]
43,189	42,243	47,800	626,324	50,000	American Institute of Physics
9,000	9,000	9,000	155,000	9,000	American Meteorological Society[3]
57,016	56,579	56,471	961,764	58,000	American Psychological Association [4]
24,000	24,000	24,000	227,608	24,000	BHA - Bibliography of the History of Art[5]
605,249	603,398	621,024	9,885,168	622,500	BIOSIS[6]
8,811	8,814	10,028	213,839	10,000	Center for Communication Programs. POPLINE
668,268	687,242	775,807	17,868,663	795,000	Chemical Abstracts Service
41,924	42,464	48,837	2,047,353	52,000	Defense Technical Information Center
8,800	8,700	8,500	125,000	9,000	Documentation Abstracts
3,381	2,723	3,749	25,314	3,600	Earthquake Engineering Research Center
372,132	368,307	373,178	5,982,981	365,000	Elsevier Science. Inc.[7]
309,000	326,066	383,682	3,813,682	398,000	Engineering Information. Inc.[8]
370,190	334,013	229,794	11,008,695	178,975	Fachinformationszentrum Karlsruhe[9]
11,181	10,424	10,079	245,830	10,400	Foods Adlibra
3,042	3,378	2,144	55,000	2,500	The Getty Conservation Institute[10]
1,017,394	2,140,895	2,309,884	22,400,000	2,500,000	Information Access Company[11]
11,760	1,200	13,051	83,139	10,000	INFO-SOUTH[12]
732,829	745,000	710,657	12,391,280	430,000	INIST/CNRS[13]
257,650	250,842	280,942	4,840,653	300,000	INSPEC
1,083,028	1,136,081	1,198,429	25,590,145	1,270,334	Institute for Scientific Information[14]
28,864	32,000	30,780		30,000	Institute of Electrical and Electronics Engineers
1,441	1,774	1,789	15,408	1,000	Migration Information and Abstracts Service
42,785	43,000	45,000	1,200,000	45,000	Modern Language Association of America
78,300	78,200	52,594	2,868,600	60,000	National Aeronautics and Space Administration[15]
115,622	89,278	89,773	3,149,130	90,000	National Agricultural Library
1,000	1,600	1,250	6,750	1,000	National Center for Post-Traumatic Stress Disorder[16]
401,000	376,312	366,595	8,157,244	380,000	National Library of Medicine[17]
18,400	14,943	16,500	390,000	17,000	PAIS - Public Affairs Information Service
4,770	4,290	4,564	121,321	4,500	SmithKline Beecham Pharmaceuticals
36,642	38,722	45,841	610,330	47,000	Sociological Abstracts[18]
1,200,000	1,400,000	1,290,000	11,790,000	1,300,000	UMI
24,332	23,466	24,030	542,482	25,200	University of Tulsa. Petroleum Abstracts
755,675	956,950	1,000,000	7,955,286	1,100,000	The H.W. Wilson Company
8,418,215	9,935,031	10,186,311	157,704,089	10,291,009	

✦ The total number of unique items contained in Members' databases as of December 31, 1994.

Normalization of the Data

One factor that tends to interfere with the interpretation of these data is the fact that NFAIS has continuous data (from 1957 forward) for only 14 of the 36 organizations listed in the table. (These organizations are: American Psychological Association, BIOSIS, CAS, DTIC, Ei, INIST, Getty Conservation Institute, INSPEC, ISI, National Agricultural Library, NLM, Smith-Kline Beecham, Sociological Abstracts, and UMI.)

Looking at just these 14 organizations produces a slightly different—but more statistically consistent—view of the growth in the abstracting and indexing sector of the information industry. The following tables compare the performance for all members against the 14 self-selected members who have supplied complete data.

Five-Year Growth Rates

	All Members	Selected Members
1957–62	59%	54%
1962–67	67%	55%
1967–72	29%	29%
1972–77	37%	26%
1977–82	31%	15%
1982–87	44%	35%
1987–92	34%	28%
Annual Growth Rates		
1992–93	18%	5%
1993–94	4%	2%

In both cases, it is possible for one large organization to create a skew in the overall data (as occurred with the 14 selected members in 1977–82 and with all members in 1992–93), due to a drastic decrease or increase in coverage from one period to the next. Readers are encouraged to use these data for general comparative purposes and to study the data for themselves to reach their own conclusions.

Footnotes to Table 1

[1] Includes Cambridge University Press's *Abstracts of Working Papers in Economics*, records since 1984.

[2] The AIAA database contains NASA records.

[3] Estimated number of abstracts published in our monthly *Meteorological & Geoastrophysical Abstracts*.

[4] Of the cumulative records, 8,974 of these items appear in the database only.

[5] Publication title: *BHA Bibliography of the History of Art/Bibliography d'Histoire de l'Art*. This publication incorporates *RILA* (International Repertory of the Literature of Art) and *Repertoire d'Art et d'Archeologie*.

[6] Coverage expanded to include BioBusiness, starting in 1985.

[7] EMBASE goes back to 1974.

[8] Data from 1991 forward include citations referenced in Ei Page One.

[9] For Fiz-Karlsruhe, only bibliographic records are shown. An additional 38,055 numeric data items have been recorded.

[10] The Getty Conservation Institute participates in a shared database with approximately 130,000 unique items, of which about 55,000 are from *Art and Archeology Technical Abstracts*.

[11] Information Access Company's total for 1993 forward includes Predicasts total.

[12] Indexing and abstracting started in June 1988, with articles going back to January 1, 1988, being indexed and abstracted.

[13] Derived from two databases: PASCAL and FRANCIS.

[14] Data reported reflect the current year's work only (articles covered) and do not include materials processed for retrospective indexes.

[15] The NASA database is maintained under contract at the NASA Center for AeroSpace Information (CASI).

[16] The National Center for Post-Traumatic Stress Disorder began its A&I operations in fall 1989.

[17] These figures include *Index Medicus* and special list citations. The cumulative total includes MEDLINE backfiles.

[18] Figures for 1993 and 1994 represent entries into *Sociological Abstracts*, *Social Planning/Policy & Development Abstracts*, and *Linguistics and Language Behavior Abstracts*.

Please Note: Where an asterisk is present in a column, we were unable to obtain the information requested from that company.

24

Growth and Change of the World's Chemical Literature as Reflected in *Chemical Abstracts*

Edward P. Donnell

Since its first appearance in January 1907, *Chemical Abstracts*, published by the Chemical Abstracts Service (CAS) division of the American Chemical Society, has endeavored to abstract and index all of the world's published literature of chemistry. The definition of what constitutes the literature of chemistry has broadened somewhat over the years. Initially, coverage focused primarily on the research literature. Coverage of the industrial applications of chemical science and technology, particularly coverage of patents, was expanded in the late 1920s and early 1930s. Patent coverage was further expanded to additional countries of issue and additional kinds of patent documents in the 1960s and 1970s.

Chemical Abstracts began with coverage of 396 scientific journals in 1907. The number reached one thousand in 1922 and two thousand in 1932. Today, material is abstracted from approximately nine thousand journals published in 97 countries; patents issued by twenty-seven national patent offices, the European Patent Office, and the World Intellectual Property Organization; and conference proceedings, dissertations, technical reports, and books published around the world.

Coverage was affected by World Wars I and II. Some German and other European publications were difficult to obtain during both World Wars, and Japanese publications were inaccessible during World War II. In most cases, missing publications were covered in the years immediately following the wars. (See Tables 1, 2 and 3.)

With the growing practice of applying for patent protection on the same invention in more than one nation, CAS began in 1961 to abstract only the first disclosure on a particular invention. Patent documents subsequently issued on

TABLE 1
Chemical Abstracts Publication Record 1907–96

Year	Vol.	Number of Abstracts Papers	Patents	Books	Total Abstracts	Total Abstracts To Date	Patent Equivalents	Total Documents Cited	Total Documents Cited to Date	Pages of Abstracts	Issue Index Pages	Vol. Index Pages	Total Pages Published[a]
1907	1	7,994	3,853		11,847	11,847				3,074		363	3,437
1908	2	11,414	3,658	97	15,169	27,016				3,416		473	3,889
1909	3	11,455	3,806	198	15,459	42,475				3,020		341	3,361
1910	4	13,006	3,754	785	17,545	60,020				3,314		727	4,041
1911	5	15,892	5,014	776	21,682	81,702				3,926		845	4,771
1912	6	15,740	6,919	535	23,194	104,896				3,544		799	4,343
1913	7	19,025	6,946	659	26,630	131,526				4,096		834	4,930
1914	8	16,468	7,920	727	25,115	156,641				3,872		725	4,597
1915	9	12,200	6,159	622	18,981	175,622				3,379		580	3,959
1916	10	10,519	5,265	324	16,108	191,730				3,180		492	3,672
1917	11	10,921	4,680	344	15,945	207,675				3,470		524	3,994
1918	12	9,283	4,074	524	13,881	221,556				2,712		503	3,215
1919	13	10,957	3,741	542	15,240	236,796				3,338		589	3,927
1920	14	13,619	4,432	1,275	19,326	256,122				3,826		846	4,672
1921	15	15,211	4,265	975	20,451	276,573				4,059		783	4,842
1922	16	18,070	5,142	886	24,098	300,671				4,365		1,156	5,521
1923b	17	19,507	4,749	1,059	25,315	325,986				3,924		1,008	4,932
1924	18	20,523	5,084	1,036	26,643	352,629				3,740		1,135	4,875
1925	19	20,951	5,475	671	27,097	379,726				3,618		1,155	4,773
1926	20	23,103	6,099	1,036	30,238	409,964				3,842		1,406	5,248
1927	21	25,037	7,872	582	33,491	443,455				4,098		1,413	5,511
1928	22	28,153	9,936	1,046	39,135	482,590				4,878		1,727	6,605
1929	23	29,082	17,867	1,344	48,293	530,883				5,614		1,821	7,435
1930	24	32,731	21,246	1,169	55,146	586,029				6,066		2,142	8,208
1931	25	32,278	18,904	1,546	52,728	638,757				6,161		2,282	8,443
1932	26	37,403	20,678	1,380	59,461	698,218				6,184		2,270	8,454
1933	27	36,139	28,051	1,963	66,153	764,371				6,024		2,172	8,196
1934c,d	28	38,371	21,824	1,375	61,570	825,941				3,798		1,157	4,955
1935	29	42,593	19,241	1,579	63,413	889,354				4,204		1,330	5,534
1936	30	41,927	20,836	1,809	64,572	953,926				4,346		1,528	5,874

TABLE 1 (continued)

1937	31	44,032	19,006	1,697	64,735	1,018,661	4,498		1,485	5,983
1938	32	45,917	19,515	1,496	66,928	1,085,589	4,782		1,542	6,324
1939	33	45,414	19,893	1,801	67,108	1,152,697	4,860		1,607	6,267
1940	34	40,624	11,635	1,421	53,680	1,206,377	4,170		1,384	5,554
1941	35	35,588	17,176	1,330	54,094	1,260,471	4,184		1,464	5,648
1942	36	30,479	14,334	833	45,646	1,306,117	3,684		1,232	4,916
1943	37	30,523	11,473	1,673	43,669	1,349,786	3,470		1,200	4,670
1944	38	30,440	11,494	1,766	43,700	1,393,486	3,306		1,175	4,481
1945	39	22,824	9,357	1,491	33,672	1,427,158	2,782		1,137	3,919
1946	40	29,943	8,810	825	39,578	1,466,736	3,853	144	1,591	5,588
1947	41	30,461	7,925	902	39,288	1,506,024	3,909	142	1,496	5,547
1948	42	35,867	7,002	1,127	43,996	1,550,020	4,623	168	1,740	6,531
1949	43	40,612	11,390	1,439	53,441	1,603,461	4,769	183	1,991	6,943
1950	44	47,496	10,063	1,539	59,098	1,662,559	5,592	210	2,350	8,152
1951[c]	45	50,657	10,417	1,959	63,033	1,725,592	5,340	242	2,534	8,116
1952	46	56,419	12,185	1,543	70,147	1,795,739	5,890	265	2,574	8,729
1953	47	61,273	11,906	1,912	75,091	1,870,830	6,444	294	2,821	9,559
1954	48	67,606	11,083	1,926	80,615	1,951,445	7,151	297	3,237	10,685
1955	49	74,664	9,926	1,732	86,322	2,037,767	8,264	324	3,721	12,309
1956	50	78,009	12,350	2,037	92,396	2,130,163	8,768	355	4,522	13,645

[a]Total includes "List of Periodicals" pages, which are not shown separately, for those years in which that list was published in *CA*.
[b]Type size decreased.
[c]Page size increased
[d]Two-column format adopted.

TABLE 1 (continued)

Year	Vol.	Number of Abstracts			Total Abstracts	Total Abstracts To Date	Patent Equiva-lents	Total Documents Cited	Total Documents Cited to Date	Pages of Abstracts	Issue Index Pages	Vol. Index Pages	Total Pages Published[a]
		Papers	Patents	Books									
1957	51	84,205	16,822	1,498	102,525	2,232,688				9,353	392	4,397	14,142
1958	52	95,736	21,920	1,274	118,930	2,351,618				10,628	486	4,873	15,987
1959	53	98,680	26,760	1,756	127,196	2,478,814				11,557	525	5,471	17,553
1960	54	104,484	27,675	2,096	134,255	2,613,069				13,014	552	6,686	20,252
1961	55	118,337	26,249	2,307	146,893	2,759,962	7,609	154,502	2,767,571	13,999	658	8,322	22,979
1962	56,57	140,168	26,467	2,716	169,351	2,929,313	5,787	175,138	2,942,709	16,725	758	9,373	26,856
1963c	58,59	141,016	26,240	4,148	171,404	3,100,717	8,400	179,804	3,122,513	15,298	1,245	9,136	25,679
1964	60,61	161,489	26,422	2,082	189,993	3,290,710	13,375	203,368	3,325,881	16,608	1,498	10,176	28,282
1965	62,63	165,770	29,225	2,088	197,083	3,487,793	19,312	216,395	3,542,276	17,963	1,820	11,074	30,857
1966	64,65	181,715	35,031	3,557	220,303	3,708,096	28,940	249,243	3,791,519	20,700	2,104	12,660	35,464
1967	66,67	202,684	36,797	3,046	242,527	3,950,623	26,766	269,293	4,060,812	22,815	2,683	14,023	39,521
1968	68,69	198,035	31,720	2,753	232,508	4,183,131	19,180	251,688	4,312,500	22,103	2,621	15,703	40,427
1969	70,71	210,344	39,424	2,552	252,320	4,435,451	33,026	285,346	4,597,846	23,533	3,220	18,071	44,824
1970	72,73	230,902	43,044	2,728	276,674	4,712,125	33,068	309,742	4,907,588	23,792	3,777	21,144	48,713
1971	74,75	262,127	43,405	3,444	308,976	5,021,101	41,129	350,105	5,257,693	24,690	5,744	21,151	51,585
1972	76,77	280,143	51,179	3,104	334,426	5,355,527	44,622	379,048	5,636,741	27,386	5,877	20,791	54,054
1973	78,79	269,711	48,683	2,611	321,005	5,676,532	35,544	356,549	5,993,290	25,865	5,708	20,123	51,696
1974	80,81	272,235	58,436	2,953	333,624	6,010,156	42,039	375,663	6,368,953	26,282	5,522	21,180	52,984
1975	82,83	317,472	68,471	6,291	392,234	6,402,390	62,011	454,245	6,823,198	31,100	6,711	25,158	62,969
1976	84,85	317,985	67,176	5,744	390,905	6,793,295	67,603	458,508	7,281,706	31,390	6,891	27,310	65,591
1977	86,87	348,059	55,441	6,637	410,137	7,203,432	68,088	478,225	7,759,931	32,253	7,263	28,980	68,496
1978	88,89	363,195	57,343	7,804	428,342	7,631,774	70,217	498,559	8,258,490	33,368	7,593	27,677	68,638
1979	90,91	370,771	58,738	7,378	436,887	8,068,661	78,854	515,741	8,774,231	34,878	8,010	30,002	72,890
1980	92,93	407,342	61,998	6,399	475,739e	8,544,400	72,937	548,676	9,322,907	38,188	8,697	32,197	79,064
1981	94,95	373,973	71,180	5,434	450,587	8,994,987	98,739	549,326	9,872,233	37,074	10,098	35,650	82,822

TABLE 1 (continued)

Year	Vol.											
1982	96,97	381,257	70,774	5,758	457,789	99,658	557,447	10,429,680	37,970	10,595	36,072	84,637
1983[b]	98,99	371,389	74,948	5,416	451,753	95,811	547,564	10,977,244	34,394	10,498	35,368	80,260
1984	100,101	380,692	73,907	5,970	460,569	111,239	571,808	11,549,052	34,876	11,216	39,135	85,227
1985	102,103	380,091	73,073	4,767	457,931	98,781	556,712	12,105,764	36,284	10,794	39,631	86,709
1986	104,105	384,141	85,767	4,521	474,429	104,453	578,882	12,684,646	37,826	11,380	42,913	92,119
1987	106,107	386,466	85,219	4,493	476,178	102,419	578,597	13,263,243	38,268	11,650	45,269	95,187
1988	108,109	389,685	80,795	4,065	474,545	103,583	578,128	13,841,371	38,968	12,048	45,711	96,727
1989	110,111	397,158	88,099	3,934	489,191	112,437	601,628	14,442,999	40,424	12,736	51,143	104,303
1990	112,113	394,945	91,082	3,490	489,517	118,113	607,630	15,050,629	41,097	13,005	54,059	108,161
1991	114,115	453,640	95,526	3,885	553,051	133,666	686,717	15,737,346	46,608	14,596	57,890	119,094
1992	116,117	430,247	98,505	3,685	532,437	135,831	668,268	16,405,614	45,394	14,716	54,394	114,504
1993	118,119	448,733	99,411	3,261	551,405	135,837	687,242	17,092,856	48,461	15,472	53,910	117,843
1994	120,121	542,511	107,226	3,318	653,055	122,752	775,807	17,868,657	58,331	17,472	66,364	142,167
1995	122,123	562,955	121,214	3,620	687,789	126,459	814,248	18,682,905	61,707	18,777	75,426	155,910
1996	124,125	579,251	121,682	5,336	706,269	141,374	847,643	19,530,548	65,481	18,635	80,114	164,230

[a]Total includes "List of Periodicals" pages, which are not shown separately, for those years in which that list was published in CA.
[b]Type size decreased.
[c]Page size increased
[d]Two-column format adopted.
[e]About 17,000 of the abstracts published in 1980 resulted from a 14-day shortening of the processing time.

TABLE 2
Sources[a] of Journal Literature Abstracted in *Chemical Abstracts*
(as percentage of total journal literature abstracted)

Nation	1909	1918	1929	1939	1943[b]	1947[b]	1951[b]	1956[b]	1962[b]	1972	1982	1993	1994	1995	1996
United States	20.1%	45.4%	25.8%	27.7%	30.6%	41.8%	36.6%	28.4%	28.4%	28.0%	27.1%	28.1%	29.2%	27.0%	27.7%
Japan	0.3	2.8	3.7	4.4	0.5	4.4	9.1	10.4	6.9	7.9	10.2	13.3	12.7	12.8	12.5
Germany	45.0	13.8	26.9	18.7	23.6	3.1	7.9	8.4	8.5			7.5	6.6	7.7	7.5
Fed. Rep. Germany										5.7	6.1				
German Dem. Rep.										0.5	1.2				
Peop. Rep. China											1.8	4.3	6.2	6.1	6.0
Brit. C'wealth	13.4	16.8	13.5	14.1	13.2	15.6	17.4	13.6							
United Kingdom									8.6	6.4	5.9	5.7	5.5	5.5	5.7
Canada									1.1	2.8	2.7	3.2	3.4	3.0	3.1
India									2.5	2.5	3.3	2.6	2.6	2.5	2.3
Australia									c	1.2	1.3	1.4	1.3	1.4	1.4
France	13.2	9.2	7.0	9.1	4.9	8.4	6.2	6.0	4.8	4.4	4.1	4.7	4.4	4.6	4.6
Italy	1.2	3.1	3.0	3.0	2.6	3.8	3.3	4.1	1.5	1.9	2.3	2.6	2.6	2.7	2.9
Spain	c	c	c	c	c	c	c	c	c	0.4	0.9	1.7	1.7	1.8	1.9
Netherlands	c	3.6	2.1	1.6	c	1.7	1.7	1.3	1.0	1.0	1.3	1.6	1.6	1.5	1.6
Poland	c	c	c	c	c	c	c	c	1.6	2.0	1.5	1.4	1.4	1.6	1.4
Sweden	c	c	c	c	c	c	c	c	1.1	1.1	1.1	1.2	1.2	1.2	1.2
Switzerland	c	1.4	1.1	0.9	c	2.8	1.9	1.9	0.9	1.0	1.1	1.2	1.1	1.2	1.2
U.S.S.R	1.2	0.7	3.4	11.1	12.8	8.2	6.3	13.5	23.0	24.0	17.6	0.6	1.0	0.1	0.0
Russia												5.4	4.6	5.0	4.5
S. Korea											0.3	1.0	1.1	1.4	1.4
All others	5.6	3.2	13.5	9.4	11.8	10.2	9.6	12.4	10.1	9.2	10.2	12.5	11.8	12.9	13.1

[a] Based on author's address.
[b]Percentages based on sample. For all other years, complete counts were made.
[c]Included in "all others' for year.

the same invention by other nations are listed in a Patent Index with a reference to the first-issued patent document and its abstract. These "patent equivalents" are listed separately in the tables and included in total documents cited for 1961 and subsequent years. (See Tables 4 and 5.)

Volume indexes to *Chemical Abstracts* were published annually until 1962, semiannually thereafter. Indexes were added to individual issues of the publication in 1946. Collective indexes were produced at ten-year intervals until 1956, when the collective indexing period was changed to five years. (See Table 6.)

TABLE 3
Language of Publication of Journal Literature
Abstracted in *Chemical Abstracts*
(as percentage of total journal literature abstracted)

Language	1961	1966	1972	1978	1984	1993	1994	1995	1996
English	43.3%	54.9%	58.0%	62.8%	69.2%	80.3%	81.9%	81.3%	83.2%
Russian	18.4	21.0	22.4	20.4	15.7	6.4	5.2	4.7	3.8
Chinese	a	0.5	a	0.3	2.2	2.9	4.6	4.4	4.2
Japanese	6.3	3.1	3.9	4.7	4.0	4.6	4.2	4.2	3.9
German	12.3	7.1	5.5	5.0	3.4	2.2	1.5	2.1	1.9
French	5.2	5.2	3.9	2.4	1.3	0.9	0.6	0.7	0.7
Korean	a	a	0.2	0.2	0.2	0.4	0.5	0.5	0.5
Polish	1.9	1.8	1.2	1.1	0.7	0.5	0.3	0.5	0.4
Spanish	0.6	0.5	0.6	0.7	0.6	0.4	0.3	0.3	0.3
Others	12.0	5.9	4.3	2.4	2.7	1.4	0.9	1.3	1.1

aIncluded in "Others" for year.

In 1965, CAS established a computer-based Chemical Registry System to provide a means for identifying chemical substances reported in the scientific literature and organizing information about the substances. Since 1965, all substances indexed for Chemical Abstracts have been recorded in a computer database, and each unique substance has been assigned a permanent identifying number, the CAS Registry Number. The number of substances registered annually has risen from just over 200,000 in 1965 to almost 1.27 million in 1996. Substances indexed in *Chemical Abstracts* between 1957 and 1965 were added to the computerized Registry in the mid and late 1980s. The total of 15.8 million substances on file at the end of 1996 represents the number of unique substances reported in the scientific literature from 1957 through 1996. (See Table 7.)

TABLE 4
Country of Issue Patents Abstracted[a] in *Chemical Abstracts*
(as percentage of total patents abstracted)

	1960	1965	1970	1975	1980	1985	1990	1993	1994	1995	1996
Japan	5.6%	6.0%	11.8%	40.4%	43.4%	54.9%	56.7%	60.3%	61.0%	57.6%	57.3%
United States	30.2	24.9	23.7	15.1	11.3	8.8	7.8	7.1	8.5	7.4	8.0
European Patent Org.	—	—	—	—	4.0	8.7	12.9	9.8	8.3	7.6	7.4
World Intel. Prop. Org.	—	—	—	—	0.4	1.4	3.4	7.2	8.0	9.0	11.2
Fed. Rep. Germany	23.6	8.3	23.5	20.3	12.1	7.7	4.8	3.9	4.6	4.1	4.8
USSR	4.8	6.9	7.7	8.8	9.7	5.3	4.7	4.9	2.8	6.7	4.2
Peop. Rep. China	—	—	—	—	—	—	1.6	1.6	1.8	3.2	1.7
France	3.3	16.0	15.3	4.0	1.7	2.1	0.7	0.7	0.7	0.6	0.5
Canada							0.2	0.9	1.1	0.8	0.7
United Kingdom	13.8	11.4	8.9	3.3	4.9	1.0	0.8	0.5	0.6	0.6	0.6
Poland	0.7	0.8	0.6	0.3	1.7	0.8	1.5	0.8	0.4	0.8	1.0
All Others	18.0	25.7	8.5	7.8	10.8	9.3	4.9	2.3	2.2	1.6	2.6

TABLE 5
Country of Issue of Equivalent Patents[a] Cited in *Chemical Abstracts*
(as percentage of total equivalent patents cited)

	1965	1970	1975	1980	1985	1990	1993	1994	1995	1996
Japan	1.3%	0.9%	19.8%	22.4%	30.4%	28.9%	32.7%	30.6%	29.9%	26.3%
European Patent Org.	—	—	—	3.3	15.0	20.6	17.6	20.1	20.5	18.6
United States	16.7	18.1	15.8	12.4	11.6	13.7	13.1	13.5	12.7	12.7
Canada	0.1	0.1	7.7	10.7	6.3	4.3	9.9	8.4	7.4	7.4
South Africa	—	4.5	4.0	2.5	3.0	2.2	1.5	0.1	1.9	5.4
Spain						0.5	2.3	5.9	4.0	5.0
Austria	—	—	3.2	1.4	3.0	3.3	4.1	3.0	1.5	4.1
Peop. Rep. China	—	—	—	—	—	4.3	1.9	2.8	3.2	3.7
World Intel. Prop. Org.	—	—	0.4	0.4	1.2	1.2	1.8	2.8	2.7	2.7
Australia	—	—	0.1	0.2	2.4	4.3	3.7	3.5	3.0	2.5
Hungary	—	0.1	0.1	0.3	2.3	2.6	1.8	1.4	1.8	1.6
Fed. Rep. Germany	14.2	32.0	2.2	3.2	1.3	1.5	1.4	1.3	1.5	1.5
Brazil	—	—	—	2.6	1.8	1.9	1.4	1.3	1.1	1.4
France	16.7	16.0	14.1	7.6	2.1	1.4	1.2	1.2	1.4	1.4
United Kingdom	27.3	23.6	16.6	13.7	6.6	2.4	1.0	1.2	1.3	1.1
Israel						0.7	1.0	0.3	1.0	0.7
Norway	—	—	—	0.4	0.9	1.1	0.8	0.3	1.3	0.6
All Others	23.7	4.7	16.4	16.9	10.1	5.1	2.8	2.3	3.8	3.3

[a]CAS abstracts the first disclosure it receives on a particular invention. Subsequently issued members of the family of patent documents on the invention are cited in the *CA* Patent Index (Patent Concordance prior to 1981).

TABLE 6
Collective Indexes to *Chemical Abstracts*

Collective Index	Years Covered	Documents Cited	Pages							
			Author	Subject	General Subject	Chemical Substance	Formula	Patent	Index Guide	Total
1 st	1907-16	191,730	1,980	2,843	———	———	———	———	———	4,823
2 nd	1917-26	218,234	2,452	4,139	———	———	———	———	———	6,591
3 rd	1927-36	543,962	3,095	4,885	———	———	———	479	———	8,459
4 th	1937-46	512,810	3,541	6,386	———	———	2,077	182	———	12,186
5 th	1947-56	663,427	5,074	13,740	———	———	2,968	144	———	21,926
6 th	1957-61	637,408	6,164	12,659	———	———	3,869	172	———	22,864
7 th	1962-66	1,023,948	9,607	24,632	———	———	7,007	352	———	41,598
8 th	1967-71	1,466,174	13,845	46,384[a]	———	———	11,769	761	2,280	75,039
9 th	1972-76	2,024,013	19,128	b	16,798	40,891	16,251	1,374	1,440	95,882
10 th	1977-81	2,601,773	24,684	b	25,508	56,112	19,904	3,643	1,605	131,456
11 th	1982-86	2,812,413	26,756	b	33,424	71,720	24,014	4,961	2,115	162,990
12 th	1987-91	3,052,700	32,659	b	42,679	97,323	34,950	5,720	2,514	215,845

[a]Includes REGISTRY-HANDBOOK—NUMBER SECTION, which was issued as part of the 8th Collective Index.
[b]The Subject Index was subdivided into General Subject and Chemical Substance Indexes for the 9th collective period.

TABLE 7
Growth of the CAS Chemical Registry System

Year	Substances Registered	Substances on file at year end	Year	Substances Registered	Substances on file at year end	Year	Substances Registered	Substances on file at year end
1965	211,934	211,934	1980	353,881	5,141,872	1995	1,186,334	14,594,302
1966	313,763	525,697	1981	424,230	5,566,102	1996	1,269,246	15,863,548
1967	270,782	796,479	1982	361,706	5,927,808			
1968	230,321	1,026,800	1983	418,905	6,346,713			
1969	287,048	1,313,848	1984	563,390[b]	6,910,103			
1970	288,085	1,601,933	1985	544,618[b]	7,454,721			
1971	351,514	1,953,447	1986	628,966[b]	8,083,687			
1972	277,563	2,231,010	1987	610,480[b]	8,694,167			
1973	437,202[a]	2,668,212	1988	602,465[b]	9,296,632			
1974	319,808	2,988,020	1989	615,987[b]	9,912,619			
1975	372,492	3,360,512	1990	663,342[b]	10,575,961			
1976	347,515	3,708,027	1991	684,252	11,260,213			
1977	369,676	4,077,703	1992	690,313	11,950,526			
1978	364,226	4,441,929	1993	680,230	12,630,756			
1979	346,062	4,787,991	1994	777,212	13,407,968			

[a]Registry III implementation added 77,650 substances.
[b]Input on substances indexed prior to 1965 added 140,760 substances in 1984; 151,431 substances in 1985; 165,705 substances in 1986; 119,888 substances in 1987; 51,253 substances in 1988; 44,112 substances in 1989; and 14,550 substances in 1990.

25

A Brief History of the Mathematical Literature

Robert G. Bartle

In the beginning, communication in mathematics presumably was mainly by word of mouth between scholar and student, and between individual scholars. Later came the schools of mathematics and the "academies", such as Plato's academy in ancient Athens, or the school of Euclid in Alexandria. Scholars there communicated orally and also by letters and manuscripts. But, since all of these early manuscripts were hand-copied, they were few in number. While many of these manuscripts have been handed down through the years, one can only wonder how much early mathematics has been lost without a trace. The invention of the printing press provided a revolution in communication and facilitated enormously the spread of ideas through the printed book. According to Eves [E;p.517], the first printed arithmetic book was published in Treviso, Italy, in 1478, the first edition of Euclid's *Elements* appeared in 1482, and the first work on mathematics printed in the New World appeared in 1556.

The academies. The great increase in scientific and mathematical activity that began to flourish in the sixteenth century led to the formation of groups of persons who met, sometimes regularly, for discussion and an exchange of ideas. Some of these groups later crystallized into what became academies, the first of which seems to have been established in Naples around 1560 [E;p.390] [St;p.101]. The Accademia dei Lincei (Academy of the Lynx-like) was founded in 1603 and Galileo became a member in 1611. According to Kline [K;p.396], in France, Desargues, Descartes, Fermat, and Pascal, among others, met privately under the leadership of Mersenne from 1630, and corresponded widely (see also [St;p.100 ff.]). This informal group led to the chartering of the Académie Royale des Sciences in 1616 by Louis XIV (and the Académie des Sciences in

1666). Similarly, an English group led by John Wallis began to hold meetings in 1645 in Gresham College, London. This group was given a charter by Charles II in 1662 and adopted the name of the Royal Society of London for the Promotion of Natural Knowledge; Wallis was a charter member. The Berlin Academy of Sciences was founded in 1700 with Leibniz as its first president. In Russia, Peter the Great founded the Academy of Sciences in St. Petersburg in 1724.

These academies were very important for the development of science and, in particular, of mathematics; indeed, many of the most important mathematicians of the eighteenth century were supported by these academies and never had a university position. The academies promoted the exchange of ideas both by facilitating the direct contact of the leading scientists and also by the publications that the academies soon started. While there were various reasons for the support of the academies by the rulers, it is clear that one reason was that the monarchs saw the importance of the emerging science and technology for the civil and military needs of their realms, and realized that mathematics was essential for this scientific development.

It may come as a surprise to the modern scientist to realize that the universities of the time played little role in the scientific development that was taking place. Instead, with a few isolated exceptions, the universities, still under the dead hand of the church, remained conservative centers of scholasticism and often taught only a meager amount of mathematics. It was not until the end of the eighteenth century that the universities began to become centers of research [K;pp.397–398][St p.101].

The scientific journals. Despite what has just been said about the academies being the centers of research the first scientific journals were organized privately. It is agreed that the first scientific periodical was the *Journal des Sçavans* (later called the *Journal des Savants*), which was first published on 5 January 1665 by D. de Sallo, a counsellor of the French court (see [G;p.115], [Sc:p.49]). It appears to have been more of a magazine reporting on scientific developments directed to the educated and curious than what we think of as a scientific journal publishing research articles. Only two months later, there appeared the *Philosophical Transactions*, launched by Henry Oldenburg, the secretary of the Royal Society of London—but it was not until 1753 that this journal became an official publication of the Royal Society. One of the most notable periodicals of its time was the *Acta Eruditorum*, published monthly at Leipzig from 1682; it was edited by O. Mencke until 1707, but Leibniz was also influential in its founding and was a frequent contributor to it. In fact Leibniz published his first paper on the differential calculus there in 1684, and his paper containing the rudiments of the integral calculus there in 1686, although he had developed this work between 1673 and 1676 [St;p.111]. (Newton's *Principia* was published in 1687.)

A number of elementary mathematics magazines were started in the early part of the eighteenth century. Some contained mathematical problems and puzzles and were aimed more at entertaining their readers than advancing mathematical knowledge. Notable among these was the English publication *The Ladies' Diary*, published from 1704–1840. G. A. Miller [M;p.38–39] quotes two problems and their solutions that were given in rhyme in early issues of this publication; he asserts that in later numbers more important mathematical questions appeared. He also asserts that the *Gentleman's Diary or the Mathematical Repository*, published 1741–1840, may be regarded as a scientific mathematical journal and contains a number of important problems and solutions relating to elementary mathematics.

Although journals published by the academies were not the first to be founded, they became among the most important and influential. The earliest academy journal appears to have been the *Miscellanea Curiosa Medico-Physica,* begun in Leipzig in 1670 by a society that (in 1682) became the Academia Caesareo-Leopoldina Naturae Curiosorum. Of enormous influence was the *Histoire et Mémoires* of the Académie Royale des Sciences in Paris, which started publication in 1699. The next few years saw the foundation of a number of academy journals in Berlin, Uppsala, St. Petersburg, Bologna, Stockholm, etc. Until 1770 it was the periodicals of the academies that provided the main vehicle of communication among researchers [G;pp.115 ff.]. But these journals were general in nature, with only an occasional article devoted to mathematical topics.

Beginning about 1770 more specialized journals began to appear in various sciences, but mathematics was not one of the first areas to have specialized journals. In 1794 the *Journal Polytechnique* (soon renamed the *Journal de l'École Polytechnique*) was founded at the famous French school; in effect it was primarily a mathematical journal. The first journal devoted exclusively to mathematics was the French journal *Annales de Mathématiques Pures et Appliquées,* founded and edited by J. D. Gergonne and published from 1810 to 1831. The next was *Correspondance Mathématique et Physique,* edited by J. G. Garnier and A. Quetelet in Gand/Bruxelles, 1825–1839. The oldest mathematics journal still in existence is the famous *Journal für die Reine und Angewandte Mathematik,* founded in Germany by A. L. Crelle in 1826 and edited by him until his death in 1855. The first British mathematical journal was *The Cambridge Mathematical Journal,* founded in 1839 by D. F. Gregory and R. L. Ellis; a continuation of this journal was later to become *The Quarterly Journal of Pure and Applied Mathematics,* which was edited for a time by J. J. Sylvester and others.

Mathematical societies. It is difficult to say where and when the first (modern style) mathematical society was founded, but the oldest one still in existence is the Mathematische Gesellschaft in Hamburg. It was founded in 1690 (and so is celebrating its tercentenary this year!) as the Kunstrechnungsliebende Societät, and has long published a journal. Another early one is the Spitalfields Mathematical Society, which lasted from 1717 to 1846, initially meeting in a pub in east London; it was ultimately absorbed into the Royal Astronomical Society in 1846. (See also [M;p.44 fn.] and especially [Cs] for an entertaining account, where it is indicated that there were at least three other "mathematical societies" in London during the early eighteenth century.)

The day of the amateurs passed, and the professionals began to take over with the formation of the national mathematical societies. The first such society is the Wiskundig Genootschap, founded in Amsterdam in 1778, but most national societies were founded considerably later: the Moscow Mathematical Society in 1864, the London Mathematical Society in 1865, the Société Mathématique de France in 1872, the Mathematical Society of Japan in 1877, the Edinburgh Mathematical Society in 1883, the Circolo Matematico di Palermo in 1884, the New York Mathematical Society (later the American Mathematical Society) in 1888 and the Deutsche Mathematiker-Vereinigung in 1890. Most of these societies commenced the publication of a mathematical journal soon after their foundation and many of these journals have played, and still play, an important role in mathematical communication.

According to Müller [Mü], before 1700 there were only 17 journals publishing articles with mathematical content, during the eighteenth century there were 210 new journals with mathematical articles, and during the nineteenth century there were another 950 new journals. (In this reckoning a continuation of a journal under a different title is considered as a "new" journal.) However, before 1900 about half of these journals had ceased publication or changed titles, so that in 1900 there were about 600 existing journals containing some mathematical articles!

The secondary journals. By the middle of the nineteenth century, mathematics had become specialized to the extent and the number of journals so large that it was not only impossible for one person to master it in its entirety, but even difficult for one to keep fully apprised of the developments in his or her area. It was clear that there was a need for a more systematic method of communication between mathematical researchers, so the bibliographic (or "secondary") journal was born.

Wölffing [W] gives an account of the various bibliographic journals founded before 1903; see also [M; pp. 275–282] for an annotated list of mathematical bibliographies and encyclopedias published before 1916. Certainly the most important secondary journal in mathematics was the *Jahrbuch über die Fortschritte der Mathematik*, founded in 1868 under the direction of Carl Ohrtmann and Felix Müller (and soon joined by Albert Wangerin) in Berlin. Among others we mention the bibliographic journal *Bulletin des Sciences Mathématiques et Astronomiques*, founded in Paris in 1870 and edited by G. Darboux; it consisted mainly of a list of publications. The journal *Revue Semestrielle des Publications Mathématiques* was founded in Amsterdam in 1893 and gave short summaries but no critical reviews.

The Jahrbuch and Zentralblatt. The format of the *Jahrbuch* was to collect reviews of all the mathematical articles published in a given year in one volume. The first volume, published in 1871, contained reviews of articles published in 1868; it contained 426 pages and there were 16 reviewers, all German and most from Berlin. The second volume, published in 1873, covering the two years 1869 and 1870, consisted of 902 pages. The third volume, published in 1874 and covering 1871, contained 588 pages and listed 33 reviewers (including

Cayley and Lie and some other non-German reviewers). Volume 31, published in 1902 and covering the year 1900, contained 970 pages and listed 59 reviewers. World War I caused considerable interference with the publication schedule of the journal, and, while efforts were made to catch up, Volume 50, covering 1924, did not appear until 1929; it contained 749 pages and listed 153 reviewers.

In the first volume of *Jahrbuch*, the mathematical universe was broken into the following twelve sections: History and philosophy, Algebra, Number theory, Probability, Series, Differential and integral calculus, Function theory, Analytic geometry, Synthetic geometry, Mechanics, Mathematical physics, and Geodesy and astronomy. One might be struck by the overall similarity with the present-day classification system used by Mathematical Reviews. There are a substantial number of "title reviews", that is, mere listing of the item without further comment, but many of the items have a critical review.

The original hope that the *Jahrbuch* might appear soon after the year being covered proved to be an illusion. Journals were slow to be published or to be received by the *Jahrbuch* office, reviewers were slow, there were difficulties with the printers, etc. In any case, by the late 1920s there was widespread dissatisfaction with the *Jahrbuch*, due largely to this time lag. Otto Neugebauer, then a young professor at Göttingen, conceived the idea of a journal that would publish the reviews of articles as soon as possible after the papers had appeared and persuaded the publishing house of J. Springer to publish such a journal. The first issue of *Zentralblatt für Mathematik und ihre Grenzgebiete*, as the new journal was called, dated April 14, 1931, had Neugebauer as its editor. It also had a very distinguished and international editorial committee (consisting of P. Alexandroff, J. Bartels, W. Blaschke, R. Courant, H. Hahn, G. H. Hardy, F. Hund, G. Julia, O. Kellogg, H. Kienle, T. Levi-Civita, R. Nevanlinna, H. Thirring and B. L. van der Waerden). The first volume consisted of seven issues plus an index, in 466 pages. (The very first item reviewed was the second edition of *Methoden der mathematischen Physik*, by Courant and Hilbert.) The classification system used was very similar to the scheme used by *Jahrbuch*.

Mathematical Reviews. Zentralblatt flourished under Neugebauer's direction and became the primary reviewing journal in mathematics. *Jahrbuch* valiantly continued until issue number 4 of its Volume 68, for the year 1942, ceasing publication in mid-1944, but it had already lost its prominence in the research community. But, just as World War I damaged *Jahrbuch*, serious harm was done to *Zentralblatt* soon after its founding by political conditions beyond its control. The anti-Semitic and anti-Soviet policies of the Nazi regime generated pressures on the editorial policies of *Zentralblatt* concerning the use of Jewish and Russian reviewers. Although Neugebauer left Göttingen for the University of Copenhagen in 1934, he had continued to edit *Zentralblatt*. But by 1938 the intrusion of politics had become intolerable and he and other members of the editorial board resigned. Despite these difficulties *Zentralblatt* continued its operation and, except for a brief suspension of publication from November 1944 until June 1948, has continued to publish to the present day.

There were other problems in 1938: the oncoming war was making publication and international cooperation difficult, particularly when the site of publication of *Zentralblatt* was Berlin. In addition, the influx of many refugee research mathematicians to the United States (which had already begun to become a power in mathematical research) helped shift the center of gravity in mathematics from central Europe. The story of the founding of Mathematical Reviews is an interesting one, but it is well presented in a chapter of the book *A history of the second fifty years* by Everett Pitcher [P]; consequently, the details of this story will not be repeated here. (See also the article by Reingold [R].) We summarize this history by mentioning that subventions were obtained from the Carnegie Corporation, the Rockefeller Foundation, and the American Philosophical Society to start a reviewing journal, to be called Mathematical Reviews, with an initial annual budget of $20,000. The Executive Committee consisted of Oswald Veblen, chairman, T. C. Fry, and Warren Weaver; their names did not appear on the cover of the new journal, and neither did the names of the co-editors, Otto Neugebauer and J. D. Tamarkin (both of whom were professors at Brown University by that time), or their technical assistant, Willy Feller. The coverage of the new journal was to start as of mid-1939, and its extent was to be the same as that of *Zentralblatt*. There has been very little basic change in the coverage of MR to the present day.

It is difficult to imagine the frenzy of activity that must have ensued in the second half of the year 1939. There were journals and books to acquire, reviewers to be recruited, subscriptions to be sold, a printer to be retained, etc. Pitcher writes [op. cit.] that, before the first issue of MR appeared, there were about 700 subscribers and 350 reviewers, with about 220 from the United States and Canada. The first issue of MR, dated January 1940, contained 176 reviews in 36 pages; the first volume contained exactly 400 pages, with 2120 reviews, written by 287 reviewers. While a number of these reviews were editorial reviews or title listings, it is clear that the panel of early reviewers were a hardworked crew.

They were also a very distinguished crew—almost every leading mathematician in the U.S. of that time is on this list. While the majority of these mathematicians were resident in the U.S. or Canada, there were a number from other countries (the U.K., the Netherlands, Switzerland, France, Japan, U.S.S.R., etc.). When one recalls the unrest and turmoil then taking place in the world, it is even more remarkable that such a project could have been started at that time and succeeded. We owe a great debt of gratitude to these persons, particularly to Otto Neugebauer, who possessed the imagination and the energy to assume this task at such a difficult time in the world's history. It is vastly to his credit that he was able to enlist a remarkable panel of reviewers and obtain the cooperation of many persons to work on this endeavor.

For the past 50 years the editors at MR have been assisted by many persons throughout the world who regard the publication of this journal as worth their support. It is with considerable appreciation that the editors acknowledge their debt to them.

References and Sources

[B] Bell, E.T, *The development of mathematics*, McGraw-Hill Book Co., New York-London, 1945.

[Cj] Cajori, Florian, *A history of mathematics*, third edition, Chelsea Pub. Co., New York, 1985.

[Cs] Cassels, J.W.S., *The Spitalfelds Mathematical Society*, Bull. London Math. Soc. **11** (1979), no.3, 241–258; MR 80k:01025. Addendum, ibid, **12** (1980), no.5, 343; MR 82f:01036.

[E] Eves, Howard, *An introduction to the history of mathematics*, fifth edition, Saunders Pub., New York, 1983.

[G] Gascoigne, Robert Mortimer, *A historical catalogue of scientific periodicals, 1665–1900, with a survey of their development*, Garland Pub. Co., New York-London, 1985.

[M] Miller, G. A., *Historical introduction to mathematical literature*, Macmillan Co., New York, 1916.

[Mü] Müller, Felix, *Über die Abkürzung der Titel mathematischer Zeitschriften*, Jahresbericht der deutschen Mathematiker-Vereinigung **12** (1903), 426–444.

[K] Kline, Morris, *Mathematical thought from ancient to modern times*, Oxford Univ. Press, New York, 1972.

[P] Pitcher, Everett, *A history of the second fifty years, American Mathematical Society, 1939–1988*, pp. 69–89, A. M. S. Centennial Publications, vol. I, American Mathematical Society, Providence, R.I., 1988.

[R] Reingold, Nathan, *Refugee mathematicians in the United States of America, 1933–1941; reception and reaction*, in *A century of mathematics in America, Part 1*, pp. 175–200, American Mathematical Society, Providence, R.I., 1988.

[St] Struik, Dirk J., *A concise history of mathematics*, Fourth revised edition, Dover Pub. Inc., New York, 1987.

[Sc] Schaefer, Barbara Kirsch, *Using the mathematical literature*, Marcel Dekker Inc., New York-Basel, 1979.

[W] Wölffing, Ernst, *Über die bibliographischen Hilfsmittel der Mathematik*, Jahresbericht der deutschen Mathematiker-Vereinigung **12** (1903), 408–426.

Appendix
TABLE 1
The Growth of the Mathematical Literature, 1940–1989*
The following table gives, for each year from 1940 to 1989,
the number of pages and the number of reviews published by MR.

Year	# pages*	# reviews**	Year	# pages	# reviews
1940	400	2,120	1965	2645	12,907
1941	419	2,275	1966	3094	15,915
1942	371	2,154	1967	3390	17,141
1943	340	1,880	1968	3148	15,179
1944	328	1,889	1969	2850	14,135
1945	334	1,967	1970	3302	16,570
1946	621	4,053	1971	3793	18,784
1947	709	4,642	1972	3333	16,558
1948	735	4,472	1973	4235	20,410
1949	857	5,059	1974	4931	23,701
1950	873	5,241	1975	5332	28,399
1951	1004	6,040	1976	5448	32,181
1952	1141	6,597	1977	4754	30,492
1953	1280	7,604	1978	4306*	32,646
1954	1141	6,700	1979	7460	52,809
1955	1338	7,822	1980	5004	34,365**
1956	1438	8,190	1981	5320	35,873
1957	1120	6,166	1982	5429	38,677
1958	1433	8,168	1983	5230	39,453
1959	1374	7,609	1984	5346	40,365
1960	1600	7,824	1985	5743	40,336
1961	2548	13,382	1986	5930	40,953
1962	2750	13,743	1987	7420	51,853
1963	2789	13,297	1988	6768	45,954
1964	2648	12,570	1989	7194	48,865

During each of the five decades the total number of reviews was:

30,511	70,137	136,093	272,550	416,694

the grand total of which is 925,985. The ratios of the number of reviews in consecutive decades are

2.3	1.9	2.0	1.5

However, during the 1980s there were very few "title reviews" published in MR; instead such articles were fully classified and listed in the MR indexes, but the titles were not published in the text of MR. Approximately 13% of all articles were treated in this way. Therefore the corresponding figure for the 1980s is more nearly 479,000, the grand total is more nearly 988,300 and the last ratio is more nearly 1.76. Thus it appears to be roughly accurate to say that the number of mathematical papers doubles each decade. This is in agreement with the findings of Derek J. Price [in "The exponential curve of science", *Discovery* **17**(1956), 240–243]. He studied the growth of the scientific literature since 1770 in a number of scientific fields and found that in almost all cases the rate of growth was to effect a doubling within 10–15 years. The experience at MR during the past 50 years bears out this finding.

However, it should be mentioned that this represents a greater rate of increase than was noted by H. S. White [in "Forty years' fluctuations in mathematical research", *Science* (N.S.) **42**(1915). no. 1073, 105–113], who reported an increase in the number of authors reviewed in *Jahrbuch* in the years 1875 and 1905 from 510 to 1880, or a factor of approximately 3.7. The graphs given in White's article do not have an exponential character.

---

*The paging for 1940–1977 includes the volume indexes but not the annual indexes (published from 1970 on as the Index of Mathematical Papers). The paging for 1978 on does not include indexes.
**The number of published reviews is listed for 1940–1979. For 1980 on, the number of items reviewed is listed (i.e.. a joint review is counted according to the number of items reviewed).

Appendix

FIGURE 1
Mathematical Reviews: Number of Pages and Reviews by Year

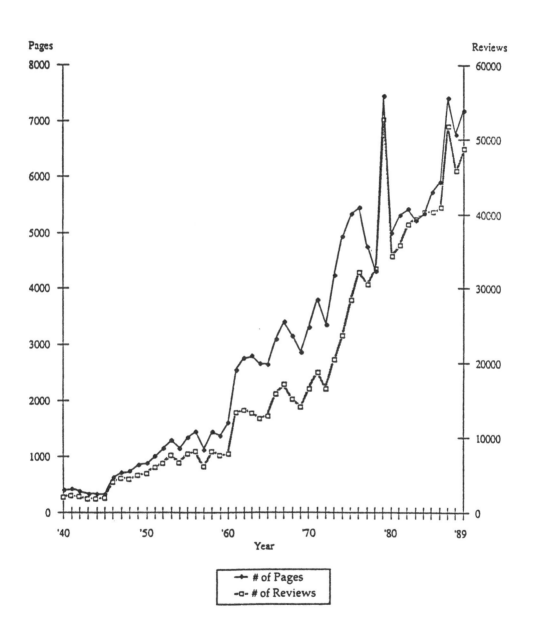

Appendix

FIGURE 2
Mathematical Reviews: Logarithm (base 10)
of Number of Reviews and Pages by Year

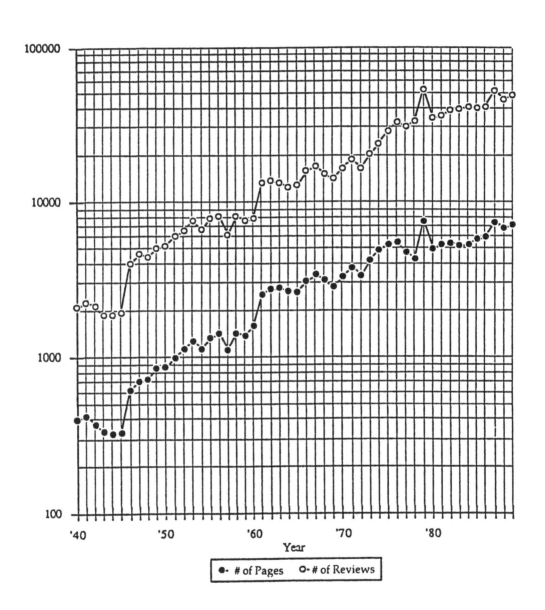

Editor's Note: In an effort to contain costs, the publishers of Mathematical Reviews decided in 1989 to keep the number of reviews at approximately 1989 levels. In order to do this and maintain comprehensive coverage of the literature within the scope of *Mathematical Reviews*, they increased the percentage of items that are not given reviews but which are included in the MR database, in the indexes of MR and in the electronic versions of MR. Thus the MR editors have been more selective about reviewing items that are borderline in scope.

The following numbers update the table in this appendix. However, they should not be interpreted as an indication of a leveling off of the number of mathematical research publications.

Year	pages	reviews
1990	7,514	50,963
1991	7,044	47,411
1992	7,194	48,651
1993	7,069	47,546
1994	7,614	47,546
1995	7,834	47,592
1996	7,940	48,021

Except for the graphs and the editor's note, which are new, this Appendix appeared as an article prepared for the semi-centenary of *Mathematical Reviews* celebrated in 1990. Published by permission of the American Mathematical Society. Copyright © Robert G. Bartle.

26

From Published Paper to MR Review: How Does It Happen?

Jane E. Kister*

The beginning of the new decade next month coincides with an important milestone for Mathematical Reviews (MR): the very first issue appeared in January 1940 and so the first issue of 1990, issue 90a, will be the 50th anniversary issue. This comes just a few months after the acquisition of the millionth item at MR [see these Notices, September 1989, 858–859]. Anniversaries are a time for reminiscence and reflection. A fascinating and informative history of MR by Everett Pitcher has already been published [A history of the second fifty years. American Mathematical Society 1939–1988, pp. 69–89, Amer. Math. Soc., Providence, RI, 1988] and that story will not be repeated here. It was in reflecting on the huge number of authors whose work has been reviewed in MR over the last 50 years that it seemed appropriate to write an article for them and perhaps answer some of the questions authors may have about reviews of their papers.

Which published papers will be reviewed in MR? "MR [provides] reviews or summaries of all articles and books that contain new contributions to mathematics at the research level" [from the Editorial Statement published in the January 1987 issue of MR]. A complex acquisition system that includes arrangements with publishers and universities all over the world is used to ensure that copies of all journal issues that might contain "new contributions to mathematics at the research level" are received in the AMS offices in Ann Arbor where MR is produced. The journals range from the Journal für die Reine und Angewandte Mathematik (Crelle's Journal, founded in 1826) and other European and US journals founded in the nineteenth century to the journal Forum Mathematicum for which the first issue was in 1989. A growing number of journals are received from the People's Republic of China (currently just over 100). Research mathematics journals are the primary source for articles but in addition many other research journals in physics, engineering and other fields where research mathematics might be applied are regularly acquired by the MR librarians. All told, about 1,800 journals are now received and of those over 400 are reviewed cover-to-cover.

Research mathematics is published not only in journals but also in volumes of conference proceedings or other collections and in authored monographs. Publishers with substantial lists in mathematics routinely send books and collections in mathematics and applied fields for possible review, and publisher catalogues from all over the world are regularly scanned for books that should be reviewed. Currently about 230 items (books or journal issues) arrive at the MR office each week.

On receipt the item is scanned by at least one of the fourteen MR editors, mathematicians who use their expertise to determine what is reviewable. The editor looks for items which contain new mathematics, either in pure mathematics or in an applied field. (Some other items of interest to research mathematicians are also covered, such as advanced-level textbooks and expository papers.) Items that are not selected are "out of scope" (do not contain research in mathematics) "too elementary" (do not contain new mathematics) or "in preliminary form" (e.g., an extended abstract); abstracts and other short papers without complete proofs are usually not covered because it is expected that the same piece of mathematics either has been or will be published in complete form and that the complete version will be reviewed. In summary, a paper published in a journal or a collection volume is virtually certain to be considered for review in MR (but note that unpublished papers such as preprints or technical reports are not covered, again because it is presumed that a published version will later be reviewed).

How are books and articles classified? Each working day the editors look at the over 200 items (books and papers) yielded by the selection process described above. At this stage a preliminary classification (which includes a unique primary classification and possibly secondary classifications as well) is made; this is the classification under which the item appears in Current Mathematical Publications (CMP). Several different criteria may be used to make the final decision. In most cases editors use their knowledge of the field and their experience in applying the classification scheme to determine the classifications from the title, summary and a scan of the whole item. In some journals classification numbers from the scheme used by MR are given for each article; this is a great help, particularly when the subject matter of an article may span several classifications and the best primary classification is not obvious from a quick scan through the article. Other pointers are the classifications used for related items listed in the bibliography or earlier papers by the author. There is a subjective element to classifying, as is evidenced from time to time by lengthy discussions among the editors about what is the correct primary classification. Although authors may not always agree with the classification selected by the editors, the classifications are selected as consistently as possible; this is essential for successful searching by classification for papers on a given topic.

Papers in the developing new areas of mathematics are sometimes the hardest items to classify; there isn't always an appropriate niche in the classification for an area that has developed since the classification system was established. The MR editors, together with the editors for Zentralblatt für Mathematik, are presently engaged in revising the classification system, balancing the need to provide classifications for new fields with the advantages of a relatively stable system that can be used for searching over long periods. The new system will probably be used in MR and CMP in 1991.

How is the reviewer chosen? The 61 areas covered in MR, as defined by the classification scheme, are divided among the MR editors, as far as possible matching the areas with each editor's expertise. So, for example, one editor is primarily responsible for Section 30, Functions of a complex variable, and other related sections in analysis, another for Section 81, Quantum mechanics, and other sections in mathematical physics. The editor responsible for a given section selects the reviewers for the papers in that section from among over 14,000 reviewers. Suppose for example that a paper written in French, has been classified in Section 20F, Special aspects of infinite or finite groups. To begin with, the editor will probably look for a reviewer among those who have expressed an interest in Section 20F (and who have indicated a willingness to review papers in French). If the paper is about decision problems for groups, then the field of potential reviewers can be further narrowed to those who have listed 20F10. The paper may also have a secondary classification in Section 03 (Mathematical logic and foundations)—03B25 if the results concern decidable problems and 03D40 if the problems are undecidable—in which case the editor may look for reviewers listing both classifications. Reviewers also provide verbal descriptions of their interests and these descriptions can be searched to match key words in the paper with the reviewers' own descriptions. A different approach will probably be used for a paper that begins: "This is a sequel to [4]..."; the editor may then check the review of the paper [4] and if appropriate assign the paper to the same reviewer. Some papers are difficult to classify at the finest level. A paper may clearly fall in Section 20F but not obviously lie in a unique subsection. In this case, the editor may scan the references of the paper; perhaps there is an item on a similar topic listed there and either the author of that item (if also a reviewer) or the reviewer of that item might be a suitable reviewer. Sometimes the most obvious choice for a reviewer cannot be used: he or she may not be a reviewer (in some areas there is a real shortage of experienced reviewers with the necessary language skills); the "obvious choice" may be the author's thesis advisor or colleague at the same institution (and so not be the best person to provide an objective review); or the chosen reviewer may already have several items to review. There is a "limit" on the number of items which may be assigned to each reviewer at any given time in order that the reviewers do not become too overloaded. MR is dependent on the good will of its reviewers and on their providing reviews in a timely way.

For a large proportion of the items sent out, the review is returned within two months. However, if after allowing the reviewer a reasonable amount of time in which to complete the review, the review still has not been returned, the editor must reconsider how best to treat the item. At this stage, because the paper is getting "old", the editor must balance the advantages of waiting even longer for a signed review with those of providing a timely description of the item. The primary purpose of a review is to give the reader a basis for deciding whether or not to consult the original paper, and to do so as soon as possible after publication. With this in mind, although occasionally the paper is sent out to a second reviewer, most often the editor will decide to use the summary or some other portion of the text as a review. This means that somewhat uneven treatment may be given to comparable papers: one may be given a lengthy evaluative review and the other a brief summary describing the main results. It is important to emphasize that the difference does not reflect a judgement on MR's part that one is more deserving of a substantive review than the other.

For some items the editor will from the start choose to review the paper by author's summary or by a brief editorial review. Summaries are very often used in the applied areas, Sections 65 through 94. This is in part because there are fewer reviewers with interests in these areas. Another reason is that journals in these areas routinely provide informative summaries.

How soon after publication of a paper will a review appear? Suppose that the paper has been published, the journal or collection in which it appears has been received at MR, the paper is within scope, and a reviewer has been selected and has returned a review. What happens then? First, the review is copy edited (the symbols are clarified for the keyboarder); the references given in the review are checked for accuracy and completeness, put into the uniform style used for references and MR review numbers are added. The review is then edited; at this stage the editor responsible for the section in which the item is primarily classified reads the review for mathematical sense; because of the volume of reviews processed by each editor (currently about 4,000 each year) it is not possible to check each review against the original paper but the editors use their expertise to identify "suspicious" reviews; if necessary, the editor will check the original paper, perhaps to clarify a formula or an obscure statement of a theorem. The editor will also check the review for clear and correct use of English; if the review contains critical statements the editor will try to ensure that the criticism is fair and in good taste and that errors are pinpointed. The editors are aware of their responsibility to the author, who does not have the opportunity to "reply" to the review in MR. The final step in the editing process is the fine classification of the item. Reviewers are invited to suggest fine (5–digit) classifications for the items they review and many do so. The editors use these suggestions together with their own knowledge of the classification scheme to modify and refine the classifications given initially. These are the classifications that appear with the review and in the MR indexes (they may not always agree with the CMP classification). The edited review is keyboarded (by experienced AMS TEX typists) and then carefully proofread (each review is read by a copy editor and two editors; usually the review is not sent back to the reviewer for proofreading). Every four weeks, the corrected keyboarded reviews are "pooled" to form an MR issue. A specially designed computer program orders and pages the electronic versions of the reviews, at the same time providing the section headings and running heads. A galley version of the paged issue is given one final check before the camera-ready version is produced and taken to the printer.

Some of the procedures described above are not entirely in MR's control. A paper cannot be processed for review until the journal or collection in which it appears has been received at MR. Some journals send page proofs (the tables of contents of these "page-proof" journals appear in the front of CMP) and this helps to get a paper into the MR pipeline early. Recently another procedure was started to speed the appearance of reviews: manuscripts which have been accepted for publication in certain journals are sent to MR as soon as they have been accepted and the manuscript version is used for the reviewing process.

A review can sometimes get delayed on the reviewer's desk. Reminders are regularly sent to reviewers but even so, some reviews are not returned until a year after the item has been sent. Once in the MR office, every effort is made to speed the review through the steps outlined above. Nevertheless, some reviews are more delayed than others. A review with several obscure references or with complicated formulas or diagrams will take longer to process than a brief review with no special notation and no references. In 1988 procedures were devised allowing reviewers to send in their reviews, coded using TEX, electronically. For the reviews sent in this way (still a rather small percentage of the 600–700 signed reviews received each week) this has eliminated the initial keyboarding described above and consequently reduced the time taken to process the review. It is reasonable to expect that, provided reviewers are prompt, most papers and books will be reviewed either in the year of publication or in the following year.

As soon as a book or paper has been selected for review and given an initial classification, the bibliographic information is processed for publication in CMP. At the time of publication of the paper copy of CMP. the information is also incorporated into MathSci, the online version of MR and CMP. Items that have been listed in CMP but not yet reviewed in MR are also included in MathSciDisc, the CD-ROM version of MR and CMP; this is updated semi-annually. Frequently. an item is listed in a CMP issue which is available in libraries before the journal issue in which the item appears.

How can authors help to make MR more useful? The author and the MR editors have the same aims: there should be a timely review, written by an expert in the subject matter of the item giving an accurate and clear description of the main results, and it should be correctly classified. As has already been mentioned, it is very useful to have the author's own assessment of the classification published with the item. It is also helpful to have a descriptive title; a paper with the title "Primitive permutation groups of odd degree" is more likely to be correctly classified than one with the title "Some problems in finite group theory". Probably the most valuable aid the author can provide is a concise (about half a page or less) succinct summary, written clearly in good English. It is much more useful if the theorems are described, as far as this is possible without introducing too many technicalities, than if the summary closes with the sentence: "We prove some results in this area." One or two key references may also be very useful. A well-written summary is an invaluable guide for the MR editors in classifying and in assigning an appropriate reviewer, and for the reviewer in placing the paper in its proper context. It is particularly helpful if a paper that summarizes earlier published work of the author or is a preliminary version of a paper to be published elsewhere contains a clear statement to that effect on the first page.

As the number of mathematicians publishing papers grows so do the chances of wrongly identifying two authors with similar names. Each author listed in MR or CMP is assigned a unique "primary" name which is used to identify that author in those instances in which the published form is ambiguous. For example, a primary name will be added for an author who uses "J. Jones" as the published form of his name. The task of sorting out, for example, the different authors named J. Jones would be considerably simplified if each author would consistently use a version that is likely to be unique; full first name and middle initial is generally sufficient although there are instances of more than one author with the same first, middle and last names (these MR distinguishes by using superscripts).

MR has been fortunate in having the services of many distinguished mathematicians as reviewers from its very first issue. In fact, a number of the reviewers for the January 1940 issue are still writing reviews today, fifty years later. However, more reviewers are needed all the time to take over from retiring reviewers and to cover the increasing number of papers published each year. Only mathematicians who are or have been active in research themselves have the skills for this crucial task. The editorial staff at MR urges those of you who are not already reviewers to consider joining your colleagues and distinguished mathematicians round the world as an "MR reviewer". If you would like to review for MR, please write with details of your mathematical interests, your publications and your language skills (by e-mail on INTERNET to MATHREV@MATH.AMS.COM or by mail to Mathematical Reviews, P.O. Box 8604, Ann Arbor, MI 48107–8604). It should be stressed that potential reviewers must be prepared to write timely reviews. In return, reviewers may find that the reviewing process stimulates their own research. MR could not function without its reviewers and the quality of the journal largely depends on them. The MR editors always welcome comments and suggestions from authors. They hope to continue the high standards of MR that have been established during its first fifty years in providing comprehensive and informed coverage of the world's mathematical literature.

27

The PASCAL and FRANCIS Databases of the Institut de l'Information Scientifique et Technique (France): Presentation and Statistics

Claude Patou

Introduction

The Institut de l'Information Scientifique et Technique (INIST) of the French Centre National de la Recherche Scientifique (CNRS) is dedicated to the collection, processing and dissemination of scientific and technical information. INIST uses its multidisciplinary collections of 25,523 journal titles and 234,548 scientific reports, doctoral dissertations, conference proceedings, reports and books as the raw material for its activities.

INIST Databases

INIST produces two multidisciplinary, multilingual (French, English, Spanish) databases, PASCAL for Science, Technology and Medicine, and FRANCIS for the Humanities, Social Sciences and Economics.

PASCAL 1995: as of 23 February 96, 11,359,731 bibliographic records dating back to 1973 are available on-line. The database is updated weekly since 1 June 1994 on QUESTEL and monthly on ESA and DIALOG. A total of 517,718 new records were loaded on these hosts in 1995.

FRANCIS 1995: 1,702,342 bibliographic records, dating back to 1973, are available online on QUESTEL. The database is updated quarterly. In 1995, 47,340 new records (excluding the Bibliography of the History of Art) were loaded on QUESTEL.

TABLE A

Years	Records	Years	Records
1995	517,718	1983	477,372
1994	654,731	1982	367,475
1993	689,918	1981	515,222
1992	693,073	1980	477,112
1991	640,605	1979	470,879
1990	383,985	1978	473,124
1989	328,464	1977	461,349
1988	451,220	1976	421,684
1987	495,548	1975	452,733
1986	423,177	1974	437,202
1985	426,013	1973	378,446
1984	456,972		

The PASCAL Database

Changes in production policy

In 1994, it was decided to enhance the basic research coverage in INIST databases by giving a new emphasis to applied research and technology. Also the quality and timeliness of data, and the general user-friendliness of the databases were targeted for improvement.

In January 1994, an Optimal Database Content working group was set up to overhaul the coverage of the PASCAL database by giving greater emphasis to applied research and technology and French language publications. Since March 1995, new input production methods have been introduced for the subject-oriented Science, Technology and Medicine (STM) resource pool. Over 4,000 titles have been selected for cover-to-cover indexing, resulting in a more comprehensive list of titles indexed in the PASCAL database.

The content of bibliographic records has been enhanced at the cataloging level with the inclusion of all authors and French author affiliations, thus providing information which is essential to any form of informetric study. All foreign author affiliations will be included by mid-1996 (at present only the first affiliation is shown).

Today, 75% of records include an abstract to enable users to conduct text word searches, which will eventually replace key-word searching. Query analysis and translation into a documentary language through the knowledge bases to be implemented in the future should result in user-friendly interfaces making it possible for users to formulate queries in natural language.

The multilingual PASCAL database is an easy-to-use first-approach tool for the nonspecialist. The organization of data by topics rather than by academic discipline is designed to simplify search procedures for the user and facilitate the preparation of subject-oriented products.

In 1995, 420,000 records were processed in this way, to which records with

TABLE B

Years	Records	Years	Records
1995	58,862	1983	80,616
1994	62,332	1982	76,722
1993	78,116	1981	79,291
1992	80,737	1980	77,502
1991	80,288	1979	71,120
1990	55,216	1978	74,457
1989	69,712	1977	72,679
1988	73,854	1976	69,668
1987	68,054	1975	72,823
1986	76,032	1974	64,225
1985	74,793	1973	54,250
1984	78,268		

cataloging data for basic research literature were added. This in-house production was completed by records supplied through national and international cooperative agreements.

PASCAL Timeliness

The Quality Assurance program implemented in 1993 resulted in shorter record production time (80% of the records loaded on the hosts in less than 2 months), indexing homogeneity and cataloging quality, and the presence of abstracts in 75% of records.

Timeliness of data is a key criterion of the quality of a database. This is why Quality Assurance has placed particular emphasis on reorganizing production circuits to ensure that bibliographic records are loaded on the hosts in less than two months following receipt of the documents at INIST.

The FRANCIS Database

FRANCIS is a multidisciplinary bibliographic database covering the Humanities and Social Sciences. It is a collection of data covering European and world literature with a special emphasis on French research. INIST produces or participates in the production of the following FRANCIS databases:

- Philosophy

- Education

- Sociology, in collaboration with the Centre d'Etudes Sociologiques sur le Droit et les Institutions Pénales (CESDIP) and the Institut d'Etudes Politiques de Grenoble (IEPG).

- History of Science and Technology

- History and Science of Literature

- Linguistics

- Prehistory and Protohistory

- Archaeology

- History and Science of Religion

- Bibliography of Administrative Science, in collaboration with the Centre d'Etudes et de Recherches de Science Administrative (CERSA), the Institut International d'Administration Publique (IIAP) and the Institut d'Etudes Politiques de Grenoble (IEPG).

- Ethnology

- Bibliography of the History of Art (BHA), with the J. Paul Getty Trust

- Economics of Energy

INIST is in charge of technical management for three databases, for the scientific content of which three other CNRS units are responsible.

- Bibliographie géographique internationale (BGI) produced by the CNRS INTERGEOPRODIG (Pôle de Recherche pour la Diffusion de l'Information en Géographie);

- Amérique Latine, a database produced by a research group formed by the Institut des Hautes Etudes de l'Amérique Latine and the University of Toulouse Le Mirail; and

- Documentation en Gestion des Entreprises (DOGE), a business management database produced by a national network of French institutions.

FRANCIS is a multidisciplinary Humanities and Social Sciences database which provides its users with a finished product (abstracts included in 85% of records, bilingual descriptors). Its strong points undoubtedly are its originality, design and range of distribution methods. FRANCIS is a collection of French language databases designed to promote French research in the international community and reflect trends in literature in Europe and around the world. It offers all the advantages of a multilingual, multidisciplinary database benefiting from fruitful cooperation programs: with CESDIP, which partners the FRANCIS sociology database, PRODIG, which has entrusted INIST with document management for its own database, and the J.P. Getty Institute, which, in association with INIST, produces the BHA database now accepted as a worldwide authority in History of Art.

Cooperation Programs

INIST conducts an active cooperation policy through its database production activities at the international level with the American Institute of Physics (AIP) and Engineering Information, Inc. (Ei) and at the national level with institutions such as the Bureau de Recherches Géologiques et Minières (BRGM) or the Institut Français du Pétrole (IFP), as well as a number of organizations producing data in the field of Public Health, and six trade associations producing data in the building and civil engineering sectors.

American Institute of Physics (AIP)

A contract with the American Institute of Physics (AIP) was signed in October 1993, and the first tapes containing bibliographic records for 64 publications were received and incorporated into the PASCAL database In April 1994. In 1995, 39,129 AIP records were incorporated into the PASCAL database: 96% of these included an author's abstract in extenso, and 99.8% were indexed using the AIP vocabulary.

Engineering Information (Ei)

Exchanges of bibliographic records between Ei and INIST were initiated in November 1995. In 1995, 2,254 Ei entries were incorporated into the PASCAL database. All records are indexed with the Ei vocabulary and they all include an abstract.

Ecole Nationale de Santé Publique (ENSP) [National School of Public Health]

The BDSP (Banque de Données de Santé Publique) is a database in Public Health coproduced by the three ministries having signed the outline agreement, ENSP, INIST, the Institut National de la Santé et de la Recherche Médicale (INSERM), ARAMIS (a network of associations producing public health data) and the Paris National Health Hospitals.

Exchanges of bibliographic records between INIST and ENSP began in 1994 and 36,698 BDSP records for the period 1972–1993 were loaded in PASCAL in that year. With the incorporation of this earlier material, the PASCAL database now contains all records in Public Health, including those previously included in the Rhesus database of FRANCIS. In 1995, some 12,000 ENSP records were loaded in PASCAL. Today, the BDSP contains 100,000 records.

Bureau de Recherches Géologiques et Minières (BRGM)

In 1995, BRGM contributed 4,357 bibliographic records to the PASCAL database.

FIGURE 1
1995 production of organizations cooperating to the PASCAL data base

Field	Organization	Number of records
Earth Sciences	BRGM	4,357
Building &	CSTB, CSTC, CETU,	
Civil Engineering	ENPC, LCPC, ATILH	2,241
Engineering	Ei	2,254
Energy	IFP	1,874
Physics	AIP	39,129
Public Health	ENSP	12,000
Total		61,855

Acronyms
AIP   American Institute of Physics
ATILH   Association Technique de l'Industrie des Liants Hydrauliques
BRGM   Bureau de Recherches Géologiques et Minières
CETU   Centre d'Etudes des Tunnels
CSTB   Centre Scientifique et Technique du Bâtiment
CSTC   Centre Scientifique et Technique de la Construction
Ei   Engineering Information
ENPC   Ecole Nationale des Ponts et Chaussées
ENSP   Ecole Nationale de Santé Publique
IFP   Institut Français du Pétrole
LCPC   Laboratoire Central des Ponts et Chaussées

FIGURE 2
1995 Production of organizations cooperating to the FRANCIS data base

Field	Organization	Number of records
Latin America	GDR 26	1,043
Administration	CERSA, IIAP, IEPG	3,958
Sociology	CESDIP, IEPG	174
DOGE	Réseau DOGE	1,427
BGI	PRODIG	3,960
BHA	J.P. Getty Trust	17,702
Total		28,264

Acronyms:
BHA   Bibliographie de Histoire de l'Art
CERSA   Centre d'Etudes et de Recherches en Science Administrative
CESDIP Centre d'Etudes Sociologiques sur le Droit et les Institutions Pénales
IIAP   Institut International d'Administration Publique
IISA   Institut International de Sciences Administratives
IEPG   Institut d'Etudes Politiques de Grenoble
PRODIG Pôle de Recherche pour la Diffusion de l'Information en Géographie

Institut Français du Pétrole (IFP)

The IFP supplied INIST with 1874 bibliographic records in 1995.

Bâtiment et Travaux Publics (BTP) [Building and Civil Engineering]

Six organizations and INIST contribute to the building and civil engineering sector of the PASCAL database.

SIGLE and WTI

INIST also contributes input to the SIGLE and WTI databases. The SIGLE database (System for Information on Grey Literature in Europe) was established in 1980 with EEC participation. It is produced by the European Association for Grey Literature Exploitation (EAGLE), which has nine member countries (France, Belgium, Germany, Italy, Luxembourg, Netherlands, UK, Ireland and Spain).

Grey literature is best defined as literature, which cannot readily be acquired through normal bookselling channels and which is therefore difficult to identify and obtain. Other terms, such as nonconventional or semipublished are also used to describe it. Examples of grey literature include technical or research reports, doctoral dissertations, some conference papers and pre-prints, some official publications, discussion and policy papers and so on.

The aim of the SIGLE database is to valorize grey literature, a type of literature often hard to locate, by collecting, indexing and supplying grey documents through national centers. By the end of 1994, SIGLE contained some 380,000 records. SIGLE is updated quarterly and 35,000–40,000 records are added each year. Records have an English title and uncontrolled indexing terms. Abstracts are not included. In 1995, INIST contributed 1,351 records to the SIGLE database.

The World Translations Index (WTI) database is coproduced by INIST and the International Translations Centre (ITC). ITC is an international awareness center for translations of scientific and technical documents, which aims to avoid duplication of translating efforts by disseminating information on existing translations. Seven European countries are members of ITC namely Belgium, France, Germany, The Netherlands, Portugal, Sweden and the United Kingdom. The WTI database is available online on ESA-IRS and DIALOG. It contains over 400,000 records dating back to 1979, of translations into Western languages. In 1995, INIST contributed 1,092 records to WTI.

Tables

Table 1 shows the distribution of PASCAL and FRANCIS records by main subject heading.

Table 2 highlights the distribution of records by document type, as of the December 1995 update.

Table 3 shows the distribution of records by publication year, as of the December 1995 update.

Table 4 shows the linguistic diversity of PASCAL and FRANCIS records.

Table 5 highlights their international journal coverage, with particular emphasis on European titles.

Table 6 gives the number of PASCAL and FRANCIS records derived from these titles.

PASCAL 1995

TABLE 1
Main Subject Headings, 1995.

Records	%	Subject Headings
176544	35.64	Medical Sciences
97262	19.63	Applied Sciences
94809	19.14	Biological Sciences
81479	16.45	Physics
28424	5.74	Earth, Ocean, Space
22066	4.45	Chemistry
9126	1.84	Mathematics
2747	0.55	Information Science

Note: Number of records by field in 1995, keeping in mind that one record can have several subject headings.

TABLE 2
Document Types as of December 1995

Records	%	Document Type
478309	96.56	Periodical
6264	1.26	Doctoral Dissertation
5348	1.08	Proceedings
4011	0.81	Book
1384	0.28	Report
38	0.01	Legislation
15	0.00	Standard

TABLE 3
Records by Publication Years as of December 1995

Years	Records	%
1995	335548	67.74
1994	146152	29.50
1993	10111	2.04
Other	3513	0.71
Undated	45	0.01

Note: Number of records by publication date as of the year under consideration. "Other" refers to publication years 3 years prior to the reference year.

TABLE 4
Records by Language, 1995

Language	Records	%
English	431643	87.14
French	44068	8.90
German	12979	2.62
Other	8255	1.34

TABLE 5
Journals Covered in PASCAL by Geographical Area—1995

Country/Region	Titles	%
Western Europe	2320	43.12%
North America	1709	31.77%
France	1318	24.50%
Asia	188	3.49%
Other	105	1.95%
Eastern Europe	69	1.28%
Africa	53	0.99%
Océania	46	0.86%
Latin America	22	0.41%

TABLE 6
PASCAL Records by Publication Country

Country/Region	Records	Percentage
North America	221371	46,28%
Western Europe	195993	40,98%
France	35130	7,34%
Asia	17693	3,70%
Eastern Europe	3023	0,63%
Océania	2736	0,57%
Other	1379	0,29%
Africa	1106	0,23%
Latin America	622	0,13%

Note: "Other" refers to periodicals published by international organizations or periodical of which the publication country is unknown.

FRANCIS 1995

TABLE 1
File names, 1995

Records	%	File Name
50	0.11	518 : Socioeconomics of labor
4375	9.24	519 : Philosophy
2583	5.45	520 : Education
3993	8.43	521 : Sociology
2055	4.34	522 : History of Sciences and Techniques
3847	8.12	523 : History and Science of Literature
2863	6.04	524 : Linguistics
3578	7.55	525 : Prehistory and Protohistory
2162	4.56	526 : Art and Archeology
6657	14.05	527 : History and Science of Religion
4094	8.64	528 : Administration
3260	6.88	529 : Ethnology
3960	8.36	531 : Geography
1043	2.20	533 : Latin America
1427	3.01	616 : Doge
1443	3.05	731 : Economics of Energy

Note: Number of records by file in 1995. 22 records belonged to two files.

TABLE 2
Document Types as of December 1995

Records	%	Document Type
44433	93.8	Serial
792	1.7	Miscellanea
750	1.8	Proceedings
570	1.2	Book
436	0.92	Doctoral Dissertation
362	0.76	Report
25	0.05	Map

TABLE 3
Records by Publication Years as of December 1995

Years	Records	%
1995	14928	31.51
1994	23046	48.65
1993	7102	14.99
Other	2235	4.72
Undated	57	0.12

Note: Number of records by publication date as of the year under consideration. "Other" refers to publication years 3 years prior to the reference year.

TABLE 4
Records by Language, 1995

Language	Records	%
French	19147	40.42
English	18715	39.51
German	3751	7.92
Spanish	2540	5.36
Italian	1765	3.73
Russian	537	1.13
Other(36)	1354	2.86

TABLE 5
Journals Covered in FRANCIS by country, 1995

Country/Region	Journals	%
France	1645	35.81%
Western Europe	1640	35.70%
North America	893	19.44%
Eastern Europe	160	3.48%
Asia	106	2.31%
Other	100	2.18%
Latin America	95	2.07%
Africa	62	1.35%
Oceania	35	0.76%

Note: "Other" refers to periodicals published by international organizations or periodicals of which the publication country is unknown.

TABLE 6
FRANCIS Records by Publication Country, 1995

Country/Region	Journals	%
Western Europe	19657	35.08%
France	18752	33.46%
North America	12488	22.28%
Eastern Europe	1674	2.99%
Asia	1071	1.91%
Latin America	776	1.38%
Other	690	1.23%
Africa	492	0.88%
Oceania	458	0.82%

Note: "Other" refers to periodicals published by international organizations or periodicals of which the publication country is unknown.

28

Information Access Company: The Evolution of InfoTrac Multi-Source Databases and Their Importance to Library End-Users

Sean Devine

Introduction

Information Access Company is one of the world's leading developers and providers of periodical and multiple source reference products. People who work or study in public and academic libraries, corporations, governments, hospitals, schools, and homes rely upon Information Access Company for useful, current information packaged in databases that are easy to access and simple to use. The company was founded in 1976 by a group of entrepreneurs. Today, Information Access employs an international force of over 1,000 employees producing, selling, and marketing a wide range of products and services that enable users around the world to make life decisions.

Besides the company's size, much has changed within Information Access and the industry as a whole, meaning major changes in the variety of databases available and the ways in which users access them. The company introduced its first product, Magazine Index™, a citation-only database, in 1977. At its debut, Magazine Index was available only on microfilm. Since then, technology has enabled the growth of databases into a variety of CD-ROM, magnetic tape, and Internet formats. Today, Information Access Company offers a full range of databases focused for business, academic, general reference, current events, legal, health, and computer research.

The growing scope of patron reference needs combined with massive technological growth has transformed both patron usage and expectation patterns. The explosive growth of the Internet and World Wide Web has increased user demand for remote access to full text resources. No matter what time of day, or where they may be, if it's a place where the computer can be plugged in, users expect to get the information they need. The availability of 24–hour remote reference systems, like Information Access Company's InfoTrac SearchBank™, is a dramatic leap forward from waiting in line at the library to use a database on microfilm or CD-ROM, the norm just a few years ago.

And serving the remote user means providing not only index, but thorough full text coverage as well. The widespread use of online services has promoted a "push the button and retrieve everything" expectation. But while Web search engines attempt to retrieve a vast array of questionable sources, Information Access has remained a reliable source in the remote reference arena, extending the library's reach to patrons outside its direct environment. For all library users, and especially those using the library remotely, information must be current, complete, and ready at a moment's notice.

The Philosophy in Creating Answers

Since its creation, Information Access has forged ahead with a basic principle to guide its development of multi-source databases: locate the most comprehensive, credible sources and incorporate them into a single database searchable with a common authority file and intuitive interface. Anyone familiar with a library knows it contains much more than just one source type for reference needs. Resources like reference books, magazines, specialized journals, and encyclopedias fill a library's shelves and offer a good balance of depth and scope to encourage thorough research. Information Access Company takes a similar approach with its databases. By integrating multiple source types and providing a search engine that seamlessly links them, users automatically uncover a range and intensity of resources that can provide complete answers to their research questions. There are several ways in which Information Access aggregates this information. They include:

- *Buying the information.* Acquiring companies or company divisions which produce comprehensive information, such as Wards Business Directory, Predicasts, Automotive Information Center, and Area Business Databank.

- *Licensing the information.* Entering into agreements with publishers or providers to include their data in exchange for royalty payments, like PR Newswire, Clinical Reference Systems, Investext, and thousands of primary publications.

- *Creating the information.* Creating bibliographic citations and abstracts for databases, and adding links and other mechanisms to make the data easily accessible.

Multi-source products dominate Information Access Company's total offerings for libraries (Fig. 1) and are the most popular choice of libraries subscribing to the company's products (Fig. 2). Information Access Company began its multi-source product offerings focusing on business information, and has expanded its collection to include general reference, health, and school research aids as well.

Multi-Source Solutions: A Series of Business Firsts

Information Access Company's business offerings are the hallmark of the company's database collection, and a popular source of business information for academic and public libraries. Leading product development for business databases is the company's belief that complete business answers are rarely contained within just one source. The perspective gained by combining business journals with newspapers is more complete than that obtained with journals alone. And, investment research reports, newswire releases, and company directories can provide a total picture of a company or industry, more complete than one in which only one of those sources is relied upon.

Information Access Company took these ideas and translated them into the first multi-source databases for library patron research. While other business databases in the market relied solely on magazines for their content, Information Access Company added the premiere source of late-breaking business news and analysis, the *Wall Street Journal*, into **Business Index™**, creating another multi-source business reference tool. **Company Intelligence™** was the first online database to deliver comprehensive company directory information blended with indexing from current business journals relevant to the listed companies.

Information Access recognizes that a complete perspective in business research is not limited to one source type. It also acknowledges that business information is not limited to business or news publications. Publications covering any industry, market segment, or population are all potential sources of relevant business information. Information Access Company developed an editorial policy incorporating this belief, which calls for any business-related article indexed by the company to be included in its business databases. For instance, *Cosmopolitan* is not a usual source for business information. However, if a current issue includes an article on Revlon's latest marketing campaign, that article would appear in the company's business databases.

All Information Access databases for library use are designed as self-service resource packages, enabling the user to find bibliographic citations, abstracts, and full text within one search. But for libraries needing more in-depth, comprehensive information, the company designs several reference center databases. These super-sized, multi-source products combine a large variety of sources into one database. **General BusinessFile ASAP™**, the company's most comprehensive business information resource, combines journal and newspa-

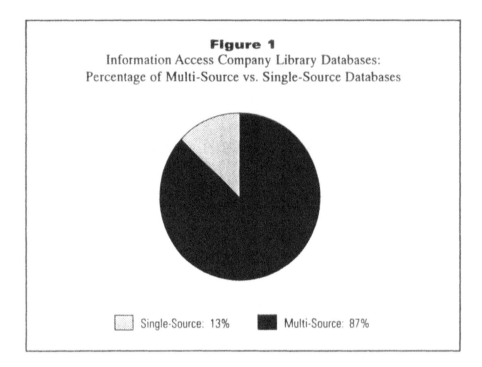

Figure 1
Information Access Company Library Databases:
Percentage of Multi-Source vs. Single-Source Databases

Single-Source: 13%   Multi-Source: 87%

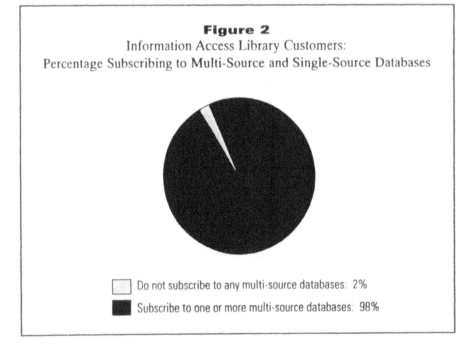

Figure 2
Information Access Library Customers:
Percentage Subscribing to Multi-Source and Single-Source Databases

Do not subscribe to any multi-source databases: 2%

Subscribe to one or more multi-source databases: 98%

Figure 3
Sample Search for Company Name "Sybase"
within General BusinessFile ASAP

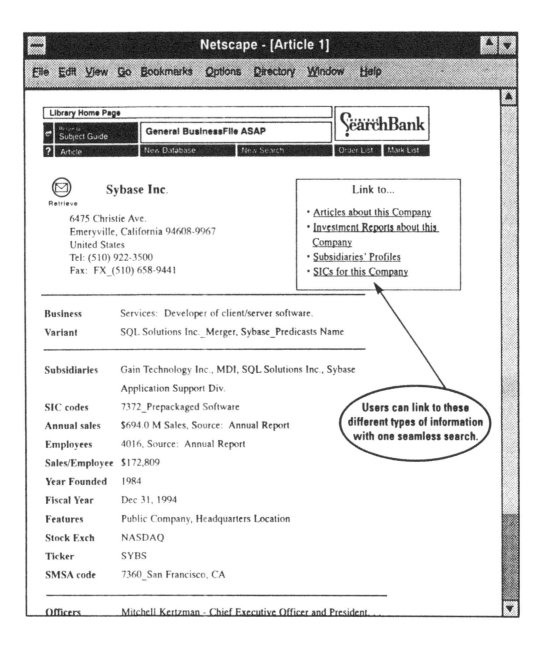

per articles, directory information, investment reports, SIC code information, and newswire releases. While each Information Access business database delivers current, complete information, the combined strengths of three databases within General BusinessFile ASAP make it the most powerful InfoTrac business research tool for users.

In public and academic libraries alike, users can search the database to locate what they need, from specific data to general overview information. A job seeker may want only contact information for a targeted search of companies in the software industry. A student may need background information for a research paper on drug marketing tactics, and concentrate mainly on journal and newspaper articles. A first-time investor may want to research everything, from investment reports to company size and industry analysis, before making any decisions. By joining all of its sources together, General BusinessFile ASAP enables the user to enter one search term, and link to articles, directory information, SIC codes, and other useful data (Fig. 3). This linking mechanism, with its ability to guide the user to appropriate and relevant data, is the central value of reference center databases like General BusinessFile ASAP.

Health Questions and Multi-Source Answers

Judging from the number of health information requests that hit public library reference desks every day, there is little doubt that this type of information is at the forefront of library patron needs. The amount and complexity of health questions has grown dramatically in the last several years, fueled by the increase in individual responsibility and interest in personal health. People no longer look to a health professional as the only source of health information. Being a well-informed consumer is key, and people expect libraries to have current, complete information to help them become knowledgeable on personal health issues.

On the heels of the success of General BusinessFile, Information Access Company's **Health Reference Center**™ debuted as the first multi-source database of its kind focused on consumer health information. While the product's initial customer base was mainly public libraries, it soon became a popular addition to academic, hospital, and patient education libraries as well (Fig. 4).

Information Access designed Health Reference Center with the consumer in mind. Database content relies heavily on periodicals, books, and pamphlets designed for those who are not medical professionals. Articles from medical journals included in the database come with abstracts written in lay language, and the inclusion of a medical dictionary provides definitions of medical terms.

As with business information, the need for health information can take a variety of forms. One user may need only a quick reference, such as a dictionary definition, while another person researching the same topic will want an in-depth description of symptoms, causes, treatments, and points of contact for more information and support. Health Reference Center responds by al-

Figure 4
Health Reference Center:
Breakdown of Customer Base by Type

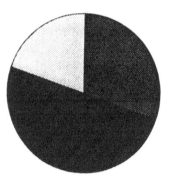

■ Public Libraries: 50%　■ Hospitals: 30%　□ College/University Libraries: 20%

Figure 5
Sample of Information Access Company
Subject Headings

Subject	Date Event Occurred (if applicable)	Date added to IAC Authority File
Kobe, Japan, Earthquake, 1995	1/17/95	1/18/95
Oklahoma City Bombing, 1995	4/19/95	4/22/95
TWA Flight 800 Disaster, 1996	7/17/96	7/18/96
Centennial Olympic Park Bombing, 1996	7/27/96	7/29/96
V-chip	n/a	7/12/95
Advanced Photo System Cameras	n/a	3/13/96
Year 2000 Transition (computers)	n/a	5/30/96
Intranets	n/a	6/13/96
Macarena (dance)	n/a	9/11/96

lowing each user to select precise information, and expand or narrow a search as needed. By combining multiple sources which are selected with the health consumer in mind, the database delivers complete, current information in one stop, eliminating the need to consult several individual print or electronic sources.

The Growing Demand for Complete Reference Solutions

The development of multi-source business and health databases proved to be a successful endeavor for Information Access, and librarians and patrons using them expressed an interest in seeing more of these databases reach out to a wider base of reference needs. Information Access Company targeted student users for the next multi-source databases, by incorporating a variety of new sources into the **TOM™** line of reference products for K–12 students. From the elementary to senior high school level, students could now access magazine articles alongside newspaper articles, books, encyclopedias, and other sources. By introducing them to multi-source research with TOM, young researchers could familiarize themselves with the library's electronic resources, and produce superior research papers and class projects using several source types rather than just one.

The latest multi-source offering, **General Reference Center™**, is also the one with the widest public library patron appeal. This database incorporates magazines, newspapers, children's titles, encyclopedias, reference books, and more into a single database. Libraries open access to General Reference Center to address a wide range of patron research needs, including personal buying decisions, job hunting, school research, and recreational topics. The database is designed to help navigate the user through a search with many options for answers. Information Access will continue to develop multi-source products like General Reference Center, products which by their size and search power can assist the greatest number of patrons and research questions possible.

How Information Access Compiles the Answers

Data Processing

Database construction and production is a complex process at Information Access Company, where one million records were compiled in 1995. A record can include up to three components—citation, abstract, and full text—depending on the rights the company acquires from its publishing partners.

Thousands of magazines arrive at Information Access headquarters in Foster City each week. These publications are tagged for database inclusion, and bundled into priority groups. The *high priority* titles for index, abstract, and full text processing include those titles libraries use the most, such as weekly news and computer magazines. Information Access makes arrangements with publishers to acquire these issues as soon as possible, and produces index/abstract coverage as early as twenty-four hours after receipt. *Second priority* titles cover city, hobby, and women's magazines, as well as other titles that are more regional or specialized in nature and coverage. The index/abstract process for these titles is complete within five to ten days. The timelines for full text inclusion vary, depending on the publication. On average, full text articles appear in the databases within three weeks of publication.

A growing trend within Information Access database production is the availability of direct electronic feed from publishers. Approximately 10 percent of journals are received electronically at Information Access. Direct electronic feed dramatically reduces production time and puts important content into the database quickly, often before the print version has hit the newsstand or library. Information Access continues to grow its direct electronic feed group, as these titles enhance the overall currency of the databases, and in turn, their relevancy for the user.

Subject Headings

The Information Access format for subject headings is based on the general style of the Library of Congress headings. However, Library of Congress headings are designed to catalog books, not magazines or other sources. As a result, these headings do not meet the specificity and currency requirements of Information Access databases.

Information Access maintains its own vocabulary management group, which monitors current news and events as reported in the publications we include in our databases. This group adds new subject headings to our databases every day, to reflect people, companies, events, products, and other topics making news. By adding these categories to our file quickly (Fig. 5), database users are able to locate the most current information on their research topic.

Search Interface

Information Access Company's InfoTrac search interface is designed to enable successful search results for both novice and experienced users. Subject and keyword searching, as well as full Boolean capabilities, guide users to the most relevant citations, abstracts, and full text for each search. Additionally, users can target searches more effectively using narrow and explore functions.

A critical strength of the InfoTrac interface lies in its extensive linking capabilities. Links are now standard technology within the Web environment, but Information Access Company pioneered the use of links in a DOS-based environment with its CD-ROM products, long before the prevalence of Web searching. With linking, InfoTrac's multi-source databases like General BusinessFile ASAP and Health Reference Center search multiple files to produce a single search result (Fig. 3). In the case of General BusinessFile ASAP, for example, a search on the company Sybase takes the user first to directory information with links to journal articles, investment reports, and more. SIC codes and

Figure 6
Total Number of Records Produced by
Information Access Company by year

Year	Number of Records
1977	1344
1982	2000
1987	1500
1992	1,017,394
1993	2,140,895
1994	2,309,884
1995	2,350,354
Cumulative through 1995	25,000,000

Figure 7
Sample of Directory, Newswire, Reference Book, and
Pamphlet Additions to IAC Databases

Source Type	# Records Added in 1995
Company Intelligence (Ward's Business Directories)	
New Company Additions	12,522
Company Updates	73,219
Newswires	
Knight-Ridder/Tribune News Service	12,835
Knight-Ridder/Tribune Business News	7,142
PR Newswire	145,306
Books	
General Reference Book Entries	83,102
School Reference Book Entries	2,849
Health Reference Book Entries	2,545
Pamphlets	
Health Pamphlets	131

mapping to a company authority file enable this type of integration and broadcast searching.

Customer Input

Information Access Company welcomes input from customer libraries. People can call a toll-free comments line, post messages on customer listservers, or speak with sales representatives and product managers to give feedback on Information Access products. The company maintains formal mechanisms to gain consistent input, including product advisory boards and focus groups. These groups meet regularly to discuss enhancements to current products and ideas for new ones, as well as current implementation strategies and usage.

The Future of the Multi-Source Answer

The future of the multi-source answer will continue to change as technology and patron needs drive libraries to incorporate new sources and methods of access for their users. Libraries will enhance their use of multi-source databases, not just for selected patrons or specialized reference needs, but to address growing general reference needs for all patron types.

Additionally, libraries will continue to seek credible, thorough resources available through the World Wide Web. The Web's ease-of-use for 24-hour searching makes it ideal for in-library and especially remote users. However, the lack of a content qualifier for the Web means that much of its content is questionable in terms of accuracy, currency, and appropriateness for a specific research need. Thus, we predict that the need for and usage of credible, multi-source, Web-accessible databases like General BusinessFile ASAP and Health Reference Center will continue to grow.

Information Access will continue to work closely with partner libraries in developing these products, to effectively meet patron reference needs in the library, at school, home, work, and anywhere research may take us in our quest for answers.

Contributors

Address for Correspondence: c/o Information Access Company, 362 Lakeside Dr., Foster City CA 94404

Ronald E. Akie is executive vice president and general manager of the Faxon Company. Address for correspondence: 15 Southwest Park, Westwood, MA 02090. akie@faxon.com.

Joan M. Aliprand, B.Sc. (Gen. Sc.), Dip. Lib., is a Programmer/Analyst at The Research Libraries Group, Inc. Address for correspondence: Research Libraries Group, Inc., 1200 Villa St., Mountain View, CA 94041-1100.

Robert G. Bartle is currently a professor of mathematics at Eastern Michigan University, Ypsilanti, Michigan. A former Executive Editor of Mathematical Reviews (1976–1978, 1986–1990, he prepared this article for the Mathematical Reviews Special Issue (50th Anniversary Celebration, 1990). It is reprinted by permission of the American Mathematical Society. Copyright © Robert G. Bartle.

Rosanna M. Bechtel is chief editor, Information Services Division, Institute of Paper Science and Technology, Inc., 500 10th St. N.W., Atlanta, GA 30318-5794.

Kim Briggs is the European marketing manager of the Secondary Publishing Division, Elsevier Science B.V., Molenwerf 1, 1014 AG Amsterdam, The Netherlands.

Miriam Chall is executive director, Sociological Abstracts, Inc., P.O. Box 22206 San Diego, CA 92191-0206.

Mark Crook is a senior consulting systems analyst at OCLC Office of Research. Address for correspondence: c/o Online Computer Library Center, Inc., 6565 Frantz Road, Dublin, OH 43017-3395.

Mark D. Crotteau is Science Cataloger and Reference Librarian, Washington State University. Address for correspondence: Holland Library, Washington State University, Pullman, WA 99164-5610.

Ian Crowlesmith is the database quality manager of the Secondary Publishing Division, Elsevier Science B.V., Molenwerf 1, 1014 AG Amsterdam, The Netherlands.

Edward P. Donnell is senior advisor for public relations, CAS division of American Chemical Society, 2540 Oletangy River Road, P.O. Boix 3012, Columbus, OH 43210-0012.

Margaret N. Eccles is AgeLine database manager, American Association of Retired Persons. Address for correspondence: c/o AARP, Research Information Center, 601 E St. NW, Washington, DC 20049.

Drucilla Ekwurzel is asssociate editor of the *Journal of Economic Literature*, 4615 Fifth Avenue, Pittsburgh, PA 15213-3661.

Bernadette Freedman is head of the Editing and Indexing Department at BIOSIS, 2100 Arch Street, Philadelphia, PA 19103.

Albert Henderson is editor of *Publishing Research Quarterly* and frequently writes about issues of concern to the publishing and library communities. Address for correspondence: P.O. Box 2423, Bridgeport, CT 06608-0423.

Darlene M. Hildebrandt is the Head of Science Libraries, Washington State University. Address for correspondence: Owen Science & Engineering Library, Washington State University, Pullman, WA 99164-3200.

Angela Hitti is vice president and managing editor at Cambridge Scientific Abstracts. Address for correspondence: 7200 Wisconsin Avenue, Bethesda, MD 20814-4823.

John F. Hood is senior vice president of CMG Information Services. Formerly known as College Marketing Group, CMG developed and introduced the first college faculty database for college text and academic publishers in 1973. Address for correspondence: c/o CMG Information Services, 187 Ballardvale Street, Suite B110, P.O. Box 7000, Wilmington, MA 01887.

John Huenefeld is Senior Publishing Consultant, The Huenefeld Company, Inc., 41 North Road, Suite 201, Bedford, MA 01730.

Olivia A. Jackson, director of INFO-SOUTH since July 1993, holds a Ph.D. in international studies with concentrations in inter-American affairs and international business. Address for correspondence: INFO-SOUTH, 1500 Monza Avenue, POB 248014, Miami, FL 33124-3027.

Richard T. Kaser is Executive Director of National Federation of Abstracting and Information Services (NFAIS). Address for correspondence: 1518 Walnut St., suite 307, Philadelphia, PA 19102.

Jane E. Kister is associate executive editor at *Mathematical Reviews*. Address for correspondence: Mathematical Reviews, 416 Fourth Street, P.O. Box 8604, Ann Arbor MI 48107-8604. Email: jek@math.ams.org

Linda P. Lerman, A.M.L.S., M.B.A., M.A., is Bibliographic Services Officer at The Research Libraries Group, Inc.

Barbara Dobbs MacKenzie is managing editor of RILM (see address under Adam P.J. O'Connor).

Adam P. J. O'Connor is editor in chief of RILM. Address for correspondence: c/o RILM Abstracts of Music Literature, City University of New York, 33 West 42nd St., New York, NY 10036.

Terry M. Owen is electronic products manager, Sociological Abstracts, Inc., P.O. Box 22206, San Diego, CA 92191-0206.

Claude Patou is Director General of INIST. Address for correspondence: inist 2, allée du Pare de Brabois, 54514 VANDOEUVRE-LES-NANCY. CEDEX FRANCE.

Barbara M. Preschel is executive director of PAIS—Public Affairs Information Service, Inc., 521 West 43rd Street, New York, NY 10036.

Peter Quimby is managing editor of history serials at ABC-Clio. Address for correspondence: c/o ABC-Clio, P.O. Box 1911, Santa Barbara, CA 93116-1911. INTERNET: editors@abc-clio.com.

Mona F. Smith. Address for correspondence: c/o NTIS, 5285 Port Royal Rd., Springfield, VA 22161

Rafael E. Ubico. Address for correspondence: Information Services Div., The University of Tulsa, 600 South College (HH 101), Tulsa, OK 74104-3184

Martha Williams is a professor at the University of Illinois, Urbana.

Glen Zimmerman is director for acquisitions and support services. Address for correspondence: Library of Congress, Washington DC 20540.